AUDUBON'S ELEPHANT

Audubon at Green Bank
Almost Happy !! —
Sep 7 1826.   Drawn by himself

Audubon's
ELEPHANT

DUFF HART-DAVIS

WEIDENFELD & NICOLSON

First published in the United Kingdom in 2003
by Weidenfeld & Nicolson
Text copyright © Duff Hart-Davis, 2003
Design and layout copyright
© Weidenfeld & Nicolson, 2003

ISBN 0 297 82967 x

Design Director: David Rowley
Editor: Marilyn Inglis
Picture researcher: Suzanne Bailey
Designed by Ken Wilson
Printed and bound in Printers SRL Trento

Weidenfeld & Nicolson
Wellington House
125 Strand
London WC2R 0BB

Contents

Return from I.st voyage to England 1829
Return from II.rd voyage to England 1831
Return from III.rd voyage to England 1836
Return from IV.th voyage to England 1839
II.nd voyage to England 1830
II.rd voyage to England & the continent 1834
III.rd voyage to England 1837
IV.th voyage to England 1830

I.st voyage to England 1826

1831

1837

1836

INTRODUCTION

THE LAST TIME a complete, double-elephant folio copy of John James Audubon's *The Birds of America* came up for sale at Christie's, New York, in March 2000, it fetched $8.8 million. Single prints, taken from dismembered copies, change hands at over $100,000 apiece, such is the fame and rarity of the most celebrated ornithological work ever published.

Many books have been written about Audubon, but none has concentrated mainly on the crucial phase of his life between 1826 and 1838 during which the woodsman from Kentucky brought his masterpiece into being. Much of this time he spent in Britain, and it was in London, after a false pregnancy in Edinburgh, that the gestation of his elephantine project took place.

Audubon was a self-taught naturalist and artist. Before he came to England he had repeatedly tried and failed to run small businesses in the frontier towns along the Ohio River, but his real interest lay in birds, and he had spent most of the past twenty years searching for and painting every species he could find, his aim being to compile a definitive, illustrated account. It was because nobody in America would publish his *magnum opus* that he sailed for the Old World in the summer of 1826.

In seeking to cover all the events of Audubon's life and his extensive peregrinations, earlier biographers have had neither the inclination nor the space to do justice to his time in England and Scotland. Yet it was in Britain that his life's work at last came to fruition: to bring *The Birds of America* into being, he had to cross the Atlantic, by sailing ship, eight times. It was a British family, the Rathbones of Liverpool, who launched him into society, and British subscribers who supported him in his project's critical early stages.

The purpose of this book is to show how, with astonishing energy and persistence, he brought his great work into being. Audubon himself wrote copiously: his letters were often enormously long and he filled numerous journals with details of his thoughts, hopes, fears, travels and negotiations. Many of his diaries were destroyed by members of his family, yet fortunately the one that charts his arrival in England has survived intact. A version of it was published by his granddaughter Maria R. Audubon in 1897, but the text was heavily cut and bowdlerised: the original – published later in America but never in England – presents a far sharper picture of an extraordinary yet endearing character, and has been used as the basis for this book's opening chapters.

CHAPTER ONE
LIVERPOOL

WHEN JOHN JAMES AUDUBON came ashore at Liverpool on the morning of Friday, 21 July 1826, after a tedious seven-week voyage from New Orleans aboard the cotton schooner *Delos*, he soon attracted attention. For one thing, he spoke with a curious accent, half American and half French; and for another, his appearance was outlandish.

A well-knit man of forty-one, he walked fast, with a springy, woods-man's stride and his habitual garb of long black frock-coat and baggy pantaloons, together with his luxuriant, dark-chestnut hair, flowing in curls on to his shoulders, marked him as an exotic bird of passage. 'My

1 page six

ARTIST'S
VOYAGES

In order to bring *The Birds of America* into being, Audubon crossed the Atlantic eight times in sailing ships between 1826 and 1838, always landing at Liverpool.

2 left

PRINCES
DOCK,
LIVERPOOL

Bales of cotton come ashore on Merseyside. When Audubon arrived in 1826, the smoke hanging over the city was so thick that it made his eyes water.

[9]

locks flew freely from under my hat,' he wrote in his journal, 'and every lady that I met looked at them and then at me until – she could see no more.' His aquiline profile was memorable, and people were struck by his bright eyes, hazel-coloured and flecked with brown, as penetrating as those of an eagle. The novelist Sir Walter Scott – a seasoned observer who met him a few months later – described his face as 'acute, handsome and interesting'.

Forty years on, an anonymous writer left this snapshot of the backwoods stranger:

> The tall and somewhat stooping form, the clothes made not by a West End but a Far West tailor, the steady, rapid, springing step, the long hair, the aquiline features, and the glowing angry eyes – the expression of a handsome man conscious of ceasing to be young, and an air and manner which told you that whoever you might be, he was John Audubon, will never be forgotten by anyone who knew or saw him.

3

HEAVY
BURDEN

The leather-bound portfolio, weighing some 100 lbs, which Audubon slung over his shoulder to carry his paintings while looking for subscribers.

The artist was by no means as confident as he seemed, and his flamboyant appearance concealed deep anxieties. Leaving his wife Lucy and two adolescent sons behind, he had crossed the Atlantic with a single, hugely ambitious aim: to arrange publication of his bird paintings in double-elephant folio – that is, in a collection of coloured engravings on sheets of heavy paper measuring 39½ by 29½ inches (100cm by 75cm). He insisted on this huge format for *The Birds of America* so that even the largest species such as the Wild Turkey could be shown at

Wild Turkey *Meleagris gallopavo* Male Americian Cane Bambusa arundinacea

4

Wild Turkey
Meleagris gallopavo

The first plate
in *The Birds of
America.* Audubon
probably painted
the original in
Louisiana during
1825.

life size, and he knew that the project would be immensely expensive and difficult to complete.

No American publisher or engraver had been prepared to handle it, and his trip to England was his final throw: he arrived with only his port-folios of paintings, a bill of exchange for £340 and several letters of introduction to prominent people who, he hoped, would help him recruit subscriptions.[1] His scheme had no beginning and no definite end, since he had not even completed his search for bird species, let alone his depiction of them, and he did not know how many plates he would need to complete his master work.

Further, he was uncomfortably aware of his own shortcomings as a businessman. His previous ventures had all ended in failure – so much so that at one stage he had been briefly imprisoned for debt – and now he was poised on the verge of a poorly defined yet enormous artistic and commercial undertaking. Having spent much of his life wandering in the woods of Kentucky and Louisiana, and having never been to England before, he was also nervous that his lack of formal education would combine with his ignorance of English customs and social behav-iour to put him at a disadvantage. Luckily his resources included two assets whose value was beyond calculation: first, his good looks, charm and liveliness made him immediately attractive to most people he met; and second, he was phenomenally energetic, with exceptional powers of endurance, able to work for twelve or fourteen hours at a stretch, and to survive indefinitely on four hours' sleep a night.

During his visit to Europe he kept a voluminous journal in which he chronicled his daily encounters. In this he constantly addressed his wife and 'beloved friend' Lucy, as if the diary entries were a series of letters; and although he often wrote to her directly, he clearly found it easiest to shape his record of events and people as though he were talking to her. His spelling and punctuation were erratic – although they improved

1. Audubon usually referred to his pictures as 'drawings', but in fact he had drawn the birds first and then painted them, mainly with watercolours. It was common practice at the time for artists to seek subscribers who would pay for each part of a work as it was published.

steadily – but he had a greater knack than many more polished writers of singling out people and incidents of genuine interest.[2]

As with everything he wrote, there arises a question of veracity. Sometimes in the past he had skated round the edges of the truth – claiming, for instance, that his father had been an admiral in the French navy, whereas in fact he was only a lieutenant, and that his mother had been a Spanish Creole, when in reality she was French. When he wrote about early episodes in his life, he often ran different events together – though whether intentionally or through carelessness, it is often impossible to tell. His grasp of history was, in any case, weak; even after several months in Britain, he thought the Spanish Armada had sailed to attack England in 1527, rather than 1588.

How much of his European journal, then, is true? The answer seems to be, 'Most of it', because he did not write it with an eye to publication, and there would have been little point in falsifying a record kept for himself and his family. Even if euphoria sometimes made him exaggerate his success, and caution led him to minimise his difficulties, the diary also contains numerous passages of painfully honest doubt, self-criticism and reproach.

In any case, there is no reason to doubt him when he says that rain was falling as he landed at Liverpool, then England's main port for transatlantic shipping, and second only to London in prosperity. The local people welcomed the downpour, for until mid-July the summer had been so hot and dry that a serious drought had set in, and many fires had broken out on the moors inland. Yet the smoke, held down by the clouds and hanging over the city, was so thick that it made Audubon's eyes water and left him hardly able to breathe.

Not knowing what to expect, Audubon was agreeably surprised by the standards prevailing at the Commercial Inn, where he and John Swift, a bibulous friend who had shared his cabin during the voyage, took lodgings:

---

2. Except in special instances, the erratic punctuation and spelling have here been tidied up to facilitate comprehension.

[13]

> We are well fed, and well attended, although, to my surprise, altogether, so
> far by females, neatly dressed and tolerably modest. I found today the per-
> sons of whom I enquired for different directions remarkably kind and
> indeed so polite that even to a man like me it was real politeness.

With characteristic financial abandon he lashed out £120 — more than a
third of his capital — on two gold watches and chains, one for himself
and one for Lucy. He probably did not have the time nor inclination to
read that day's issue of the *Liverpool Mercury*. If he had, he would have
seen the numerous advertisements for ships sailing to New York, Canada
and Philadelphia, 'copper-fastened and newly coppered'. He might also
have noticed that Oliver Goldsmith's comedy *She Stoops to Conquer* was
playing at the Theatre Royal, and he would have been startled by an
unusual advertisement near the top of the front page – 'To be sold. Two
fine young eagles, not yet full grown, and each measuring from tip to tip,
seven feet' – for he had something of an obsession about eagles, and had
once bought a captive bird with the express purpose of killing it so that
he could set it up and draw it.

On Saturday morning he went to the Customs House to recover his
drawings and was not pleased to find that he had to pay duty on them:

> The officers were all of the opinion that they were free of duty, but the law
> was looked at because it is not every day, it seems, that such portfolios as
> mine are presented at the Custom House, and I was obliged to pay two
> pence on each, [these] being water-coloured drawings ... My book being
> American, I paid fourteen pence per pound weight.

As he was unused to life in cities, he kept being startled by 'the noise of
pattens' on the flagstones as he wandered about. If the sound was behind
him, he would turn his head, expecting to see a horse running 'full speed
with open mouth, intent on taking my head for fresh grass'; but instead
he would observe 'a neat, plump-looking maid, tripping as briskly by as a
killdeer [a form of plover]'.

He had unwittingly reached England at a time of widespread social
unrest, brought on by unemployment and shortages of food, especially

in the industrial towns of the north. Only a week before Audubon's arrival *The Times* had reported that 'the state of the country in general, and more particularly of the manufacturing districts, is such as to excite much anxiety, not unmixed with alarm'. There were rumours of imminent hunger strikes in Manchester, where bacon, oatmeal and peas were being distributed to the poor, and with thousands of men out of work, the question was 'how to prevent the disorder and tumult which great and general distress inevitably produces'. On the very day he landed, a leading article in the *Liverpool Mercury* gloomily pronounced: 'All appears to be stagnation and despondency.'

Had his reception reflected the state of the economy in general, he might well have abandoned his quest and returned promptly to America; but fortunately his contacts were not among the poor. Rather, they were in the upper echelons of Liverpool society, and one of the first letters of introduction that he delivered – as it turned out, by far the most important – was from his friend in New Orleans, Vincent Nolte, to Richard Rathbone, a member of the family that had founded and built up the powerful merchant trading firm Rathbone Brothers & Co.

Nolte's letter was excellent – down-to-earth and persuasive. Audubon's 400 drawings, he wrote, 'I should think convey a far better idea of American birds than all the stuffed birds of all the museums put together,' and the writer promised the recipient that he would 'derive much gratification' from the artist's conversation.

The artist could not have been furnished with a better contact, for the Rathbones knew everyone worth knowing in Liverpool, and were renowned as much for their philanthropic, political and social endeavours as for their commercial success. Audubon's initial approach elicited a polite note inviting him to dine on the following Wednesday; but in the event he did not have to wait that long to meet the clan who at once accorded him magnificent support and friendship.

On Sunday – a beautiful day – he noted that the thermometer in the sun read 65° Fahrenheit, and in the shade 41°. Then he added, 'I would have wrote 40° but I love odd numbers. I have been told that they are the fortunate ones at lotteries, or at making a choice among a set of females for a wife.'

On Monday morning he slept late, then leapt up and walked to 87 Duke Street, Richard Rathbone's home, only to find that he had gone to his counting-house. There the artist soon ran him to earth:

> My name was taken to the special room of Mr Rathbone, and in a moment I was met by one who acted towards me as a brother ought to do! How truly kind and really polite. He did not give his card to poor Audubon. He gave the most polite invitation to call at his house at two o'clock that I ever received since I left America ...
>
> See me leaning against a window from the inside of a handsome dining-room ... Mr Rathbone entered the room. With both arms extended he advanced towards me with, 'My Dear Sir, I regret that I suffered you to wait thus.' I dined — but no, I did not dine, I feasted my eyes and heart on the delightful picture before me, the mellow picture of a happy family, the Rathbones. Oh sweet children, oh amiable woman, oh hospitable man! ... Mrs Rathbone is, my dearest Lucy, as amiable a lady and as learned a one as — but come, what shall I say? Well then, as thy sweet self!!!

After lunch Richard took his visitor to the Exchange Buildings, where 'introduction followed introduction'. Audubon — acutely self-conscious — felt certain that anyone who looked hard at him was trying to gauge his intelligence from the shape of his head. The next day brought such excitements that he began his journal entry: 'Burst my brains, burst my coarse skull, and give the whole of your slender powers to enable me to describe my feelings.' Richard invited him to bring his portfolio round to Duke Street and from there the party travelled out by horse-drawn coach to the Rathbone family's home, Greenbank, their country house three miles east of Liverpool.

As Audubon quickly discovered, for several generations the family had bestowed the same Christian name on its eldest son, with the result that there were a bewildering number of Williams. At Greenbank the visitors were greeted by Richard's mother, Hannah Mary, a widow of 65 (her husband William IV, had died in 1809). As always in new company,

Audubon felt 'painfully awkward' at first, but he became calmer when he was greeted 'with all kindness and with natural ease that I thought had deserted this earth with the Golden Age'.

> I saw as I entered this happy dwelling a beautiful collection of the birds of England, well prepared … What sensations I had whilst I helped to untie the fastening of my Folio Book! I knew, by all around me, that all was full of best taste and strong judgment, but I did not know if I would at all please … I was panting like the winged pheasant … [but] ah Lucy, these friends praised my birds, and I felt the praise, yes, breathed as if some celestial being succoured me in Elysium!

Audubon's gushing reports reflect the relief and delight he felt, not only at being greeted with such immediate kindness, but also at being taken seriously. He promptly decided that Greenbank was 'the habitation of Philemon and Baucis' – the humble couple who, in Greek mythology, offered hospitality to Zeus and Hermes when the gods were visiting the earth incognito, and were rewarded by having all their wishes granted.

It is small wonder that he fell in love with Greenbank, for the house and its surroundings formed a most harmonious ensemble, with the dwelling perched comfortably at the head of a gentle slope that ran down to an ornamental lake, and then up again on the opposite side. William Rathbone IV had bought the 24-acre property in 1788, and later his sons remodelled the old house, giving it a saucy Gothic front on the lines pioneered by Horace Walpole at Strawberry Hill in Twicken-ham, with windows set in steeply pointed arches, They also added a fine entrance porch and an elaborate cast-iron screen forming a two-storey verandah along the side.

There, on Sundays, they held open house for the young men from their counting house, and Greenbank became a favourite port of call for visiting ships' captains. Generous entertainers, the family often invited fifteen or twenty people to dinner. One of the guests remembered the grounds as 'a garden of paradise' for children: here was a sundial set into the sloping lawn, a walk beside a sunken fence that looked out over fields, beehives, a rose garden, and behind the house a favourite large horse-chestnut tree. In 1819 the poet Henry Chorley described the dwelling and its denizens in glowing terms:

> The library was copious, and novels and poems were read aloud in the parlours. There was a capital garden; there was a double verandah . . . and there was a pianoforte. There was water and a boat; but more, there was true fire from heaven in the owner of all these delights.

It was the fire from heaven that warmed Audubon's heart. Within hours he had fallen in love with the whole Rathbone family. William V, the eldest son (then thirty-nine), and Richard (thirty-eight) were almost his exact contemporaries. The clan had been trading in Liverpool since 1742, originally in timber and ship-building, but the brothers had established a business of their own as commission agents in 1809, and their activities as ship-owners, merchants and social reformers had made them highly regarded in Liverpool.[3]

William V (known in the family as 'Willie') was always the dominant partner: Richard was good at detail, but on his own admission lacked initiative, whereas his brother – like Audubon – was a man of high principles, strong will and ebullient energy, inclined to be impulsive, but also fearless. 'If he thought he saw meanness or tyranny,' Willie's son wrote of him, 'he was not very measured in his judgement or expression.'

Both brothers treated their American guest with a warmth far beyond anything he had hoped for – one small favour that impressed him being Richard's insistence on paying the coachmen who drove him back to his lodgings in the evenings. Whenever Audubon tried to give a driver money, the man would reply, 'Sir, I have been paid.' Soon, in Audubon's

---

3. The Rathbone family included nearly as many Hannah Marys as it did Williams. Hannah Mary I (1761–1839), the Queen Bee, was the wife of William IV (1757–1809) and mother of William V (1787–1868). Hannah Mary II (1798–1878), originally Reynolds, was the wife of William V's younger brother Richard (1788–1860). Hannah Mary III (1791–1865) was William V's younger sister, and Hannah Mary IV his second daughter (1816–60). Hannah Mary III, who fascinated Audubon, married William Reynolds in 1831. In her edition of *The 1826 Journal of John James Audubon*, that great authority Alice Ford confused the generations, mistakenly calling the artist's main benefactor William IV instead of William V.

eyes, old Mrs Rathbone became 'the Queen Bee', ruling her 'honeyed mansion' of a hive with energy and grace. Yet for him the most captivating member of the family was William's unmarried sister, Hannah Mary, then thirty-five, with her 'brilliant and yet mild' black eyes. Night after night in his journal Audubon extolled her charms, calling her an angel; he addressed his entries to Lucy (as always), but seems not to have realised what apprehension his remarks might arouse the other side of the ocean.

Barred Owl. Male adult.
STRIX NEBULOSA.

5 facing page

BARRED OWL
Strix nebulosa now
Strix varia

At first there was
no grey squirrel
in the picture.
Audubon painted
it separately, and
Robert Havell
Jnr, the engraver,
later incorporated
it into the print.

CHAPTER TWO

WANDERER

Until he came to England, Audubon's life had been extraordinarily lacking in direction. In every sense of the phrase, he had been all over the place, and it had taken him many years to focus his enormous energy on the project which eventually made his name.

Because he knew he was illegitimate, he liked to cloak his origins in mystery. He would pretend not to know his exact date of birth and sometimes, when rumour suggested that he might be the Dauphin — the long-lost son of Louis XVI of France and Marie-Antoinette — he did not refute the idea. More often, he claimed that his mother had been his father's first wife, a Spanish Creole woman of exceptional beauty, and that she had died in an insurrection on the Caribbean island of Saint Domingue (now Haiti), which was then a French colony.

The truth was more prosaic. The artist's father was Jean Audubon, a French merchant, planter, slave-dealer and naval officer, who came from Nantes. In 1785, when he was forty-one, he had been married for twelve years to Anne Moynet, a well-to-do widow in Nantes; he had no legitimate offspring, but he had already fathered two daughters with a local woman in the Caribbean, and on the night of 26 April 1785, in the little town of Les Cayes, his son was born to Jeanne Rabin, an illiterate French chambermaid of twenty-five who had gone out to the Caribbean to work for another French family. The baby, born out of wedlock, was never baptised, and on 11 November that same year, when the boy was only six months old, Jeanne died of a fever. It is not clear who cared for the child during the next three years of his life; but during that period relations between blacks and whites on Saint Domingue deteriorated so rapidly that his father, who had built up a profitable business trading in wine and sugar, sold most of his property and in July 1788 asked a friend to carry his young son to France, where Anne took charge of him. She must have been exceptionally broad-minded, for she not only tolerated Jean's infidelities, but brought up the boy (also called Jean at first) and his mulatto half-sister Rose Bonnitte.

Jean Senior had moved none too soon. In 1789 echoes of the revolution in France reached Saint Domingue and set off violent clashes, in which free coloured people demanded that French revolutionary principles should apply to them – a struggle which culminated in a slave revolt two years later. Jean meanwhile returned to France and – sight unseen – bought Mill Grove, a 200-acre farm in eastern Pennsylvania, some twenty miles north-west of Philadelphia, drawn both by the attractive sound of the property and by the rumour that a valuable vein of lead ran beneath it.

Although married to and in amity with a rich French woman, Jean was

6

MILL GROVE

Audubon's first home in America, built in 1762, stands on a shelf in a commanding position above the fast-flowing water of the Perkiomen Creek.

a fervent radical and supporter of Napoleon. Back in France, he joined the National Guard and later the French Navy, and this meant that during the next few years he was often away from home; but in March 1794 he and Anne took young Jean and his half-sister to the town hall in Nantes to have them legally adopted. Because of his frequent absences, the boy had been brought up largely by Anne – and in later life he never ceased to extol her virtues as a surrogate mother. To her he was 'the handsomest boy in Nantes, but perhaps not the most studious'.

He grew up mainly at La Gerbetière, the family home near the village of Couëron, some ten miles west of Nantes; and although he was sent to school, he harboured what he himself called an incurable 'tendency to follow nature in her walks'. This made him constantly play truant:

> Almost every day, instead of going to school when I ought to have gone, I usually made for the fields ... My little basket went with me, filled with good eatables, and came back full of birds' eggs, nests, lichens, flowers and pebbles.

At home private teachers sought to make him proficient in drawing, geography, maths, fencing, music (he learnt to play the violin and flute) and dancing. He grew very fond of his stepmother – and no wonder, for she spoilt him outrageously, giving him *carte blanche* at all the confectionery shops in Nantes and repeatedly saying, in his presence, that he was the best-looking boy in France.

As for his father: although the boy saw relatively little of his parent, he looked back on him from later life with reverence and affection. Just as he tried to enhance his father's reputation by promoting him posthumously from lieutenant to admiral, so he sought to increase his physical stature. 'My father and I were of the same height and stature,' he wrote, 'say about five feet ten inches, erect, and with muscles of steel'. Other sources record that Jean Senior was powerfully built but stocky – only about 5 feet 4 inches (1.6 metres) tall – and surviving garments suggest that his son was about 5 feet 8 inches (1.7 metres) tall.

'In temperament,' the younger man believed, 'we much resembled each other also, being warm, irascible and at times violent; but it was like the blast of a hurricane, dreadful for a time, when calm almost instantly returned.' The father set great store on good education, and one of his favourite maxims was that although fortunes could be lost overnight in revolutions, 'talents and knowledge, added to sound mental training, assisted by honest industry, can never fail'.

It was at Couëron that young Audubon began drawing the birds of France. Before the days of binoculars or cameras, the only way an ornithologist could study a specimen closely was by shooting or catching it, and he became highly skilled with his muzzle-loading shot-guns.[1] By the time he was seventeen, he had completed 200 studies. He seems to have been largely self-taught, but later in life he encouraged people to believe that he had received instruction from Jacques-Louis David, court painter to Louis XVI and later to Napoleon, and had spent many hours drawing 'eyes and noses belonging to giants and heads of horses represented in ancient sculptures'. David did visit Nantes in 1802, when Audubon was sixteen or seventeen, yet no evidence survives to show that he ever gave the boy lessons. It may be that in the course of time Audubon came to believe his own invention, as many fantasists do.

In the autumn of 1803 Jean gave his son new forenames – John James Laforest – made him swear always to keep his illegitimacy secret and sent him off to America on board a friend's ship. The aim was threefold: to put the young man beyond the reach of Napoleon's recruiters who were scouring France in search of new blood for their armies; to make him learn English; and to teach him the basics of farming, which he could pick up at Mill Grove.

There the eighteen-year-old found a handsome house made of rough-hewn, red-brown stone, built in 1762, looking out westwards from a natural shelf over the fast-flowing waters of the Perkiomen Creek. After a spell learning English in exchange for drawing lessons in nearby Norristown, he moved out to lodge with William Thomas, a Quaker who rented the Mill Grove land, and whose own farm lay close by.

---

1. By then telescopes did exist, but they were scarce and extremely inefficient.

The dark-red soil of the region was excellent for growing cereal crops, but agriculture held little fascination for the budding naturalist who preferred to spend his days on solitary forays into the surrounding woods and open country, armed with gun or fishing rod, exhilarated by the wildness of his surroundings. In some instinctive way he seemed to identify with the wildlife of the frontier. 'Hunting, fishing, drawing and music occupied my every moment,' he wrote. And although neighbours began to think him fairly eccentric and reckoned he was wasting his time, he was, in fact, starting to build up the immense store of knowledge that later enabled him to produce his masterpiece. He later claimed that the earliest drawings which appeared in *The Birds of America* were done in 1805 – and indeed, during his early days at Mill Grove his favourite resort was a cave hollowed out of the rocks above the Perkiomen, which he made into an outdoor study, bringing pencils and paper to draw the Pewees that came to nest there every spring.

In seeking to increase the realism and animation of his paintings, he made various unsuccessful experiments, some of which he described in his paper 'My Style of Drawing Birds', written in 1828. Having tried tying dead birds up in different attitudes with heads and wings held by thread, he tried to make a three-dimensional model:

> I laboured in wood, cork and wires and formed a grotesque figure which I cannot describe in any other terms than by telling you that when sat up it was a very tolerable looking 'Dodo'! A friend present laughed heartily and raised my blood by assuring me that, as far as I might wish to represent a tame gander or bird of that sort, my model would do. I gave it a kick, demolished it to atoms, walked off and thought again.

He then developed the method which he used ever after, of fixing a freshly shot bird with pins, skewers and wire to a board of his own design, in the attitude he wanted to depict. He also put a grid or graph behind the specimen, and another on his sheet of paper, so that he could capture proportions accurately. Thus equipped, he would immediately set to work, drawing and painting before the living colours began to fade.

Immersion in the largely Quaker society of Pennsylvania gave him the

habit, which he kept for life, of using 'thou' and 'thee' in his speech and writing. A few months after his arrival at Mill Grove, he heard that an English family named Bakewell had bought Vaux Hill, the neighbouring property, a much grander house, with a pillared portico on the entrance front, which commanded twenty-mile views.

7 far left

BLUE JAY
Corvus cristatus
now *Cyanocitta
cristata*

One male, with wings half-open to show their colouring, and two females are grouped on a dead tree. Painted around 1825.

The news did not please him, because his father, who had twice been imprisoned by the English, had instilled in him a deep dislike of the island race, and he himself entertained 'the greatest prejudices against all of his [William Bakewell's] nationality'. The result was that when the newcomer called and left a card with an invitation to go shooting, young Audubon boorishly did not reply – even though he heard that Bakewell 'had several handsome and very interesting daughters, and beautiful pointer dogs'.

Years later, he squirmed with embarrassment at his lack of manners, but at the time fate smiled on him, for that winter, when frost set in and 'grouse were abundant along the fir-covered ground near the creek,' he ran across Bakewell out shooting, and was at once struck not just by the man's polite manner, but also by the fact that he was an excellent marksman. Having apologised for his rudeness, he promised to call on the Bakewell household – and when he did, there, 'snugly seated at her work by the fire,' was the eldest daughter, Lucy.

8 left

BLUE JAY

A modern reconstruction of how the artist mounted birds on a wire frame to draw and paint them.

Audubon was at once transfixed by her good looks and by the liveliness of her features and discourse. 'Her form … seemed radiant with beauty,' he wrote later, 'and my heart and eyes followed her every step.' Lucy, equally, was fascinated by her close encounter with the strange

[27]

French neighbour about whom, until then, she had heard only rumours. So well did their conversation flow that he stayed to lunch and then invited the whole family back. After a meal they repaired to the ice on the creek, where, 'in comfortable sledges, each fair one was propelled by an ardent skater'.

Skating was one of Audubon's most stylish accomplishments — and showing off at it nearly killed him. One day when the ice was 'in capital order', he took a party duck-shooting up the creek. On the way home in the dusk he was leading, holding up a white handkerchief on a stick as a marker for the others, when he suddenly dropped through an air-hole into the freezing water. He could easily have drowned, but his luck held; the current carried him downstream until he bobbed up through another air-hole and was dragged clear — 'a singular and extraordinary escape from death'.

The Bakewells soon renamed their house Fatland Ford, echoing the early settlers who had called the fertile terrain 'the fatlands of Egypt Road'. Their home was in sight of Mill Grove and signals could be passed from one to the other, chalked on boards hung outside windows. However, Audubon's courtship of Lucy was tiresomely interrupted by the arrival of Francis da Costa, an acquaintance of the Audubon family in Nantes who had some knowledge of mining, and had been sent out by Audubon's father to oversee the opening up of the lead vein under Mill Grove.

Before long it became clear that da Costa had designs on the entire property, and John James took violently against 'this covetous wretch, who did all he could to ruin my father, and indeed swindled both of us to a large amount ... A greater scoundrel probably never existed, but peace be with his soul.'

Da Costa was crafty and tenacious, and to get rid of him Audubon decided he must secure his father's permission. That meant a trip to France, no easy journey in those days. Audubon lacked the money to pay for a passage and it must have been humiliating for him to ask da Costa for a loan. The response was a sealed envelope addressed to Mr Kauman, an agent and banker in New York, which Audubon supposed was a letter of credit.

Taking it with him, he walked through the winter snows to the city – a distance of some 150 miles, which he covered in less than three days – and presented his document, only to find that it recommended Kauman to have the bearer arrested and deported by force to China. 'The blood rose in my temples,' Audubon remembered, 'and well it was that I had no weapon about me'. He left the agent feeling 'half bewildered, half mad,' planning to return to Philadelphia at once and murder da Costa. Luckily, he was persuaded out of such lunacy; instead, in March 1805 Lucy's uncle Benjamin Bakewell lent him the money for a passage to France.

He took ship in the *Hope* and must have been direly frustrated when, almost at once, the captain put into New Bedford, claiming that repairs were necessary, when in fact wanting to spend time with his wife, whom he had recently married. After a week's delay they departed, and nineteen days later Audubon was sailing up the Loire. His sudden reappearance at La Gerbetière amazed his father, who had had no warning of his approach, but was delighted to see him. So was his stepmother Anne, by then in her seventies. Yet Audubon's homecoming was far from comfortable, for the threat of being seized and conscripted into the Napoleonic army limited his movements, forcing him to hang around close to home.

At the same time, he and his father were all too well aware that da Costa was continuing his machinations in Pennsylvania, and presently they adopted new tactics. To raise some money, Jean Audubon sold his share in the Mill Grove plantation to a friend, Claude Rozier, and set up a partnership between his own son John James and Claude's son Ferdinand. The plan was that the two young men should go out to Pennsylvania together and settle matters with da Costa. If necessary, they would sell their interest in Mill Grove and set up business on their own in some promising frontier town. Audubon was naturally eager to return to Lucy, but it was not until the following summer that he saw her again. On 12 April 1806 he and his new partner went aboard the American ship *Polly* at St Nazaire, he claiming to be an American from Louisiana, Rozier posing as a Dutchman. That was the last time Audubon saw his father and step-mother, for he did not return to Europe for twenty years and by then both were dead.

On the way home the *Polly* was intercepted and ransacked by an English privateer, but Audubon and Rozier landed safely in Manhattan on 28 May, and after a pause in New York to seek advice from Benjamin Bakewell on possible commercial ventures, they went on to Fatland Ford. Thrilled as he was to be back with his sweetheart, Audubon annoyed her father by declining to deploy his physical strength on the hard work of the harvest. While hired hands sweated at cutting and carrying the wheat and oats, he wandered in the woods, sketching birds and wild flowers, or swam in the mill pond, and Rozier loafed about with an equal lack of application. 'Don't like their being here in idleness,' William Bakewell noted in his diary. 'Mr Audubon did not bring his father's permission to marry nor the $150 I lent him [the passage money advanced by Benjamin Bakewell in New York].'

Gradually, bit by bit, the partners sold Mill Grove to da Costa and moved into commerce. For a few months both worked as apprentice clerks, Audubon in New York, Rozier in Philadelphia. Audubon made some spectacular mistakes, his mind distracted by thoughts of birds and hopes of marriage. 'My dear Father,' he wrote during April 1806 in his improving but still stuttering English:

I am allways in Mr Benjamin Bakewell's store where I work as much as I can and passes my days happy ... Mi Biloved Lucy ... constantly loves me and makes perfectly happy. I shall wait for thy Consent and the one of my good Mamma to marry her. Could thou but see her and thou wouldst I am sure be pleased of the prudency of my choice ... I wish thou would wrights to me ofnor and longuely. Think by thyself how pleasing it is to read a friend's letter.

In 1807 Audubon and Rozier set off to make their fortunes in the west, drifting down the Ohio River on a primitive flatboat to Louisville, then a bustling frontier-town of some 1300 souls. There they set up a log-cabin store, which for a while did reasonably well. Yet Audubon was never greatly interested in commerce; much of the land round about had been settled by planters, but it was alive with birds and animals and these attracted him irresistibly. Leaving Rozier to manage the store, he hunted, shot, stuffed and drew birds insatiably.

Nevertheless, it was the business on which his plans and hopes were based, for only by showing that he possessed a solid asset and some knowledge of commerce could he persuade Lucy's parents that he would make a fit husband for their daughter. In this he somehow succeeded, and the couple were married at Fatland Ford on 5 April 1808. Three days later they set out with Rozier for Louisville, which they reached after an uncomfortable twelve-day voyage down the Ohio. Their quarters in Louisville, at the hostelry known as the Indian Queen, were none too comfortable either: but Lucy seems to have made light of the privations, and their first son, Victor, was born there on 12 June 1809.

One of the most important – if least agreeable – days of Audubon's life came in March 1810, when into his store, unannounced, walked the Scottish weaver, pedlar, poet and ornithologist Alexander Wilson, who was then forty-three. An obstinate, irritable little man, who hated to be told that he was wrong, Wilson had criticised the Scottish weavers' em-ployers so fiercely with his satirical ballads that in 1794, at the age of twenty-eight, he had been forced to flee from his native Paisley and emigrate to America. Penniless, he walked from New York to Phila-delphia and there in 1802, after eight

10

ALEXANDER
WILSON

Audubon's great rival, the diminu-tive exiled Scot began publishing his nine-volume *American Ornithol-ogy* in 1808.

[31]

years of desultory, short-term jobs, he had taken over the school at Gray's Ferry, some four miles out of town.

He had long suffered attacks of depression, and it was to combat these that two old friends – William Bartram, an older schoolmaster, and Alexander Lawson, a Scots-born engraver – persuaded him to take up drawing. This he did, and his increasing skill coupled with a growing interest in birds, led him to conceive the idea of producing his *magnum opus, American Ornithology*, which eventually ran to nine volumes.

Apparently unknown to Audubon, who until then had never heard of the project, Wilson's first volume had been published in 1808; yet the arrival one morning of this small, scruffy stranger, who carried two large portfolios under his arm, created an indelible impression on the mind of the store-keeper:

> His long, rather hooked nose, the keenness of his eyes, and his prominent cheek-bones stamped his countenance with a peculiar character. His dress, too, was of a kind not usually seen in that part of the country; a short coat, trousers and a waistcoat of grey cloth … As he approached the table at which I was working, I thought I discovered something like astonishment in his countenance.

The purpose of Wilson's visit quickly became apparent: he was seeking subscribers for his huge project. Audubon turned over a few of the plates, admired what he saw and had picked up his pen to sign his name when Rozier asked him 'rather abruptly' in French why he was proposing to subscribe, as his own drawings were 'certainly far better' and his knowledge of birds at least as great as Wilson's.

'Vanity and the encomiums of my friend prevented me from subscribing,' Audubon wrote later. Wilson, clearly annoyed, asked if his host had any drawings of his own. When Audubon brought them out, 'his surprise appeared great, as he told me he had never had the most distant idea that any other individual than himself had been engaged in forming such a collection. He asked me if it was my intention to publish, and when I answered in the negative, his surprise seemed to increase.'

According to Audubon, he showed Wilson every civility; he presented him to his wife and friends, and took him out shooting to see if they could procure any of the birds the Scot was lacking. He also offered him the use of any of his own drawings that might fill gaps in the *Ornithology*, provided their provenance was made clear, and suggested that they should 'open a correspondence'. But Wilson allegedly made no reply to either proposal, and from the start Audubon sensed something unsatisfactory in this spiky fellow's character:

> It happened that he lodged in the same house with us, but his retired habits, I thought, exhibited either a strong feeling of discontent or a decided melancholy. The Scotch airs which he played sweetly on his flute made me melancholy, too, and I felt for him.

Later the two men met again briefly in Philadelphia. Audubon, arriving in town, immediately paid Wilson a visit and found him drawing a White-headed Eagle:

> He received me with civility, and took me to the exhibition rooms of Rembrandt Peale, the artist, who had then portrayed Napoleon crossing the Alps. Mr Wilson spoke not of birds or drawings. Feeling, as I was forced to do, that my company was not agreeable, I parted from him, and after that I never saw him again. But judge of my astonishment some time after when, on reading the thirty-ninth page of the ninth volume of [his] *American Ornithology*, I found in it the following paragraph:
>
> '23 March 1810. I bade adieu to Louisville, to which place I had four letters of recommendation, and was taught to expect much of everything there; but neither received one act of civility from those to whom I was recommended, one subscriber, nor one new bird; although I delivered my letters, ransacked the woods repeatedly, and visited all the characters likely to subscribe. Science or literature has not one friend in this place.'

It may well be that Audubon exaggerated the efforts he had made on Wilson's behalf; but there was never much personal animosity between the two, for after a short illness Wilson died prematurely in 1813, aged only fifty. It was his friend, editor and biographer George Ord who later revived and exploited the feud in his attempts to promote Wilson's work and attack Audubon's. It was Ord who edited the eighth and wrote the ninth and last volume of Wilson's work, both of which appeared after his death. It was also Ord who claimed to have seen Wilson's original diary entry for that fateful day – although the document has never come to light.

Whatever the truth of the meetings in Louisville, the Scot's visit did have a profound effect on Audubon – for the sudden appearance of a competitor who had already established a commanding lead galvanised him into action and for the first time began to focus his own ambition. Until then – as he told Wilson – he had drawn only for his own edification, and had had no thought of publishing his pictures, but from now a new idea smouldered in his mind.

Meanwhile, business was slack and soon the restless partners were on the move again, seeking their salvation farther to the south-west at Henderson, a cluster of log houses with a population of only 200, some 125 miles down the Ohio River, where they opened another store. There, too, it was the wildness and beauty of the surroundings, rather than the possibility of making money, that captivated Audubon.

Six months later, in December 1810, leaving his wife Lucy and small son Victor at the home of a hospitable physician, Dr Adam Rankin, two miles outside Henderson, he and Rozier again set off for the west with a cargo of whisky and gunpowder, aiming for the small settlement of Ste Geneviève on the Mississippi River. At Cash Creek, near the mouth of the Ohio, they were caught in the ice – a mishap that delighted Audubon, as it enabled him to spend several weeks hunting with the Shawnee Indians and

II

EATEN BY RATS

Japanese woodblock print, 1875, illustrating the disaster when Norwegian rats invaded Audubon's box of paintings and shredded the contents to make their nest.

joining in their slaughter of wild swans, whose feathers they were selling to traders for export to Europe. When at last the partners gained the Mississippi, they warped their way laboriously upstream, hauling against the current at the rate of ten miles a day, until again halted by ice — another six-week delay ensued, during which they lived largely on the meat of bears, opossums and wild turkeys.

Ste Geneviève was full of French people; this suited Rozier, who wanted to settle there, but not Audubon, who hated the place immediately and had already become more American than French. In April 1811 the two amicably agreed to dissolve their partnership, and Audubon set off back to Henderson, claiming in one later account that he covered the 165 miles on foot in four days, but in another that he bought 'a beauty of a horse' on the way.

In Kentucky he was reunited with his family, and his exceptional resilience was demonstrated as never before in the way he overcame yet another disaster. He found that in his absence the wooden box containing all his bird paintings, which he had left in the care of a relative, had been invaded by Norway rats, which had shredded the pictures to make their nest, thereby destroying nearly 1000 'inhabitants of the air'. Audubon's reaction was characteristic:

> The burning heat which instantly rushed through my brain was too great to be endured . . . I slept not for several nights, and the days passed like days of oblivion until, the animal powers being recalled into action through the strength of my constitution, I took up my gun, my notebook and my pencils and went forth to the woods as gaily as if nothing had happened. I felt pleased that I might now make better drawings than before; and ere a period not exceeding three years had elapsed, I had my portfolio filled again.

The young couple's existence was far from easy. They lost two daughters, Rosa and Lucy, in infancy, and although they were overjoyed when their second son, John Woodhouse, was born on 30 November 1812, they were often critically short of money.

Audubon tried to go into business with his brother-in-law, Thomas W. Bakewell, but the enterprise failed in a few months, and early in the spring of 1812 he went back briefly to Ste Geneviève, hoping to collect funds that Rozier still owed him. He returned empty-handed, and again made the journey on foot, splashing through the flooded prairies to complete the 165 miles in little over three days.

That summer war broke out between America and England, and in spite of the economic difficulties which the conflict engendered, Audubon began to prosper. Once more he opened a store in Henderson and acquired some land with the idea of settling there permanently. The family lived in a log-cabin next door to the shop and for a time all went well, although the naturalist would disappear into the woods for weeks on end, pursuing birds to shoot and draw.

It was another venture with his brother-in-law that brought final commercial ruin. In March 1817 he and Thomas rented a parcel of land on the river front and built a steam-powered mill for sawing timber and grinding grain. This enterprise limped along for a couple of years, and while it was still in existence, Audubon got into a violent quarrel with a man called Samuel Adams Brown, who swore he would kill him. Luckily, Lucy became so alarmed that she made him carry a dagger, so that when his enemy came at him from behind, he was at least armed. As he himself recorded:

> On turning, I observed Mr B marching toward me with a heavy club in his hand. I stood still, and he soon reached me. He complained of my conduct to him at New Orleans, and suddenly raising his bludgeon laid it about me. Though white with wrath, I spoke nor moved not till he had given me twelve severe blows, then drawing my dagger with my left hand (unfortunately my right was disabled and in a sling, having been caught and much injured in the wheels of the steam engine), I stabbed him and he instantly fell.

Brown was not fatally injured, and when the case came up in court, the judge told Audubon he had committed 'an exceedingly serious offence, in failing to kill the damned rascal'.

One day late in the summer of 1818, walking by the river, Audubon saw an extraordinary figure disembarking from a boat:

> A long loose coat of yellow nankeen, much the worse of the many rubs it had got in its time, and stained all over with the juice of plants, hung loosely

about him like a sac. A waistcoat of the same, with enormous pockets, and buttoned up to the chin, reached below over a tight pair of pantaloons, the lower parts of which were buttoned down to the ankles. His beard was as long as I have known mine to be during some of my peregrinations, and his lank black hair hung down loosely over his shoulders ... His words impressed an assurance of rigid truth, and as he directed the conversation to the study of the natural sciences, I listened to him with as much delight as Telemachus could have listened to Mentor.

In spite of the stranger's outlandish appearance, the Audubons gave him shelter in their house and so got to know the deeply eccentric, itinerant naturalist Constantine Samuel Rafinesque. Of French and Greek parentage, born in Constantinople, he was then thirty-five, and had led an even stranger life than Audubon. After his father had died of yellow fever in 1793, his mother took the family to Italy where young Constantine showed a remarkable facility for languages, and in 1802 he was sent to America to become a shipper's clerk in Philadelphia. Three years later he went to Sicily, where he made a great deal of money by discovering the medicinal properties of squill, or sea onion. He also managed a whisky distillery, explored the island, studied its fish, acted as editor and writer for various learned men, and fathered two children with a Sicilian woman. In 1815 he returned to America, but his ship went down in Long Island Sound and he lost all his worldly goods.

If Audubon had known what a difficult time Rafinesque had been through, he might not have pulled his leg in the way he did; but the appearance of the stranger was so outlandish that Audubon played a cruel practical joke on him, describing and even drawing ten species of fictitious fish which he claimed were native to the Ohio River. Swallowing the bait, Rafinesque wrote accounts of these imaginary creatures in articles which were first published in an obscure magazine, but which in 1820 were collected into a slim volume, *Ichthyologia Ohiensis*. For years these caused serious confusion among specialists — and no wonder, since much of it was outrageous: for instance, the author's description of the Devil-Jack Diamond Fish, which he claimed was

One of the
fictitious fish said
to inhabit the
Ohio River, drawn
and described by
Audubon to tease
the naturalist
Constantine
Samuel
Rafinesque.

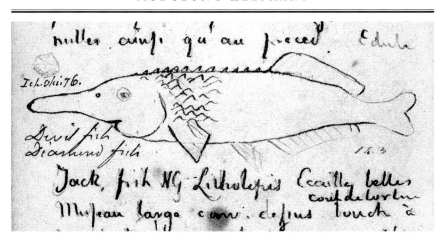

between four and ten feet long, weighed up to 400 lbs, and was covered with bullet-proof scales 'cut like diamonds'. Even if he was mischievous, Audubon can hardly be blamed for the fact that his joke succeeded so well. Rafinesque himself does not seem to have resented it.

In 1819 the mill closed, leaving Audubon heavily in debt; he was thrown into gaol and obliged to secure his release by declaring himself bankrupt in court. Penury forced him to abandon his idea of going to France to see his step-mother and sister; instead, he sold everything he owned except his drawings, his gun and the clothes he was wearing and, leaving Lucy and the children behind, he departed from Henderson for good, walking miserably to Louisville:

> I left my dear log house, my delightful garden and orchards, with that heaviest of burdens, a heavy heart, and turned my face towards Louisville. This was the saddest of all my journeys, the only time in my life when the Wild Turkeys that so often crossed my path, and the thousands of lesser birds that enlivened the woods and the prairies, all looked like enemies, and I turned my eyes from them, as if I could have wished that they had never existed.

Yet his final humiliation in business proved the catalyst which set him on the road to eventual success; for, admitting at last that he was not made for commerce, he vowed instead henceforth to rely on his 'poor talents' as an artist to keep the family going. His aim was to collect 'all the birds of America' – no less – and for the next five years he wandered restlessly about the southern and western states, earning a crust by executing portraits in pencil and charcoal, mainly of the living, but sometimes also of the dead, and whenever he could adding new birds to his portfolio. His looks were undoubtedly an advantage. To Mrs Nathaniel Wells Pope, the wife of his clerk in Henderson, he was:

> One of the handsomest men I ever saw. In person he was tall and slender, his blue eyes[2] were an eagle's in brightness, his teeth were white and even, his hair a beautiful chestnut colour, very glossy and curly. His bearing was courteous and refined, simple and unassuming.

He spent some months at Shippingport, then a village on the Falls of the Ohio, two miles out of Louisville, where steamers and lesser river boats were built. He stayed at the home of his brother-in-law Nicholas Berthoud, but felt 'straitened to the very utmost,' and was obliged to draw portraits in black chalk for the rock-bottom fee of five dollars apiece. Next, after another sojourn in the woods, he moved on to Cincinnati, becoming resident taxidermist at the Western Museum. When Lucy and the boys joined him, he helped feed the family by shooting wild turkeys and partridges; once again he drew crayon portraits for money and started a drawing school.

Then in October 1820, again leaving his loved ones behind, he set out for New Orleans on a further quest for new species, drifting down the Ohio on a flatboat. With him he took Joseph Mason, a promising young artist whom he described as 'of good family and naturally an amiable youth,' and whose task was to paint backgrounds for the bird portraits, filling in trees, leaves and flowers.

Staccato entries in Audubon's journal give a vivid idea of the journey downriver. By then his English had improved a good deal, but it still carried unconscious echoes of French ('remarquable', 'desagreable', 'femelle' and so on) and included some inspired spelling: 'emased',

---

2. Perhaps Mrs Pope was overexcited. Other witnesses reported that his eyes were hazel-coloured.

'oppolent' and 'a bad head hake' (brought on by too much wine). Well capable though he was of living rough, Audubon liked to maintain certain standards of personal hygiene:

> When we left Cincinnati we agreed to shave and clean completely every Sunday – and often [I] have been anxious to see the day come for certainly a shirt worn one week, hunting every day and sleeping in buffalo robes at night, soon becomes soiled and desagreable.

Almost every day some members of the party went ashore with their guns to shoot for the pot and to procure specimens. When cooped up on board by bad weather, Audubon sank into deep depressions, but his ornithological curiosity was boundless, and he revived whenever presented with a chance of securing new species. The rarer the bird, the more eagerly he pursued it, never apparently worrying that by killing it he might hasten the extinction of its kind. The abundant partridges were often on the menu – the shooting parties killed as many as thirty a day – and sometimes less common species also found their way on to the table. A rare hermit thrush, for instance, Audubon pronounced 'very fat and delicate eating', and twenty-six starlings made a 'good and delicate' supper, but some grebes proved disappointing, 'extremely fishy, rancid and fat'.

Food remained a preoccupation throughout the trip. On board the boat, table manners were rough and ready. 'Having not used a fork and scarcely even a plate since I left Louisville,' wrote the artist after an evening ashore, 'I involuntarily took meat and vegetables in my fingers several times.' One evening they landed and walked to the only tavern in the country, arriving 'wearied, muddy, wet and hungry'. Supper was 'soon called for, and soon served, and to see four wolfs tearing at an old carcass would not give you a bad idea of our helping ourselves'. Another evening, at dinner, the company was surprised at 'the astonishing leaps that some maggots took about our table. They issued out of a very good piece of cheese.'

At Natchez he had the luck to fall in with Lucy's brother-in-law, Nicholas Berthoud. The settlement of Natchez-under-the-Hill, crowded against a bluff on a bend of the river, was a notorious slum of drinking dives, gambling dens and brothels, but the town above was well laid out, and Nicholas put Audubon up at Garnier's, the best hotel, at his own expense. Even so, the artist desperately needed money, and again drew portraits at five dollars a head. More important, he managed to borrow the volumes of Alexander Wilson's *American Ornithology* – all except the last – and so was able to discover what birds his rival had that he did not.

Then, however, he made a dreadful mistake. On 31 December, as he started down-river again – this time on Nicholas's own keel-boat which was towed by the steamer *Columbus* – he suddenly realised that he had left his portfolio of fifteen finished drawings and a portrait of Lucy lying on the shore. A journal entry reveals his despair:

> No hopes can I have of ever seeing it [again] when lost amongst 150 or 160 flatboats and houses filled with the lowest of characters. No doubt my drawings will serve to ornament their parlours or will be nailed on some of the steering oars.

On New Year's Day of 1821 he reached Bayou Sara, a settlement where the river of that name joins the Mississippi, reflecting that it was twenty-one years since he had left France, and that what he had seen and felt since 'would fill a large volume'. His lack of confidence came out in a gloomy journal entry: 'Not willing to dwell on ideal futurity, I do not at present attempt to foresee where my poor body may be this day twelve months.'

In New Orleans at last, he and Mason scratched about for a living, dashing off portraits and giving drawing lessons. 'I rose early tormented by many disagreeable thoughts,' he wrote on 13 January, 'nearly again without a cent in a bustling city where no one cares a fig for a man in my situation.' He found some consolation in the superabundance of birds – Golden Wing Woodpeckers, Carolina Wrens, Fish Crows, Marsh Hawks, Winter Falcons, Hermit Thrushes, Canada Geese, Bluebirds – and shot many in order to draw them.

Towards the end of February 1821 he was temporarily distracted by a mysterious and erotic commission. A beautiful, sophisticated young woman accosted him in the street and invited him – almost ordered him

— to come round to her house and draw her naked; a task which he performed during hour-long sessions over the next nine days. His journal for 21 February recorded only that he 'met with one of those slightly discouraging incidents connected with the life of artists,' and it was not until the middle of May that he set down a full account of the highly charged episode: even then, he evidently felt that the story was too hot to remain where it was, and he tore out twelve and a half pages.

By his own account, Audubon never laid a finger on his demanding model, but their relationship became intense and intimate, especially when she insisted on adding a few touches to his portrait, 'because she liked mingling her talents with mine'. Only when the job was done and the sitter was satisfied, did she make any physical contact: 'Taking me by the hand, she gave me a delightful kiss … I begged leave to kiss her hand. She extended it freely. We parted, probably for ever.' Instead of payment, he accepted a good new gun on which he had the maker inscribe a grateful message from his benefactor: *'Ne refuse pas ce don d'une amie qui t'est reconnaissante, puisse qu'il t'égaler en bonté.'* (Do not refuse this gift from a friend who is beholden to thee. May it equal thyself in goodness.)

News of these encounters — which he dutifully passed on — naturally did not please Lucy who was still in Cincinnati, and as the summer wore on, relations between the two deteriorated. She was earning some money of her own by teaching, but, irritated by his failure to bring in a reliable income, she complained about lack of funds, and went so far as to say that she did not wish to see him again until he had some positive achievement to report.

'I am very sorry that thou are so intent on my not returning to thee,' he wrote in his hurt reply. 'Your great desire that I should stay away is, I must acknowledge, very unexpected.' In a reference to his idea of going to England, he went on, 'If you can bear to have me go on a voyage of at least three years without wishing to see me before, I cannot help thinking Lucy would probably be better pleased should I never return — and so it may be.' Before sending the letter, he softened his strictures with a loving postscript, but his tone showed what a low ebb he had reached.

Early in April, to his intense relief, he recovered his lost portfolio. A crewman from a north-bound steamboat had stopped at Natchez-under-the-Hill, searched through the slums on the river bank, found the bundle of pictures and taken it to the office of the local newspaper, whence it was forwarded to New Orleans. Miraculously, only one painting was missing

Trade in New Orleans remained so poor that at the beginning of June Audubon decided to head back to Shippingport. By chance, on board the steamer *Columbus* was Mrs James Pirrie, whose husband owned Oakley, a large cotton plantation five miles from St Francisville, on the hill above Bayou Sara. So favourable was the impression that Audubon made on his new friend that she hired him to teach her fifteen-year-old daughter Eliza drawing at the rate of $60 dollars a month (he had demanded $100) with the special dispensation that half his time should be free for hunting and drawing his own pictures.

For four months that summer he and Mason lived with the Scottish Pirries at Oakley. For the woodsman-artist, the forests of magnolia, oak, beech and poplar, alive with birds, were paradise; falling in love with that fine, wild country with its hills and red clay soil rising above the alluvial plain of the Mississippi, he came to think of Louisiana as in some way his own state, almost believing he had been born there.

Having arrived in June 1821, he worked furiously at his pictures, producing many of the originals from which his plates were later engraved, while Mason painted local plants and trees for the backgrounds. One of the most striking images from this time was his painting of the Barred Owl, which he showed poised on a sloping branch with wings extended and beak gaping as it menaces a squirrel (see page 20). By giving the bird this animated posture, he was able to show the pattern of its rounded wings which, with their softly rayed feather edges, form part of its armament, enabling it to fly in silence, and so helping to make it a lethal predator. (He drew the squirrel separately, on 22 July 1821 in Louisiana, and later incorporated it into the picture for the engraving made in London.) Audubon rarely showed any favouritism in his enthusiasm for the feathered tribes – he admired them all. Yet he did have a special liking for owls, and Barred Owls in particular:

> I have observed that the approach of a squirrel intimidated them if one of these animals accidentally jumped on to a branch close to them, although the owl destroys a number of them during the twilight. It is for this reason that I have represented the Barred Owl gazing in amazement at one of the squirrels placed only a few inches from him.
>
> How often have I seen this nocturnal marauder alight within a few yards of me, expose his whole body to the glare of my fire, and eye me in such a curious manner that, had it been reasonable to do so, I would gladly have invited him to walk in and join me in my repast, that I might have enjoyed the pleasure of forming a better acquaintance with him. The liveliness of his motions, joined to their oddness, have often made me think that his society would be at least as agreeable as that of many of the buffoons we meet with in the world.

On 25 August 1821 Audubon finished a splendidly vibrant picture of a rattlesnake, coiled round the stem of a tree, attacking a nest of young mocking-birds amid jasmine flowers, while the parents scream defiance at the intruder. This drawing later proved among the most controversial and troublesome of all, for other naturalists claimed that rattlesnakes never climbed trees, and sought to show that Audubon was not only ignorant, but positively dishonest.

Profitable though it was in terms of birds portrayed, his stay at Oakley was far from easy, for James Pirrie, though 'truly a good man' when sober, was liable to degenerate into 'a state of intoxication,' during which he exhibited 'all the madman's actions ... under its paroxysm' and his wife sometimes gave way 'to the whole force of her violent passions'. Nor did Audubon much care for his pupil Eliza, 'of a good form of body, not handsome of face, proud of her wealth and of herself, cannot well be too much fed on praise – and God knows how hard I tried to please her in vain.'

He remained with the Pirries until 21 October, but after a series of rows, mainly about money, had to depart ignominiously. His departure was accelerated by the enmity of the young doctor who was treating

facing page 13

TROUBLE IN
THE MAKING

Among the most controversial of Audubon's paintings was his picture of a rattle-snake attacking a nest of Mocking Birds (*Mimus polyglottos*). Rival naturalists claimed that rattlers never climbed trees, and that the artist had invented the whole episode.

PLATE 21.

The Mocking Bird. 1. Male. 2. F.
TURDUS POLYGLOTTUS.

Plant Vulgo. Yellow Jessamin.

Rattlesnake.
CROTALUS HORRIDUS.

Drawn and Published by John J. Audubon, F.R.S.E. M.W.S.

Engraved, Printed and Coloured by R.Havell & Son, London.

Eliza for a recurrent fever. The physician, who was in love with his patient, resented the presence of a good-looking artist, and created such difficulties that his pupil was allowed to learn drawing only at certain times and under close supervision. The atmosphere became so strained that, when he looked back, Audubon could not remember once laughing in her presence.

He therefore returned to New Orleans, where he found enough new pupils to keep himself going, and to send some money to Lucy, who was still teaching in Cincinnati. By then he had realised all too clearly that his most formidable competition was the pioneering work done by Alexander Wilson. The diminutive Scot had been dead for eight years, but his *American Ornithology* had won wide renown, and his cause was being vigorously promoted by George Ord. Audubon had difficulty obtaining any of the volumes because they were scarce and expensive, and he knew that criticism of the contents would stir up trouble – but in his journal for 20 October he wrote:

> The great many errors I found in the work of Wilson astonished me. I tried to speak of them with care, and as seldom as possible, knowing the good wish of that man, [and] the hurry he was in and the vast many hearsay accounts he depended on.

Every day Audobon was extending his own knowledge, shooting birds, drawing them, recording minutely detailed observations in his notebook and journal – as of the Brown Pelican on 7 November 1821:

> The upper plumage of the neck assuming a silky appearance and much worn by resting on the back and shoulders of the bird. Shoulders and back covered with pointed small feathers, light ash in their centers edged with rufous and some with brown – the latter silvery in the center edge, with deep black to the rump ... The tail rounded, composed of 18 feathers quills, black shaded silvery ash. The wings extended measured 7 ½ feet, the second joint 9 inches closing on the body reaching to the beginning of the neck.

By the autumn of 1821 he had been separated from his family for more than a year, and he had no small difficulty in persuading Lucy to leave her friends and job, to join him in the south. In New Orleans, early on the morning of 11 November, he suddenly heard that she was about to depart from Louisville on a small steamboat, on her way to join him. 'This news,' he wrote, 'kept me nearly wild all day. Yet no boat arrived. No wife no friend yet near.' Five weeks passed, punctuated by many false reports of sailings, before Lucy and the two boys appeared, all in good health, on 18 December – and when they did, his relief and joy knew no bounds: 'After 14 months' absence the meeting of all that renders life agreeable to me was gratefully welcomed, and I thanked my Maker for this mark of mercy.'

Somehow they scraped through the winter in New Orleans, so poor that Audubon stopped writing his journal because he could not afford $1.25 for a new notebook. Throughout that hard time and the years of haphazard research that followed, Lucy remained his rock. A wife less devoted, or of less strong character, might well have lost patience and cast him off. Not she; never wavering in her belief that his genius would one day be recognised, she forgave all his failings and provided the moral and financial support without which he could not have achieved his aim. While he scoured the wilderness, she worked as a teacher – head of a private school or governess in a well-to-do household – and earned enough to keep the family going. Audubon also taught – drawing, music and French – and somehow they kept afloat.

Lucy's character is not easy to discern. Clearly she was intelligent, efficient and independent-minded – but perhaps she lacked warmth. In one of the few surviving portraits, made in 1835, she looks every inch the school marm, with her hard, uncompromising stare and firm mouth. When Audubon reached England, his constant refrain was that he would not dream of bringing her over until he could provide her with the standard of living to which she was accustomed. What, then, did she demand in the way of accommodation? Earlier, she had buckled down to the primitive facilities at the Indian Queen in Louisville, but as she grew older, she seems to have become less flexible.

There is no doubt that Audubon loved her, nor any doubt that during their long separations he missed her severely. His letters to her were full of endearments – often embarrassingly fulsome – but for months after their despatch he had no means of telling whether or not they had reached their destination, and he was much downcast when he received no reply.

In the spring of 1822 he returned to Natchez where he landed a job teaching in a school, and after some initial reluctance and delay, Lucy followed him. She too found a job, as governess to a minister's children; the boys were at school and for once the family enjoyed a period of relative stability. But during the summer Audubon suffered a serious blow with the loss of Joseph Mason, who for the best part of two years had worked diligently to create backgrounds for the bird portraits, skilfully filling in trees, leaves and flowers. 'We experienced great pain at parting,' Audubon wrote, and when the boy decided to go off on his own, he gave him 'paper and chalks to work his way with, and the double-barrelled gun'. As if to compensate for this loss, there arrived in Natchez a travelling portrait-painter called John Stein who began teaching Audubon to paint in oils – a skill which earned him badly needed funds when he came to England.

Early in 1823 Lucy established a school known as Beechwoods on a prosperous cotton plantation belonging to the Percy family, some fifteen miles from St Francisville, and there she remained for the next five years, teaching her younger son John among the other pupils. Perhaps it was the security which this job offered that encouraged Audubon to write:

> I had finally determined to break through all bonds and follow my ornithological pursuits. My best friends solemnly regarded me as a madman, and my wife and family alone gave me encouragement. My wife determined that my genius should prevail, and that my final success as an ornithologist should be triumphant.

For the time being he continued to drift about: along with Stein he bought a horse and wagon, and taking his elder son Victor with them, began touring the southern states, trying to make money as portrait painters. This venture quickly failed and Audubon spent the summer of 1823 at Beechwoods, teaching the young ladies drawing and music – until he quarrelled with Mrs Percy, whereupon he went back to Natchez taking Victor with him. There in the autumn father and son both fell ill with yellow fever, from which Lucy nursed them back to health, and when he had recovered he set off for Kentucky by boat, again taking Victor with him. When low water grounded them at Trinity, Victor, aged fourteen, suggested they should walk the rest of the way to Shippingport, Kentucky – some 250 miles. Their two companions, both grown men, were convinced that the boy would not last the course, but in the end it was they who gave up on the seventh morning of the marathon, leaving father and son to carry on alone.

Audubon spent the winter of 1823–24 in Shippingport, but already his sights were set on Philadelphia; even though his portfolio of birds was far from complete, he hoped there to find a sponsor who at least would help him start to publish his pictures.

As always, his resilience was remarkable. Sensitive as he was, and wounded by repeated failure, he always bounced back. Later his grand-daughter Maria wrote that 'even to the end he kept the freshness of childhood; he was one of those who had the secret of youth; he was old in years only, his heart was young. The earth was fair; plants still bloomed, and birds still sang for him.'

Nevertheless, ornithology at that date was a fiercely competitive activity which bred high passions among its practitioners. The bird-men vied with each other in discovering and describing new species – and when a novelty did turn up, its finder enjoyed the pleasure of naming it, often after a friend or benefactor. As Audubon soon discovered, he was moving into a hostile environment.

Having left Victor to work as a clerk in the Berthoud counting house in Shippingport, he reached Philadelphia on 5 April 1824. With its hand-some public buildings, its streets set out in a regular grid pattern, its brick houses and brick-laid sidewalks shaded by wide awnings, the city was already a Mecca for artists and men of science. Until 1800, when the seat of government was moved to Washington, it had been the capital of the United States – and in the 1820s it was still very much the Quaker capital; religious observance was so strict that on Sundays chains were slung across the streets to stop horses and carriages passing.

Audubon's visit proved both disastrous and invaluable; a disaster, in that he was met with critical hostility from friends and allies of the late Alexander Wilson, but an incalculable benefit, in that his work was not published locally in some second-rate form, and that his energy was not siphoned off into projects unworthy of his originality.

His most rewarding new contact was young Charles Lucien Bonaparte, Prince of Canino and Musignano, a nephew of the Emperor Napoleon and also of Joseph Bonaparte, the former King of Spain, who had settled in Philadelpia. Charles was then twenty-one, stocky and dark-eyed, with a strong resemblance to his notorious uncle which he modified to some extent by cultivating a goatee beard. A member of the city's Academy of Natural Sciences, and a rising star among the bird-men, he was working on his own major project, the four-volume *American Ornithology, or the Natural History of the Birds of the United States, Not Given by Wilson*. He was thus a natural successor to Wilson, but endowed with a spirit of generosity markedly lacking in the Scot and his other allies: he was immediately entranced by Audubon's paintings, and hoped that the wandering naturalist might help with his own work – which he did, by giving him much information about the Wild Turkey.

Others, however, saw Audubon as a dangerous rival, and did everything they could to damage his cause. His most determined opponent was Wilson's editor and biographer George Ord, a churlish fellow of about his own age, the immigrant son of an English chandler and rope-maker. Ord was a curious character. A man of some means, he was well-known in Philadelphia, and delighted friends with his sparkling conversation; yet he was shy and awkward with strangers and could fly into towering rages. Perhaps because he himself lacked any creative spark, he had latched on to Wilson's work and reputation and set himself up as their guardian.

Goaded by jealousy and the threat to Wilson's supremacy that the boastful newcomer represented, Ord became an implacable enemy; he detested Audubon on sight and launched a long campaign of denigration by black-balling him when Bonaparte put him up for membership of the Philadelphia Academy of Natural Sciences. Siding with Ord was Alexander Lawson, the engraver who had taught Wilson to draw birds and now was making plates for the later editions of his work.

Ord criticised Audubon's habit of including leaves and flowers as background in his paintings, and Lawson told a friend that the pictures were 'ill-drawn, not true to nature, and anatomically incorrect'. When Bonaparte stood up for them and said he would be happy to buy them, the garrulous Scot replied scornfully, 'You may buy them, but I will not engrave them ... because ornithology requires truth in the forms and correctness in the lines. Here are neither.'

Other local naturalists joined the fray. The French artist Charles-Alexandre Leseur saw the originality in Audubon's paintings and suggested that France might be the best place to have them published. The Quaker doctor and zoologist Richard Harlan also stood up for the woodsman. But his most congenial new acquaintance was Edward Harris, a young land-owner with a strong interest in natural history who bred horses and lived a civilised life of leisure. Not only did Harris buy all the pictures that Audubon wanted to sell, he also pressed on him an extra $100 bill, saying, 'Men like you ought not to want for money.' In return, the artist gave him all his pictures of French birds, and thereafter Harris rendered unstinting help, sending him rare specimens and accompanying him on research expeditions. Years later Audubon looked back on the start of their friendship with heartfelt gratitude. 'I would have kissed him,' he wrote, 'but that it is not the custom in this icy city.'

> When I publish my life, and let the world know that Audubon like Wilson was at Philadelphia without the half of a dollar, and that had it not been for benevolent generosity of a certain gentleman whose name is Edward Harris, Audubon must have walked off from one of the fairest of our cities like a beggar does in poor Ireland ... my dear Harris, will not the world stare!

Another valuable friend in Philadelphia was the portrait painter Thomas Sully, who gave Audubon lessons in oil painting. Born in Lincolnshire and brought out to America by his theatrical family as a boy, Sully had himself been through a struggle for recognition very much like the one in which the naturalist was engaged. But his portrait of John Quincy Adams, done in 1824, a year before Adams became president, had established him among the country's leading artists. Like Harris, he saw that Audubon had immense talent and urged him to develop it, predicting that he would eventually triumph.

For the time being, however, all was acrimony – not least when Joseph Mason, who was working at some gardens outside Philadelphia, came in to call on his former master. When the young man asked to see the pictures on which they had worked together, he was disconcerted to find that Audubon had signed the paintings in ink, but that his own signature had been either erased or left in faint pencil. Obviously, the bird-man intended to claim all the credit. Mason demanded that his name, also, should have a clear showing, but his requests were brushed aside, leaving him furious.

Whatever it was that drove Audubon to such selfishness – perhaps simply the fact that after years of failure he was desperate for recognition – he made a dangerous mistake; for Mason, living in Philadelphia, was able to pass damaging information to Ord and his cronies, confirming that Audubon claimed to have done work which in fact had been executed by another artist, and so was to some extent a fraud.

After exhibiting his drawings for a week and finding that the show did not pay, Audubon left Philadelphia in disgust at the end of July. He was chagrined by the hostility he had met, and persuaded by the advice of his friends that he must go to Europe to find a publisher capable of doing justice to his work.

From Philadelphia he went to New York, which he described in a letter to Sully as 'now an immense city'. Huge it was, but many of the people who might have helped him had fled the August heat and none of the publishers he met showed interest in his project; they may well have been put off by poisonous whispers sent ahead by Ord and Lawson. A letter of recommendation from Sully, praising his work most generously, arrived too late to be of avail. His one success was at the New York Lyceum, where he exhibited his pictures and gave a talk on the migration of swallows. This went down so well that the members ordered the lecture published, and the paper became Audubon's first writing to appear in print.

He found some solace in watching the ocean-going ships, 'tossing over the foaming billows with the grace of the wild swan,' but soon he was off again on his wanderings, this time to paint the Niagara Falls. Wherever he went, he was haunted by dreams of success: at Niagara, after eating a good dinner for twelve cents, he went to bed:

> Thinking of Franklin eating his roll in the streets of Philadelphia, of Goldsmith travelling by the aid of his musical powers, and of other great men who had worked their way through hardships and difficulties to fame, and fell asleep, hoping, by persevering industry, to make a name for himself among his countrymen.[3]

As he made his erratic way back towards Lucy at Beechwoods, he had to borrow $15 for a passage on a boat bound for Louisville, and even then he had to sleep on deck on a pile of shavings. He claimed he was not ashamed of the fact that he had no money, or, as yet, success. He arrived at Beechwoods 'with rent and wasted clothes, and uncut hair, and looking altogether like the wandering Jew,' to find that in his absence the little school had prospered and Lucy had accumulated a useful amount of money. Having re-established good relations with Mrs Percy, he settled down for the whole of 1825 to teach drawing, music, French, fencing and dancing. His fame as a dancing-master spread, and soon he was teaching the villagers of Woodville, fifteen miles away. By spring he had earned about $2000, and felt able to set off on his transatlantic quest.

Throughout all his vicissitudes, he had steadily developed his artistic - abilities, using a variety of techniques to make his birds seem three-

3. The statesman Benjamin Franklin, born in Boston in 1706, went to Philadelphia in 1723 and worked as a printer. Oliver Goldsmith, the poet and dramatist, was educated at Trinity College, Dublin, and after studying medicine at the universities of Edinburgh and Leiden wandered through Europe, playing the flute and begging.

dimensional, with the textures of feathers, feet, beaks and eyes as true to life as possible. He seems generally to have started a picture with an out-line drawn in graphite (pencil), and then to have painted over it with watercolour, oil, pastel, chalk or gouache, sometimes scraping away colour to make white lines and highlights, or applying natural gum or gelatin to increase depth of colour and gloss. Often he used several different techniques and materials in the same work; for instance, in his picture of the Bald Eagle, which he painted in 1820, the head and claws of the eagle are done in watercolour, but the landscape and the rest of the bird are pastel (which is applied from sticks). To achieve his most intense colours, he applied layer after layer of watercolour, with the result that the pigments, instead of fading, as most watercolours do, have survived almost unchanged.

Highly skilled though he had become, the spectre of financial ruin would not leave him. He may have hoped that at some stage he would receive legacies from his father and step-mother, but in the event he got nothing. He did not know for some time that his father had died at Nantes in 1818, and extraordinarily, it seems that he did not learn of his step-mother Anne's death in October 1821 at the age of 92, for at least five years after the event.

So it was that he took his tremendous gamble. On 26 April 1826 he said goodbye to his family at Beechwoods, caught a steamboat for New Orleans, which he reached next day, and there contracted to sail for Liverpool in the cotton ship *Delos*, with captain Joseph Hatch. But when he found that the vessel was not going to leave for a week, he returned up the Mississippi, landed at Bayou Sara, borrowed a horse and rode through the dark woods, reaching home at three in the morning. His sudden arrival surprised Lucy, but, as he wrote in his journal, 'the moments spent afterwards full repaid me'. He stayed with his family for two more nights, then dropped back down the river on his way to the Old World.

Chapter Three
LIONISED

MANY FACETS of Audubon's character and behaviour can be inferred from his own writing. A devout Quaker, he said his prayers out loud every night, kneeling beside his bed, and firmly believed that the natural world, along with all its creatures, had been created by the Almighty. He once wrote that whenever he set eyes on a Red Indian, he felt 'the greatness of our Creator in all its splendour, for there I see a man naked from his hand and yet free from acquired sorrow'. His admiration of nature, in all its forms, was unbounded, and he was haunted by the fear that mankind had already begun to destroy the environment.

He was vain about his looks, especially his hair, his profile and long, straight nose, but he was racked by doubts about his competence as an artist and his lack of formal education. He was ambidextrous, usually writing with his right hand in a small, neat, strongly sloped italic script, but able to use his left nearly as well, and extending the lines to the very edges of the page. He disliked heights and suffered from vertigo.

He was clearly a good trencherman, and enjoyed his food; breakfast was particularly important to him – no doubt because his habit of walking for miles at dawn sharpened his appetite in the morning. It is a pity that he so rarely gives details of what he ate in England and Scotland; one breakfast, of which he thought nothing, included beefsteak, tea, toast and buttered bread, another (which he commended) mutton, ham and good coffee. He also recorded that once, lunching on his own, he had herrings, mutton chops, cabbage and fritters, and for another solitary meal 'fried oysters and vinegar and Scotch herrings'; but usually he refers simply to enormous meals with many courses. No matter what delicacies were put before him in great houses, he hankered after the roasted eggs of the soft-shell turtle which he had put away on the banks of Thompson Creek, and the 'well roasted and jellied venison' which he had eaten in Kentucky, to the accompaniment of wolves howling.

Before he arrived in England he had generally avoided alcohol, but soon he succumbed to the blandishments of his hosts, and was drinking wine with the best of them. When he walked about, in towns or in the country, he carried a swagger cane that concealed a small sword. As for his clothes – at first he deliberately sought to attract attention by cultivating a strange appearance, but within a few months he had taken to shaving every day and wearing black silk stockings.

In spite of his lack of schooling, he had a good knowledge of literature. Partly because, at home, Lucy had often read to him in the evenings, he was familiar with stories from Greek and Roman myths; he also knew some of Shakespeare's plays, the romances of Sir Walter Scott, the poems of Lord Byron and the novels of James Fenimore Cooper. He was fond of music, played the flute well, and was endowed with unquenchable energy. He dreaded having nothing to do, and once, during a period of enforced inactivity, wrote in his journal: 'Fatigued of being idle, so powerful are habits of all kinds that to spend a month thus would render me sick of life.' In all his writing – letters, journals, books – he never resorted to swear-words, even when severely provoked, still less to obscenities. Nor did his language ever become scatological. His most extreme exclamation was 'Fudge!', borrowed from Mr Burchell, one of the principal characters in Oliver Goldsmith's *The Vicar of Wakefield*.

By sheer chance Audubon came to England at a time when interest in ornithology was growing rapidly, and several outstanding bird artists were at work. Chief among the native practitioners was Prideaux John Selby, the owner of a substantial estate based on Twizell House in Northumberland. A genial, likeable fellow, not given to jealousy, Selby was working with a dashing young Scottish baronet, Sir William Jardine, already well known as a naturalist, on a large-scale publication entitled

Illustrations of British Ornithology. In the south, the precocious John Gould, at only twenty-three, was already an accomplished taxidermist, and was about to be appointed the first Curator and Preserver of Specimens at the newly formed Zoological Society of London. Another budding bird artist, the melancholic Edward Lear, was still in his teens, yet already drawing birds and animals with exceptional delicacy.

The study of birds was by no means new in England, but after the pioneering work of Willoughby and Ray, who, in 1676 produced their *Ornithologia*, it had lapsed for much of the eighteenth century. Gilbert White's immortal *The Natural History of Selborne* first came out in 1769, but that was essentially the work of a gifted amateur, and no specialist observer appeared until the emergence of the master wood-engraver Thomas Bewick, whose two-volume *History of British Birds* was published in 1797 and 1804.

The renewal of activity was auspicious for the American visitor, as it had raised general awareness of ornithological illustration. Yet the knowledge that such competition existed inevitably increased Audubon's apprehension. Would he be able to challenge the native practitioners?

The worst frustration of his first days in England came in his failure to meet Lucy's sister Ann, who was married to Alexander Gordon, another cotton broker, whom he had met in New Orleans. Ann's home was in Liverpool, but several times, when Audubon tried to call on her, he was told that she was out and when he did finally run her to ground, she seemed by no means thrilled to see him. His journal entry about the meeting was edgy and odd:

> I saw and kissed thy sister Ann Gordon. I kissed her, I thought, more than she wished; at all events, she did not kiss me ... However, she became more sensible that I was yet Audubon; perhaps, too, recollected that I never injured her; perhaps indeed she might have recollected that I always loved her as my sister. Whatever might be her present reasons, she returned to old times with more familiarity than I expected. She talked a good deal ... I thought ... she had acquired a great deal of the Scotch stiffness.

Chez Rathbone, in contrast, he felt so secure that one evening, to ease his homesickness, he began to read out extracts from his journal. The performance raised his emotions to such a pitch that he recorded the scene in the historic present:

> I am astounded. Mr Richard Rathbone, who was reposing on a sofa, has approached the table. All are listening to me. My eyes are burning. They conceive the situation of my heart! But, Dearest Friend, they call my tottering essays, at giving thee the thoughts that act upon my absence from thee, quite agreeable to them. I am not now so much choked. I drink, and I read on – perhaps half a dozen of my days.

How much did he tell his solicitous hosts about his own background? He must surely have described his life-long obsession with birds and given some account of his endless hunting in the woods of Kentucky and Louisiana, his forays with Red Indians, his ability to speak the language of the Osage tribe, his prodigious feats of perambulation. Certainly to the Rathbones 'there was a halo of romance about Mr Audubon', with his 'amiable character ... tinged with melancholy by past sufferings and beautiful, expressive face'.

But did he have the sense to withhold details that might have made people wonder about him? Did he describe how he had revelled in massacres of bison and swans? Did he confess that as a young man he had been 'ridiculously fond of dress', and had gone shooting in black satin breeches, silk stockings and the finest ruffled shirts that money could buy? Perhaps he realised that this sort of revelation might have undermined his attempt to create the impression of a serious artist.

The truth was that he was on the run from failure. 'Remember that I have done nothing, and fear that I may die unknown,' he had written two years earlier. 'I feel I am strange to all but the birds of America. In a few days I shall be in the woods and quite forgotten.'

His best ambassadors were the drawings themselves, which he carried about in a huge portfolio, weighing nearly a hundred pounds, slung over his shoulder. One early contact, introduced by the Rathbone family, was the entomologist André Melly, often referred to by Audubon as 'the intelligent Swiss,' who made himself very useful on the artist's behalf (and later married William V's sister-in-law, Ellen Greg). A still more valuable ally was the veteran author William Roscoe, well known as an historian and poet, and a leading patron of the arts in Liverpool, with several books, including *Lorenzo de Medici* and *Leo the Tenth*, to his name. The Rathbones had backed him in his campaigns for the abolition of slavery and for the establishment of reading rooms and a botanical garden for the people of Liverpool. They had also rescued him from financial disaster when his bank failed — for, as a friend remarked, although a fine writer, 'he was a very bad banker'. Now he was able to return their favours by supporting their new friend. Audubon described him as 'tall, with a good eye under a good eyebrow, all mildness . . . one of those come-at-able persons that are just what is necessary for me to have to talk to'.

Having declared himself 'filled with surprise and admiration' by the bird pictures, Roscoe performed the priceless service of introducing Audubon to F.J. Martin, Secretary of the Royal Institution of Liverpool, who arranged for the drawings to be exhibited for two hours on the mornings of Monday, Tuesday and Wednesday following.[1]

This was the move that set Audubon's carriage rolling. He spent the morning of 31 July pinning out his 250 drawings on a purple background, and when the doors were opened at midday, 'the ladies flocked in'. Word of the extraordinary exhibition — like nothing the intelligentsia of Liverpool had seen before — spread so fast that on the next day 413 people came to see the pictures. 'I broke down bowing and scraping to all the new faces I was introduced to,' Audubon reported. 'It was, in a word, a business to bow.'

The paintings were so big, so bold and so blazingly coloured, so full of energy and violence, that they caused a sensation. Until then birds had been portrayed in static poses, usually in profile; but here were

---

1. The Institution had opened in 1817 to promote literature, science and the arts — one of several such bodies created early in the nineteenth century by leading industrialists, merchants, bankers and so on, for the 'advancement of knowledge' in provincial centres which lacked a university.

birds twisting in flight, birds climbing, diving, screeching, birds fighting; owls, herons, falcons and eagles all the size of life, seizing prey or ripping their victims apart.

The artist's fame travelled so fast that on the third day 'persons of wealth' came from Manchester — a journey of several hours by coach — to see the show. Several 'gentlemen attached to the Institution' told him that he should charge for admission, and although at first he baulked at the idea, because the room had been given him free, in due course he came round to it and, rather against his better instincts, inserted a notice in local newspapers. To make him feel easier, the Committee positively asked him to make a charge — whereupon he wrote: 'This request must and will, I am sure, take off any discredit attached to the tormenting feeling of showing my work for money.' On the first ticket-only day 164 persons were admitted, and in the end he cleared £100.

Less than a fortnight after arriving in England, he had become the darling of Liverpool society, constantly entertained by the Rathbones, the Roscoes and sundry other 'persons of distinction,' among them Dr Thomas Traill, the scientist and editor of the eighth edition of *Encyclopaedia Britannica*. Audubon was a rewarding guest, a lively raconteur who sang for his supper not only by talking about America and telling stories of his time in the woods, but also by playing the flute, making quick portrait sketches and causing ladies to clutch at their throats with his imitations of the Barred Owl hooting and his Red Indian war cries.

His hosts can have had scarcely an inkling of the difference between their own comfortable, sophisticated surroundings and the world from which their visitor had come — but startling glimpses of it appeared in *Domestic Manners of the Americans*, the best-selling account by Frances Trollope (mother of the novelist Anthony) published in 1832. The fastidious Frances crossed the Atlantic in 1828, and when she went up the Mississippi on a steamboat, she was horrified by the habits of her fellow travellers, particularly in the dining-room:

> The total want of all the usual courtesies of the table, the voracious rapidity with which the viands were seized and devoured, the strange uncouth

> phrases and pronunciation; the loathsome spitting, from the contamination
> of which it was absolutely impossible to protect our dresses; the frightful
> manner of cleaning the teeth afterwards with the pocket-knife ... we never
> tarried there a moment longer than was absolutely necessary to eat.

Such were the habits of the mess-mates to whom Audubon was accustomed – and now he was being waited on by liveried footmen.

Several of his contacts suggested that he should meet Lord Stanley (later the 13th Earl of Derby), a Member of Parliament and a passionate naturalist, whose palatial home of Knowsley Hall lay in a fine park, encircled by a wall, just beyond the outskirts of the city. The prospect of coming face to face with a nobleman threw Audubon into a fever of anxiety. 'I am a very poor fool, to be sure, to be troubled and disturbed in mind at the idea of meeting an English gentleman, called, moreover, a lord,' he wrote. 'But that confounded feeling is too deeply rooted ever to be extricated from my nature.' When the encounter finally came about, at the home of his new friends, the Hodgsons:

> I have not the least doubt that if my head had been looked at, it would have
> been thought the body, globularly closed, of one of our largest porcupines.
> All my hair (and I have enough) stood straight on end.

In spite of the artist's apprehension, his fears were quickly soothed. Stanley, who himself painted birds, went down on his knees to look at the drawings spread out on the floor, and, although praising them highly, pointed out a fault. This pleased the artist, as he saw that Stanley's interest was genuine, and he was delighted to receive an invitation to 'call on him in Grosvenor Street in town (thus he refers to London)'. After shaking hands again, Stanley mounted an elegant hunter and 'moved off at the rate of twelve miles an hour'. The artist joyfully reported to Lucy that the noble lord had called his work 'unique', and said that it deserved the patronage of the Crown.

Never before had people made so much of Audubon. Although still cursing his own shyness, and wishing that he had been 'flogged out of this miserable way of feeling and acting when young', by 6 August, with a touch of incredulity, he was writing:

I am well received wherever I am known. Every object known to me smiles as I meet it, and my poor heart is at least relieved [of] the great anxiety that has for so many years agitated it, [by the feeling that] I have not worked altogether in vain.

In a letter to Lucy dated 7 August he took up the same theme:

I have many comfortable nights at gentlemen's seats in the neighbourhood, and the style of living is beyond all description. Coaches call for me, and waiters in livery are obedient to me as if I myself was a lord of England ... If I was not dreading to become proud, I would say that I am, in Liverpool, a shadow of Lafayette and his welcome in America.[2]

Not that he entirely enjoyed the continuous entertainment which the society hostesses offered him. He claimed that until he got married (in 1808) he had:

lived on milk, fruits and vegetables, with the addition of game or fish at times, but never had I swallowed a single glass of wine or spirits ... The result has been my uncommon, nay iron, constitution ... Pies, puddings, eggs, milk or cream was all I cared for in the way of food ... I was fair and as rosy as a girl, though as strong, indeed stronger, than most young men, and active as a buck.

Now in England politeness was forcing him to eat one heavy meal after another, and to sit up half the night drinking. At first he tried to preserve his teetotal habits, but gradually he succumbed to the pressure of relentless hospitality, and after a while he was drinking alcohol with enthusiasm. 'It is a singular thing,' he remarked, 'that in England dinner, dessert, wines and tea-drinking follow each other so quickly that if we did not remove to another room to partake of the last, it would be a constant repast.' As far as possible he avoided meat, except for game, and one night at Greenbank he amused his neighbour at dinner, Lady Isabella Douglas, by eating some tomatoes raw: 'Neither she nor any of the

---

2. Marie Joseph Paul Lafayette, reforming French politician and general, was a hero in the American War of Independence (1777–82), distinguishing himself in several campaigns, especially at Brandywine in September 1777, when troops under George Washington tried to stop the British advance on Philadelphia, and during the defence of Virginia in 1781 and the battle of Yorktown in 1782.

company had ever seen them on the table without being cooked.' His remedy for excessive consumption was robust: to get up at or before dawn and walk hard for several hours. Staying with the Hodgsons, he reported:

> I arose to listen to the voice of an English blackbird, perhaps just as the day broke. It was a little after three of the morning. I dressed, and silently as in my power, carrying my boots in one hand and the house key in another, I moved down the stairs and out of the cottage, and pushed off toward the fields and meadows. I walked a good deal — went to the sea-shore, saw a hare, and returned to breakfast.

A few days later, on a beautiful morning, he was again out at daybreak, this time in the middle of the city. 'The watchmen have, however, ceased to look upon me with suspicion, and think, perhaps, I am a harmless lunatic.' Goaded by his habitual need to work, he bought watercolours and brushes and started painting local birds: one study of a pair of flycatchers he presented to the elder Mrs Rathbone.

Several times as he walked across fields outside Liverpool he was dismayed to see signs proclaiming, 'Any person trespassing on these grounds will be pursued with all the rigour of the law.' This, he decided, 'must be a mistake ... this cannot be English liberty and freedom.' He was also outraged by the obvious disparity between rich and poor in privilege and standards of living:

> Is it not very shocking that whilst in England all is hospitality within [large houses], all is aristocratic without? No one dares trespass, as it is called, one foot on the grass. Signs of large dogs are put up [to warn] that further you must not advance. Steel traps and spring guns are set to destroy you, should you prove foolhardy ... Beggars in England are like our ticks of Louisiana: they stick to one, and sting our better feelings every moment. England is now rich with poverty, gaping, aghast, every way you may look.

No amount of hospitality could cure his homesickness. He was yearning not for any particular house — for as an adult he had never stayed in any fixed abode for long; rather, he longed to see his family, and to be back in the land to which he was so attached. The British countryside fell far short of what he was used to, and he was missing the birds, the woods, the wildness of Louisiana. 'I cannot but long with unutterable longing for America,' he wrote.

He was much troubled by the fact that no letter from Lucy had reached him: again and again he went to the post office in vain, and one night he had a sudden, horrible vision of her 'covered in such an attire as completely destroyed all my powers.' It seems that he saw her in grave clothes, and the terror which seized him was so chilling that he was stupefied for a full hour. 'Oh do write,' he besought her, 'or I will not be able to write at all.'

For some time the compilation of his journal was the only means he had of relieving his feelings. Entries became very long – he often wrote 1500 or 2000 words each night – and veered from facetious, high-spirited jokes and reports on English life to the gloomiest expressions of despair ('the winds impart dismal tokens in their howlings'). Some of the entries were not exactly tactful: what would Lucy, thousands of miles away, have made of this?

> A neat young girl stopped me in the middle of a principal street and delivered a paper to me of a most extraordinary nature. I cannot, really, mention its contents to thee … My dear wife, the number of abandoned and daring prostitutes is wonderful. What a world! Good God! Good night: half past one.

Undeterred by the possibility that such remarks might cause alarm 4000 miles away, he had retained the services of a copier, to make a second version of the journal as it went along, and he sent it off to Lucy via the brig *Isabella*, bound for New Orleans.

On the afternoon of 17 August, he began to paint a picture of an otter caught in a trap, which he planned to present to Richard's wife, Hannah Mary II, herself an accomplished artist. The resumption of creative activity evidently absorbed much of his intellectual energy, and for the next few days his diary entries became much shorter. He finished the picture on 21 August, and presented it, along with a flowery letter of thanks for all the kindness he had received. He had first painted the subject in

14

OTTER
CAUGHT
IN A TRAP

This oil painting,
done in 1826, did
not find favour
with its intended
recipient, Mrs
Richard Rathbone,
whose husband
presented it to the
Royal Institution
in Liverpool.

watercolour nearly fifteen years earlier, and he was so pleased with it that he later painted at least six more versions in oil.

On about 20 August he moved out to Greenbank – invited not merely for a night or two, but to stay as long as he wanted. Much as he loved being there, he was dismayed to find that Hannah Mary disliked his otter from the start: although she accepted it politely, she hated seeing the animal with its claw clamped in the jaws of the trap, and in due course her husband gave the painting to the Royal Institution.

On 1 September, in a letter to Lucy, Audubon described some of his more admirable discoveries:

> Victor [their elder son, then fifteen] would have profited by this voyage immensely. The young gentlemen here have a superiority of education that bears no parallel with our young countrymen. The ladies are still more remarkable for their plainness of manners and superior acquirements. All those I have the pleasure of visiting possess the French, Italian and Spanish languages, draw beautifully, are good musicians and as fresh as roses!

Writing to Victor on the same day, Audubon told his son that the proceeds of his exhibition were 'far beyond my expectations, and it seems that I am considered unrivalled in the art of drawing even by the most learned of this country'. His dislikes were remarkably few, his main complaint being of ignorance about America:

> I cannot help expressing my surprise that the people of England, generally speaking, are so unacquainted with the customs and localities of our country. The principal conversation about it always turns to Indians and their ways, as if the land produced nothing else.

In terms of food, shelter and local recognition, he was capitally provided for, and socially he had scored a bull's-eye; but as yet he had no proper plan of action. He had formed a vague idea of trying to 'procure a solid place in one of the Royal Institutions here, as an ornithologist and artist to form a collection of drawings for whoever may employ me' – and this, had it come off, might have given him some breathing-space. But his urgent need was to find somebody able to tackle the huge job of engraving and publishing his paintings, and as the days slipped past his spirits fluctuated wildly between optimism and despair.

Contradictory advice came at him from all sides. The Intelligent Swiss urged him to proceed at once to Paris, rather than waste time in England. Other 'men of learning and excellent judgment' told him to visit Manchester, Birmingham, London and Edinburgh before trying France – and this he decided to do.

So it was that he left Greenbank – 'this enchanted spot' – with a heavy heart. 'It reminds me of parting with my own family again,' he told Lucy. 'When I left America, I did not feel worse.' The day before, he had drawn a small but striking self-portrait in pencil for his beloved Hannah Mary III, apparently at her request: he made the most of his aquiline profile and endorsed the picture, 'Audubon at Greenbank, Almost Happy!! Sepr 1826. Drawn by himself.' It is impossible to tell how much, if any, of his feeling she reciprocated; but when the time came for him to leave – at 8am on 9 September – she insisted on accompanying him into Liverpool. She had first proposed that they should walk into town together,

but because the weather was unsettled, they decided to go by coach.

After breakfast with the 'Intelligent Swiss' at which his head was 'all full of the Rathbones', Audubon fell in with Mr Munro, Curator of the Royal Institution in Liverpool; he paid £1 for two inside seats and set off by coach No 11335 for Manchester. He felt depressed at leaving all the good friends he had made: thinking back over his stay in Liverpool, he feared that he would never be able to express, 'much less hope to repay', his indebtedness to all those who had helped him. Apart from the self-portrait, and the large study of the turkey cock presented to the Royal Institution, Audubon had distributed many smaller drawings to friends 'as mementoes of one who will always cherish their memories'.

The most heart-felt of these gifts went to the unmarried Hannah Mary III – she of the dark eyes – with whom he had become so dangerously infatuated. In the picture of a robin which he gave her, done in pencil, black chalk and watercolour, the subject was perched on a mossy stone, but the model for it was almost certainly the bird which came in to call through the window of Greenbank. On the back of the paper the artist wrote:

> It was my greatest wish to have affixed on the face of this drawing my real thoughts of the amiable lady for whom I made it, in poetry divine! But an injunction from Hannah Rathbone against that wish of my heart has put an end to it – and now I am forced to think only of her benevolence! Of her

15

WOODSMAN IN LOVE

Smitten by admiration for the unmarried Hannah Mary Rathbone, the artist drew this self-portrait in September 1826 and signed it 'Audubon at Greenbank. Almost happy!!' See frontispiece (page 2) for inscription.

filial love! Of her genial affections – her most kind attentions and friendly civilities to all who come to repose under this hospitable roof – to the stranger who must now bid her farewell, who will pray for her, her mother and her friends, and who will be forever her most devoted and obedient humble servant,

John J Audubon.

Thereafter he was bitterly disappointed that – whether out of caution or distaste – she never answered his letters. In 1831 she married William Reynolds, but – perhaps because she was already forty years old – she never had children.

16 facing page

WILD TURKEY
Meleagris gallopavo

Audubon disliked painting in oils, however, he completed numerous studies in the medium, usually to earn immediate cash. The engraving appears on p. 11.

Chapter Four

MANCHESTER

AS THE COACH rolled towards Manchester, Audubon was entertained by the sight of a boy of about twelve who ran beside the vehicle and 'suddenly tumbled five or six times repeatedly, heels over head, exhibiting this feat to procure a few pence'. The artist's companion, Mr Munro, assured him that such lads, if properly rewarded, would take any letter thrown out of a coach and deliver it 'with great security'.

Manchester may have become, in the view of the statesman Benjamin Disraeli, 'a modern Athens', but it depressed Audubon acutely. With its dark, satanic cotton mills clustered along the rivers and canals, which were no more than open sewers, it had established itself as the centre of the English textile industry, the epitome of the Industrial Revolution. On his first night there he reported his position to Lucy as 'thirty-eight miles from Liverpool, and nearly six thousand from thee,' and was long kept awake by the racket in the streets.

Things improved next day, when he delivered his thirteen letters of introduction, and everywhere met 'a most amiable reception'. He also obtained the use of a good room in the Exchange Buildings and had it cleared for his exhibition; but still he was in a mean mood, claiming that much of the day had been

> largely spoiled by one of those uncomfortable busybodies that think of all other persons' affairs in preference to their own ... a dealer in stuffed specimens — and there ends his history. I wished him at Hanover, or in [the] Congo, or New Zealand, or at Bombay, or in a bomb-shell on his route to Eternity.

17 facing page

CANADA
GOOSE
Anser canadensis.
now *Branta canadensis*

The standing male was painted in 1821, then cut out and pasted on to the picture of the female sitting on her nest.

[71]

He hired a man inauspiciously named Crookes, 'well recommended', to take money at the door of the show-room and to copy letters, and rejected the offer of a band from two men who, 'by their noses and large mouths', he thought must be Italian.

> My exhibition being neither Egyptian mummies or deathly looking wax figures, I do not conceive it necessary in the company of so many songsters as I have; and if my songsters will not sing or be agreeable by themselves, other music would only diminish their worth.

Yet the city dismayed him, for it seemed 'a miserably laid out place, and the smokiest I ever was in'.

> I think I ought not to use the words 'laid out' at all. It is composed of an astonishing number of small, dirty, narrow, crooked lanes, where one cart can scarce pass another. It is full of noise and tumult ... The vast number of youth of both sexes, with sallow complexions, ragged apparel and downcast looks, made me feel they were not as happy as the slaves of Louisiana.

At a dinner given by the American Consul, Mr Brookes, he was delighted to be offered a dish of Indian corn, but amazed his fellow guests by the way he tackled it: '[That] I ate it buttered and salted, held by my two hands as if I intended gagging myself with the ear, I took [to be] a matter of much wonder to the English gentlemen, [who] did not even like the vegetable in any way.'

Business proved poor, with few people coming to see the pictures, but the artist's circle of friends continued to expand, and on 16 September his spirits leapt when he received two letters from Lucy, one dated 28 May and one 3 June. News from home, even though more than three months old, relieved his anxieties and encouraged him to pass remarks about his kind but gigantic landlady, Mrs Hedge, whose 'hams, if cured well, would turn out ... extraordinary bacon'.

Writing in answer to Lucy, he could give only a vague outline of his plans. He said he intended to travel through England and Scotland 'very slowly', exhibiting his work, until the beginning of March, when he hoped to reach London 'and there exhibit on a larger scale and for a long time'. If the exhibition brought in less than he needed, he might go to

London sooner, or to Paris, and establish himself 'under the patronage of some person of importance'. As for Lucy, the best thing of all would be for her 'to come over with John only, and travel with me, or remain with me either in London or Paris, where I think I may reside a long time'. The more distant future was still harder to discern. Good as his portfolio of birds was, many species were still missing: he wished he had had two more years in America, hunting and painting, and he knew that, before his great work could be completed, he would have to return.

With Lucy's letter he enclosed a note to 'My Dear Beloved Son, John,' exhorting the lad to improve himself. 'Draw, my dear boy, and study music. You will soon now be able to assist your father very much in rendering our good friend your Mamma quite comfortable. Oh what pleasure you will feel then.'

No wonder he was homesick, and that he told Lucy how his blood 'congealed' at the thought that he might never see her again. Even as he wrote, he knew that he would not see any of the family for months to come, and that he must pursue his quest alone. Only exceptional fortitude and determination kept him going.

That same evening Audubon also composed a very different kind of letter, whose hesitations and sudden changes of direction betrayed the agitation he was feeling:

My dear Miss Hannah,

If Manchester is a dull town of itself, I can now boast that it contains at least one happy individual at present! This morning I had the pleasure and comfort of reading two long letters from my beloved wife ...

I have been longing to write to you ever since I left your delightful Greenbank, but my spirits were low ... My little son John Woodhouse enclosed me from America a couple of small [drawing] essays of his on rice paper. I have taken the liberty to put one in this, with hopes that perhaps you would give it a place in the little red portfolio ... John is only twelve years old, and is my son.

The sun is now set, I see you all at tea, kind to each other as ever you were. I alone am speaking with my pen only. I have just drank a glass of wine to the health and continual happiness of all the inhabitants of Greenbank.

Many, many such will I wish again if a longer life is granted me ...

My letter is composed of different effects of feeling. Please to excuse it. But, between the pleasure of having heard from home and the disagreeable sensation of being thirty-eight miles from you, it would be impossible for me just now to collect one better deserving your attention ...

Believe me, with the sincerest sentiments of highest respect, my dear Miss Rathbone,

Forever your truly obedient servant,
J.J. Audubon.

For the time being, he was still making new friends. On 19 September 1826 he met Samuel Greg, William V's father-in-law, and drove out with him some twelve miles in his carriage to his home, Quarry Bank, 'a most enchanting spot' on the banks of the little River Irwell. There he found an establishment not unlike the one he had left behind at Greenbank – a comfortable country house and a large family, which included two sons and four daughters. As always, he had an eye for the girls, particularly Ellen, whom he found 'so very attractive of looks and manners, and so polite'. The fact that she was deeply enamoured of, if not actually engaged to, André Melly, 'the intelligent Swiss', did not deter him, and he had the sauce to tell Lucy, 'I do not miss a miss, if fair, wherever I go.'

Next morning dawned cloudy and wet, but he rose early and took 'an immense walk, up and down the river, through the gardens, along the ponds, about the woods, the fields and the meadows'. The sight of some partridges made him propose a shooting party, which duly went out in the afternoon, accompanied by Mr Shaw, Lord Stamford's head game-keeper. Although pheasants were not yet in season, a bird was specially shot for Audubon's benefit, as he wanted to draw one, and he was thrilled by the vividness of its plumage: 'Beautiful creature, his eye was yet all life, his crest all crimson, his coat all brilliance.' He much enjoyed the outing, not least because he could see the hills of Derbyshire, Lucy's birthplace; yet, used as he was to the wide open spaces of Louisiana, he felt restricted by the small scale of the English countryside and its many boundaries. He recorded dismissively that every tree of Lord Stamford's 'that we would scarcely call a sapling' was marked and numbered, and that if a partridge crossed the river or any other boundary, to alight on ground other than his lordship's, it was 'as safe from his attacks as if it were in Guinea.'

He bore off the shot pheasant, and spent much of the next two days drawing it. Between bouts of work he got an unsettling glimpse of the Industrial Revolution during a visit to George Murray's cotton mills, which employed 1500 people.

> These mills consist of a complete square area of about eight acres, built round with five, six or seven storey houses. In the centre of this square is a large basin of water that flows through the tower. Two engines of forty and forty-five horsepower are kept going from 6 am to 8 o'clock each day ... This is the largest establishment owned by one single individual in Manchester. Some others, belonging to friends or co-partnerships of several, have as many as 2500 working hands — as poor, miserable, abject wretches as ever worked in the mines of Golconda [once a centre of diamond production in Hyderabad].

The wealthy natives continued to entertain him nobly — and none more so than Mr and Mrs Thomas Lloyd, who lived a couple of miles outside the city. Audubon was entranced by their park, gardens and hothouses: 'The coffee tree was bearing. The bananas were ripening under the juicy grapes of Spain and Italy'; and he revelled, up to a point, in the luxurious appointments of the house. Three men-servants in livery trimmed with red on a white ground waited at table, and many toasts were drunk in wine; but the company sat at table for five hours, and Audubon grew restless, itching to get back to his work.

Next morning, in Manchester, there appeared a 'handsome Quaker', who asked if he and his friends might view the exhibition early, as they had to leave town. Audubon, glad to see a kindred spirit, agreed to meet him in the lobby of the Exchange at 8.55 am; but as he stood waiting, two men came in and held the following conversation:

> —'Pray, have you seen Mr Audubon's collections of birds? I am told it is well worth a shilling. Suppose we go now.'

—'Puh! It's all a hoax. Save your shilling for better use. I have seen them. Why, the fellow ought to be drummed out of town.'

He was uncomfortable again that evening, when he went to a concert and sat at the side of the hall, where he thought he would not be noticed. Inevitably, his long hair and unfashionable garments attracted attention, and between the pieces of music he felt himself being 'gazed at through lorgnettes'. Extravagant praise from the Quaker group restored the artist's morale a little, but by then he had decided that Manchester was not advancing his grand design fast enough, and, leaving the exhibition in place, he set off back to Liverpool.

CHAPTER FIVE

EDINBURGH

OCTOBER 1826 came in with crisp, autumnal weather: frosts had started to turn the leaves yellow and swallows were flying south. On Merseyside once more, Audubon 'bounced onto the pavement' and felt he was again in a land not of strangers but of friends.

In Manchester he had conceived the idea of starting a 'Book of Subscriptions', open, as he modestly put it, 'to receive the names of all persons inclined to have the best illustrations of American birds yet published'. Now Thomas Traill introduced him to Henry Bohn, a bookseller from London, a 'handsome, well-formed young gentleman', who kept a huge warehouse with 200,000 volumes regularly in stock. Bohn advised him to proceed at once to the capital and there meet the principal naturalists of the day, and through them to see the best engravers, lithographers, colourists, printers and paper-merchants, and thus form some idea of the cost of the enterprise. Then, said Bohn, he should go on to Brussels and Paris, to test the possibilities of each country and decide where the work could best be undertaken. Once Audubon had thus tested the water, he should issue a prospectus and bring out the first Number of his *Birds*.

Bohn was emphatic, also, about the size of the book, sensibly insisting that it must not be too large for the English market. 'Productions of taste', he told Audubon, 'are purchased with delight by persons who receive company, particularly, and that to have your book to be laid on the table as a pastime piece of entertainment is the principal use [to be] made of it.' If it were so big 'as to bring shame on other works or encumber the table,' he went on, 'it will not be purchased by the set of people who now are the very life of the trade.' If only large institutions and a few noblemen bought it, he warned, a hundred copies, at most, might 'find their way out of the shops,' instead of the thousand or so that a smaller volume would sell. Bohn further told Audubon that exhibiting his pictures, as he had been, would get him nowhere, and he advised him to have his book printed in Paris, but then to bring over 250 copies, 'to be issued to the world of England as genuine English production'. He estimated that 100 copies could be sold in Paris, 250 in London, 100 in Holland, 100 in Russia and 450 in America – a total of 1000 copies.

Like Traill, Audubon was impressed by Bohn and at first agreed to follow his advice; but soon he reverted to his own ideas about size. For him, it must be double-elephant or nothing. Yet he was hugely gratified by Bohn's praise of his artistic ability: the bookseller told him that although the undertaking was 'greatly laborious', he could rest assured that success would eventually crown it, as his drawings were 'very superior'.

He was delighted to be back among his old friends, the Rathbones especially; but when Mary Hodgson, 'a Quaker of great benevolence, smartness and solid understanding,' took him to visit Liverpool gaol, Audubon was considerably disturbed. He particularly deplored the use of tread-mills, which he thought were both morally degrading and destructive of health:

> Conceive of a wild squirrel within a round wheel, moving himself without progress. The labour is too severe, and the true motive of correction destroyed, as there are no mental resources attached to this laborious engine of shame only, if viewed by strangers. Why should each individual not be taught different trades, enabling them, when thrown again upon the vile world, to support themselves more honestly?

He was horrified by the 'sallow, withered, emaciated, thin visages and bodies' of the prisoners, and sickened by the gaol's foul air, especially in the women's quarters, which were thick with smoke: 'Suffice it to say that through the want of tobacco the ladies there smoke their petticoats [in pipes].'

It is not clear how long Audubon planned to stay in Liverpool before returning to Manchester, but when old Mrs Rathbone proposed that she and her daughter Hannah should accompany him, in their own carriage, his joy was unbounded. During the journey they picnicked off their knees in the carriage, trying not to spill glasses of wine, and finishing their meal with melon, grapes, pears and apples.

At the exhibition Audubon found his door-keeper incapable with drink, and dismissed him on the spot, but his spirits revived when he looked closely at his own paintings, for he thought the birds 'were fresh and as gay in appearance as their originals in our woods'. Bohn the book-seller, appearing again, changed his mind about the size of Audubon's intended publication: after lengthy examination of the paintings, he decreed that they should be published 'full size of life'. But he strongly reaffirmed his advice to clear out of Manchester and go to London, assuring Audubon that there he would be 'cherished by the nobility', and was bound to succeed.

Once more he stayed with the Gregs at Quarry Bank, while his companions went to lodge with the Rathbones' cousin Abigail Dockray and her husband David. Audubon was keen to meet Mrs Dockray, because she was a Quaker minister and a prison reformer — and when he did, he was delighted to be chided for not having come to the family, with its nine children, even earlier. Going from Greenbank outside Liverpool to Quarry Bank outside Manchester, he remarked, was like moving 'from one pleasure to another, not like a butterfly that skips from flower to flower and merely sees their beauties, but more, I hope, as a bee gathering honeyed knowledge for older times!'

It was Mrs Rathbone who suggested an expedition into the wilds of Derbyshire, and Audubon leapt at the chance of visiting Bakewell, the source of Lucy's family name. So it was that on the morning of 11 October a party of seven, including several children, set off in two chaises, accompanied by a servant and two postillions, through Stockport and Whaley Bridge to Chapel-en-le-Frith and on to the small market town of Bakewell. During the journey he got his first glimpse of what he called 'the railways'; these must have been the lines of the Peak Forest

Tramway from Buxworth to Dove Holes Dale, a novelty at the time. yet the embryonic form of transport apparently did not interest him, for he merely mentioned it in passing.

Bakewell delighted him with 'its ancient look, its peaceable quietness, and the simplicity of its cottages crowded together as if needing the support of each other.' Via his journal he told Lucy, 'I am at last, my beloved wife, at the spot that has been honoured with thy ancestors' name.' Yet when he walked round the churchyard, with Hannah leaning on his arm, emotional stress sent him into a peculiar reverie:

> [I was], neither very happy nor very sad, perhaps feeling a kind of vacancy about me, and undetermination, a kind of restless dreaming, illusion-like, that made me doubt if I lived and walked. If I saw and felt. If thou were present or not. If the place was called Bakewell or Audubon.

He was so taken with the scenery of the Derbyshire dales, so thrilled to be on Lucy's home territory, that for a couple of days he seems to have forgotten his commercial and artistic worries. From a comfortable base at an inn the travellers explored by chaise and on foot, passing the Duke of Devonshire's groom ('What whiskers, mustachios and strange-looking spotted horses, going tandem, too!'), ascending the Heights of Abraham, to look down on Matlock, and visiting a spectacular cave, in which Audubon 'imitated the owl's cry and the Indian yell'.

During the day the weather was changeable, but the evening proved so calm and inviting that the whole party went out in a boat on the River Derwent, and Audubon rowed them up and down, singing at the oars. At the inn the town baths, lined with white marble and vaulted, were immediately beneath the party's sitting room, and he reckoned them to be 'completely secure from noise and splashes.' But when he returned from his ablutions, he was told he had been heard all over the house – 'a great proof indeed that walls are no safeguard for secrecy'. In spite of his embarrassment, he found the whole excursion extremely agreeable.

Back in Manchester, as he packed up his paintings and prepared to leave for Edinburgh, he was surprised to receive a large book presented by Mrs Rathbone, and was moved to write in his journal, 'Will this good friend adopt me for one of her sons, I wonder? For positively there is no end to her generosity.'

The 212-mile journey to the Scottish capital took two days. On the first day the coach left Manchester at 5 am and stopped long enough at Preston for the passengers to snatch a quick breakfast. But then, after the next change of horses, such a 'shocking smell' invaded the coach that the guard announced that he could not remain in his seat. Audubon was outraged to be asked if his trunk belonged to him, 'and if it did not contain a dead body intended for dissection at Edinburgh.' When he denied it,

> The guard smiled as if quite sure my trunk contained such a thing, and told my companions that he would inform against me at Lancaster ... I offered to open my trunk, and would certainly have done so at Lancaster; but, whilst we were proceeding, the guard came to the door and made an apology. [He] said the smell had been removed, and that it was positively attached to the inside of the man's breeches who was on the seat by him. This caused much laughter and many coarse jokes.

Other incidents enlivened the journey. At one point two passengers were left behind during a change of horses, and had to run nearly a mile to overtake the coach, which reached Carlisle at 9.30 pm, having travelled 122 miles. Audubon was plagued by a cold and cough, which he exacerbated by riding outside the coach for thirty miles so that he could observe the scenery. The next day he was much vexed at being charged an extra twelve shillings (on top of the fare of £3 15s, and tips to drivers and guards) for his trunk and portfolio.

At Hawick he dined on 'excellent sea fish', and for the first time tasted Scotch whisky, which he found too strong for him, although liking its taste. He was incited to drink more by a young man called Pattison, who, with his father, had been most friendly during the journey. When Audubon said he suspected the boy was trying to make him drunk, the father replied that it was probably to see if he would prove as good-natured drunk as sober — which Audubon took for a compliment, and forgave the young fellow. As they passed close by Abbotsford, the home of his hero the novelist Sir Walter Scott, he rose from his seat and stretched his neck 'some inches' in the vain hope of setting eyes on the house.

Even though they reached Edinburgh in the dark, he was immediately delighted by the 'splendid city', which over the past half-century had grown and changed amazingly. An entire New Town, begun in 1767, had sprung up to the north of Princes Street Gardens, and had gradually spread westwards from St Andrew Square, in a grid pattern of what Robert Louis Stevenson called 'draughty parallelograms'. The Old Town, beneath the high mound of the castle, was still a maze of filthy alleys and tenements, but most well-to-do citizens had moved up to the straight, wide, clean streets and elegant squares and crescents of the New Town, with their fine houses and Neo-classical buildings, faced with grey granite. Writing to his son Victor, Audubon described Edinburgh as 'the most beautiful, picturesque and romantic city probably in the world'.

> The Castle I should conceive impregnable; two sides of it are protected by an almost perpendicular rock 300 feet high. It looks like an eagle perched on a bold naked cypress ready to fall and crush all about below.

His favourable first impression was enhanced by the discovery of excellent lodgings at No. 2 George Street, where Mrs Dickie charged only a guinea a week for a good bedroom and well-furnished sitting-room, with a pair of stuffed pheasants on a cabinet, and views out over the Firth of Forth. There he unpacked his paintings and looked at them 'with pleasure, and yet with a considerable degree of fear that they would never be published'.

Fine architecture, he knew, was merely the outward sign of Edinburgh's sophistication. During the past hundred years, the period known as the Scottish Enlightenment, the city had become a centre of law, art, medicine, science, engineering and literature, producing a stream of distinguished men, among them the architects Robert and James Adam, the painters Sir Henry Raeburn and Allan Ramsay, the economist Adam Smith, the philosopher David Hume, the chemist Joseph Black (who discovered carbon dioxide), and the historian William Robertson. In 1815 alone 565 books were published there. William Smellie, who edited the first edition of the *Encyclopaedia Britannica*, and wrote large sections of it, recorded a remark made by Mr Amyat, 'King's Chymist', who said: 'Here I stand at what is called the Cross of Edinburgh, and can, in a few minutes, take fifty men of genius and learning by the hand.'

Inevitably, the newcomer was nervous about how he would fare in such a highly charged intellectual atmosphere. His first few days in the city were frustrating, for the eminent citizens to whom he had introductions were either away or too busy to see him immediately. Depression threatened, and to ward it off he resorted to his usual remedy of walking vigorously about. His surroundings pleased him enormously:

> The great breadth of the streets, their good pavement and foot ways, the beautiful uniformity of the buildings, their natural grey colouring and wonderful cleanliness ... A high castle here, another there, a bridge looking at a second city below, here a rugged mountain, and there beautiful public grounds, monuments, the sea, the landscape around, all wonderfully managed indeed ... There is a wildness expressed in all its component parts as well as in its tout ensemble that agrees precisely with the ideas of a man of the woods.

He was fascinated by a visit to the royal Palace of Holyrood, and remarked that the furniture was all decaying fast, as were the pictures, which were 'encrusted into the walls'. Although disappointed by the size of the room in which the Scottish Kings had held audiences, he reckoned that the hangings of bright scarlet cloth had 'a very warm effect', and that the chamber would be a capital place in which to exhibit his drawings.

One morning he walked to the port of Leith, then a large village, three miles along the Firth to the east, and in the evening went to a performance of *Rob Roy*, an adaptation of Scott's novel, which he knew and loved. The play was so well done that he vowed never to watch another production of it in America, where performances tended to be burlesques, and 'we do not even know how the hardy mountaineer of this rigid country [the Highlands] throws on his plaid or wears his cap, or his front piece [sporran] beautifully made of several tails of the red deer'.

The people of Edinburgh impressed him less than the architecture.

The women of the lower classes, he thought, resembled Indian squaws, and waddled through the streets in the same way, with large leather straps passed over their foreheads to take the weight of their baskets:

> Their complexion, if fair, is beyond rosy, partaking indeed of purple – cold and disagreeable. If dark, they are dark indeed. Many of the men wear long whiskers and beards, and are extremely uncouth of manners, and still more so of language.

One of his potentially valuable contacts, to whom he had an introduction was Robert Jameson, Professor of Natural History at Edinburgh University, founder of the Wernerian Natural History Society[1] and founder-editor of the *Edinburgh Philosophical Journal*. At first this prominent intellectual seemed rather cool: he told his American visitor that Sir Walter Scott was busy with a novel and his life of Napoleon, and that he probably would not see him. 'Not see Walter Scott!' trumpeted Audubon in his journal. 'By Washington I shall, if I have to crawl on all fours for a mile!'

18

ROBERT JAMESON

The Professor of Natural History at Edinburgh University amazed Audubon with his hair, which the artist reported was arranged in 'three distinct, different courses'.

He was disconcerted to find that Jameson was already collaborating with two other ornithologists, P.J. Selby and Sir William Jardine, on a major work about British birds. Soon he met and liked both these avid ornithologists; and at first, when a friend suggested that he might join forces with them to further his own plans, he thought it a good idea. 'As I find I am a useful man that way, it is most likely that I shall

1. The body of distinguished naturalists named after the German geologist Abraham Gottlob Werner. Counterpart of the Linnean Society in London.

be connected with them with a good share of the credit and a good deal of cash.' Later though, he had second thoughts:

> My independent spirit does not turn to the idea with any pleasure, and I think if my work deserves the attention of the public, it must stand on its own legs, not on the reputation of men superior in education and literary acquirements, but possibly not so in the actual observation of Nature at her best, in the wilds, as I certainly have seen her.

A warmer approach came from the one-eyed Dr Robert Knox, who taught in his own private school of anatomy and arrived straight from it 'dressed with an overgown and bloody fingers'. Having bowed, washed and dried his hands, he read the letter of introduction that Dr Traill had given Audubon in Liverpool, and promised 'all in his power' in the way of help. Did he, in the course of conversation, reveal that few bodies were available for dissection, and that in consequence there was a thriving illicit trade, operated by body-snatchers or 'resurrectionists', who exhumed recently buried corpses?[2]

For the time being Audubon exhibited his paintings in his lodgings, where he received visitors and, in the intervals, wrote letters and kept up his journal. But, deprived of the merry Rathbones' company, he felt 'very much alone again', and longed for someone in whom he could confide. Lack of progress made him increasingly irritated, and towards the end of October he had decided he must head for London.

Then – thanks to Patrick Neill, a naturalist and gardener who ran a printing works in the city, and was a member of the Wernerian Society – he made a vital breakthrough. When he first met Neill and explained that he was looking for a publisher, the printer was very civil and promised to help; but then for three days nothing happened, and on the morning of 30 October, exasperated by the lack of action, Audubon walked to his office in Fish Market Close. There Neill listened to his

---

2. Two years later Dr Knox was caught up in the nefarious activities of the murderers William Burke and William Hare, who suffocated their victims and sold at least 16 bodies to Knox for amounts varying from £8 to £14, claiming they had died of natural causes. Hare escaped prosecution by turning King's evidence, but Burke was hanged on 28 January 1829. Although Knox denied knowledge of any impropriety, his reputation and business were ruined.

19
WILLIAM
HOME LIZARS

*Self-portrait
in chalk of the
engraver whose
firm in Edin-
burgh made the
first ten plates in
The Birds of
America.*

worries and took him to 'one of the most scientific men,' who looked at the artist coolly, wrote down his name and address, and 'promised to send amateurs'. This was not good enough for Neill, who immediately led Audubon to James Square to meet William Home Lizars, the city's leading engraver (and Sir William Jardine's brother-in-law), who had been making plates for Jardine and Selby.

For the first few minutes Audubon thought little of this new contact. As they proceeded through the rain towards the artist's lodgings, Lizars 'talked of nothing else … besides the astounding talent of his employer [Selby], how quick he drew, and how well, had I seen the work? etc. etc.' Walking along in silence under the same umbrella, Audubon almost lost hope. But once they had gone up the stairs to his rooms, and Lizars' eye fell on the huge portfolio, everything changed:

> I slowly unbuckled the straps, and putting a chair for him to set, without uttering a word I turned up a drawing … Mr Lizars, quite surprised, exclaimed, 'My God! I never saw anything like this before' … Mr Lizars was so astonished that he said Sir Somebody [Sir William Jardine] must see them, that he would write immediately (and so did he), that Mr Selby must see them, and to him also he wrote. And, going as it grew dark, he called, it seems, on a Mr W. Heath, a great artist from London, who came immediately to see me. I had, however, made my exit.

Next morning Lizars brought along the enigmatic Robert Jameson, having told him of his amazing discovery. Now the professor seemed 'very kind,' but Audubon still felt that he did not 'understand the man clearly'. He dared to hope, nevertheless, that he might prove a good friend, especially when Jameson promised to announce the drawings 'to the world'. The engraver, on the other hand, made an immediately favourable impression on Audubon, who referred to him as 'the warm-hearted Mr Lizars', and, when he saw some of his work, was abashed to discover that he was 'a most wonderful artist'.

Invited by him and his wife Henrietta to dine, the American found the evening 'extremely pleasant', not least because he took a fancy to Mrs Lizars, with her fine, large eyes, 'well coloured with burnt umber, or perhaps Vandyke brown'. Henceforth in his journal he referred to her as 'Lady No 1' – and he was further comforted by the sight of some drawings by Selby and Jardine, instantly deciding that his son Johnny could 'do as good'. Writing to Lucy, he said that he considered Lizars 'an excellent good man', and that the Rathbones had congratulated him on 'the happy rencontre I have made of him'.

Next morning he breakfasted with Professor Jameson in his 'most splendid house, splendid everything, a good breakfast to boot', and reported that his host wore his hair :

> in three distinct, different courses. When he sits fronting the south, for instance, those on the upper forehead are bent westwardly, towards the east, those that cover both ears are inclined; and the very short sheared portion behind mounts directly upward, perhaps somewhat like the sister quills of the 'fretful porcupine'.

A contemporary portrait does not quite bear out this extravagant description – but the professor was friendliness itself, chatted 'with an uncommon degree of cordiality', and promised Audubon every assistance. The artist spent the rest of the day showing his paintings to a stream of visitors, then again called on Lizars, who uncorked a bottle of 'warmed London porter' and presented him with a copy of his own engraved *Views of Edinburgh*, embellished on the first page with the flattering inscription:

> To John J. Audubon as a very imperfect expression of the regard entertained for his abilities as an artist, and for his worth as a friend.

After a glimpse of Lizars' workshop in James Square, where his colour-ers were working by gaslight on prints taken from engraved copper plates, Audubon returned to his lodgings and read. As he went to sleep, he put the book under his pillow, 'like children are wont do at Christmas Eve,' hoping that his subconscious would continue with the story; but his 'senses all operated another way. I dreamed of the Beechwoods, of a house there! Of a female there! Of — !'

The more Lizars saw of Audubon's pictures, the more enthusiastic he became. The Mocking Birds and rattlesnake, the Hen Turkey and her brood, the Hawk pouncing on seventeen partridges, the Whooping Crane devouring baby alligators — all these appealed to him most strongly:

> but when the Great-footed Hawks came with bloody rage at their beaks' ends and with cruel delight in the glance of their daring eyes, he stopped mute for perhaps an instant. His arms fell … then he said, 'I will engrave and publish this.'

Lizars began to stir up prominent citizens on the artist's behalf. 'Mr Audubon,' he said, 'the people here don't know who you are at all. But depend on it, they shall know.' Accolades came from every side. The distinguished artist John Syme, a pupil of Raeburn, arranged to paint Audubon's portrait.[3] The phrenologist George Combe asked if he might take a cast of his head. Such was the press of distinguished visitors to the artist's rooms that he could hardly get any painting done — and he made an indelible impression on all who saw him, 'When we first set eyes on him in a party of literati,' wrote John Wilson, the editor of *Blackwood's Magazine*, 'in "stately Edinburgh throned on crags", he was such an American woodsman as took the shine out of us modern Athenians'.

Effusive praise was showered on his pictures, and so hectic was his social round of breakfasts, lunches and dinners that when he came to

---

3. The original, now in the White House, Washington, shows Audubon in hunter's garb; he is wearing his wolfskin coat (which he put on at Lizars' suggestion) with fur showing at the neck and cuffs, and he holds a double-barrelled shotgun across his chest. The face is long and strong, with bold eyes gleaming from under highly arched brows, and curls of hair flowing down his back (see p. 92).

write up his journal, late on the night of 2 November, his imagination soared to dizzy heights:

> Then Fame, expand thy unwearied pinions, and far, far and high, high soar away! Yet smoothly circle about me wherever I go, and call out with musical mellowness the name of this child of Nature, her humble but true admirer! Call out, call out, call out — LOUD, LOUD, LOUD, AUDUBON!!!

By then he was referring to Lizars as '*mon bon cheval de bataille*', and soon a deal was struck: Lizars agreed to engrave and publish the first number of *The Birds of America*, and on about 10 November 1826 began work on the first copper plate. The subject was the Wild Turkey Cock — the magnificent great creature which, by its size alone, demanded the double-elephant format. Subscribers were not to know that when Audubon shot the bird on which he modelled his drawing, at Beechwoods in 1825, he set its 28-pound body up against a wall and left it for several days as he sketched it. 'The damned fellow kept it pinned up there till it rotted and stunk,' recalled Robert Percy, who was with him. 'I hated to lose so much good eating.'

Then, as now, the process of engraving was laborious and slow. Using

a tool called a burin, the artist incised the design on to a sheet of copper. The plate was then inked and wiped clean, so that ink remained only in the incised lines, after which it went under the press. Audubon's plates were printed in black only, and the colours were added later by a team of colourers or copyists, working from the original paintings. Watching the men at work, the artist was thrilled to see how faithfully his designs were copied, 'and scarcely able to conceive the great adroit required to form all the lines in a sense contrary to the model before them.'

Lizars handed Audubon a first proof of the turkey print on 28 November – and so the mighty enterprise got under way. In a letter to William Rathbone, with which he enclosed a copy of his prospectus, the artist described the launch of his 'enormously gigantic work'. From what he had seen of Lizars' execution, the plates would be 'equal to anything in the world at present', and he intended to superintend the engraving and colouring himself. His plan was to publish the first Number, of five prints, at his own expense, travel with it under his arm, and beg his way round the country. He thought that if he could procure 300 good subscribers, be they individuals or institutions, he could not fail to do well for his family, even though he might have to abandon his life to the success of the project, 'and undergo many sad perplexities, and perhaps never see again my own beloved America'.

He also sent the prospectus to William Roscoe, together with a letter which revealed what stress he was suffering:

> To tell you all my feelings would be quite impossible. My head can scarcely be said to be on my shoulders. I never before felt so wild, and at a loss to

speak or to act as I do now. I may perhaps become reconciled and habitu-
ated to all my present perturbed situation, but I scarce can conceive it possible, and I fear often that the woods only were intended for me to live in.

Lizars' undertaking to publish the first Number was enough to put all
his 'powers of acting and of thinking in a high paroxysm of fever'. The
newspapers also began to praise him and his pictures, so that altogether
he 'felt quite dazzled with uncertainties of hope and fear.' Another letter
– to the portrait painter Thomas Sully in Philadelphia – echoed the same
theme: 'I am thrown into a vortex of business that I never conceived I
could manage.'

He knew that, although Bohn had come round to the double-elephant
format, some of his friends were worried by the dimensions of the
sheets, and he himself admitted that the published work was going to be
'rather bulky', but his heart remained bent on presenting even the biggest
birds at life-size. 'If I do not succeed,' he added with a characteristic
touch of self-pity, 'I can always return to my woods and there in peace
and quiet die, with the thought that I have done my utmost to be agreeable, if not useful to the world at large.'

So far he appears to have given little thought to the question of
providing text to go with his pictures. For him, the illustrations were
everything – indeed the Numbers appeared without any account of the
birds portrayed. But gradually he realised that he ought to deploy the
immense stock of natural history which he had acquired from his observations in the wild, and, in a letter to Lucy he declared that he would
'proceed with a firm resolution to attempt being an author'.

The trouble was that, for all his fluency in keeping his journal and
dashing off family letters, he had frightful difficulty composing anything
more formal, for the thought of publication seemed to turn his brain to
jelly. 'It is a terrible thing to me,' he admitted, 'far better fitted to study
and delineate in the forests than to arrange phrases with sensible gram-
marian skill' – and again: 'Writing is very irksome, and of no benefit to
me whatever.'

One morning, as daylight was coming up, he sat down to write a description of the Wild Turkeys which he had just finished painting. His breakfast arrived, but his pen carried him on along the Arkansas River, and he felt for his 'beloved country' so intently that he could not swallow a morsel. Yet when he read out what he had written to David Bridges, an Edinburgh newspaper editor, and said he intended to lay the document on the table in the exhibition room, his visitor advised him to take it to John Wilson, editor of *Blackwood's Magazine*, to have it put into good English. This he did, and Wilson agreed to sort out the article for him. Not that he took kindly to rigorous editing: when he gave an essay on the carrion crow to the optician and scientific writer Dr David Brewster, he was 'quite shocked' to find how much it had been altered. 'It made me quite sick,' he reported. 'He [Brewster] had improved the style and destroyed the matter.'

For the first weeks of his stay in Edinburgh, he exhibited his pictures in his own lodgings, and was much harassed by the press of visitors who came to see them, thereby making it impossible for him to paint. Then at last, 'through the astonishing perseverance of some unknown friends,' the Royal Institution invited him to show the pictures in one of its fine rooms, free of charge, and again, as in Liverpool, the display made a tremendously strong impression. 'The effect was like magic,' John Wilson recorded:

> The spectator imagined himself in the forest ... birds in motion or at rest, in their glee and their gambols, their loves and their wars, singing or caressing or brooding or preying or tearing one another into pieces.

The switch enabled Audubon to work 'from day to night' on an oil-painting of a Wild Turkey cock, a hen and nine chicks. But on 5 November there arrived an unpleasant reminder that, even before any of his work had been published, his enemies were out to destroy his reputation: he received what he called a 'scrubby' letter from Charles Waterton', the squire of Walton Hall, near Wakefield in Yorkshire, an eccentric English naturalist who by chance had met George Ord in Philadelphia and become an admirer of Alexander Wilson's work.

Waterton, a relentless exhibitionist, had been showing off all his life.

In 1817, aged thirty five, during a stay in Italy, he had climbed the dome of St Peter's in Rome, ascended the cross and left his gloves on the tip of the lightning conductor above it. He also climbed the roof of the Castle of St Angelo and posed on one leg on the head of the Guardian Angel which crowned it. In South America he had travelled widely and experimented with *wourali* poison (curare). A firm believer in the efficacy of bleeding, he drew his own blood more than eighty times when far from medical aid, and this, 'with calomel and jalap mixed together as a purgative, with the use of rhubarb in occasional cases of dysentery, and with vast and often-repeated potations of powdered Peruvian bark as a restorative,' enabled him to overcome sickness.

He had inherited Walton Hall, a fine, three-storey house which stood on an island in the middle of a lake, and during the 1820s he ordered the construction of a mile-long stone wall, between nine and ten feet high, which enclosed his park and formed a wildlife sanctuary.

At 5.30 am on 18 May 1829 he married Mary Anne Edmonstone (who at seventeen was thirty years his junior) in the chapel of the English convent in the Rue des Carmes at Bruges, and in April the following year she bore him a son, only to expire of puerperal fever three weeks later. What she made of Walton Hall will never be known, but she must have had strong nerves, for the house was packed with grotesque taxidermical jokes: at the foot of the stairs, for instance, was 'The Nightmare', a hideous composite creature with a grinning human face, wild boar's tusks, a man's hands, satanic horns, elephant's ears, bat's wings, one foot cloven, the other that of an eagle, with talons outstretched, and the tail of a snake.

Shocked by his loss, and never remarrying, Waterton occupied himself with travelling abroad, running his estate, writing about natural history, and squaring up for verbal fisticuffs with anyone who presumed to disagree with him. When not provoked or seeking to annoy, he wrote about birds with knowledge and good sense, advocating protection rather than persecution, in a manner far ahead of most contemporaries, and his letters to friends were full of amusing little stories. Yet his habits were far from conventional. For the last thirty-five years of his life –

from the moment Anne died in 1830 – he slept on bare boards, with a hollowed-out block of beech (or, some said, oak) for a pillow, rose at 3am, performed an hour's devotions in his private chapel, read Latin and Spanish texts and wrote letters, all before breakfast at eight. In his seventies he was still climbing trees barefoot, and demonstrating to visitors how he could scratch the back of his head with his big toe.

His main claim to fame was his book *Wanderings in South America*, published in 1824, which described a series of journeys made in search of native fauna, mainly through British Guiana (he was attracted to the wilds of South America because for a time he managed the family's sugar plantations in Demerara). Ostentatiously peppered with quotations in Latin from Virgil, Ovid and other classical authors, intolerably boastful, reeking of false modesty, yet lively and entertaining, the narrative included many stirring episodes whose veracity seemed dubious, to say the least.

The most notorious, for which the author later took heavy verbal punishment, was his account of how he had ridden on the back of a ten-foot cayman (or alligator) as it was being dragged ashore out of a river by his native henchmen. The book also included a description and

23

CHARLES
WATERTON

The Squire of
Walton Hall is
towed ashore
on the back of
an alligator: the
alleged incident,
depicted by
Captain Edward
Jones, for which
Waterton was
widely mocked.

drawing of a mysterious ape-man, unknown to science, which Waterton claimed to have discovered in the jungle and which he called 'The Non-descript'. The fact that his sketch of its stuffed head and torso bore a strong resemblance to one of his principal enemies in London did not pass unnoticed, and word soon went round that the unfortunate creature had been a red howler monkey. This hoax, which he thought tremendously amusing, had the unfortunate effect of making its perpetrator into a figure of fun among serious naturalists.

Waterton's own travels gave him a wide knowledge of fauna and flora, but he was blinkered by his own prejudices, and by the inability to admit that he could be wrong – witness the intemperate scorn which he poured on another naturalist who maintained, quite correctly, that a young cuckoo evicts the chicks and eggs of its host from the nest. This claim, he thundered, 'carries its own condemnation, no matter by whom related, or by whom received.' As a naturalist, then, he was not taken seriously by most contemporaries. Yet, armoured as he was with arrogance and conceit, he was a dangerous enemy, and in his determination to support George Ord by denigrating Audubon's work, he harassed the artist for the next dozen years. If he and Ord had been able to kill off the embryonic elephant before it ever drew breath, they would have been delighted.

Audubon himself was capable of a fine turn of sarcasm: in private he referred to Waterton as 'the alligator *maquignon* [coper],' and in his journal he described Ord as 'the venomous tallow chandler of Philadelphia, possessor of three Greek words, seven of Latin – none belonging to what ought to be his usual language – and describer of objects yet unknown to the Almighty.' In spite of numerous vexations, he never answered Ord's or Waterton's diatribes in public; yet he was profoundly irritated by their sniping, and once, describing how young English ladies kept asking him about his adventures on the frontier, wrote to Lucy:

> They all appear very much surprised that ... I, so much in the woods, have not been devoured at least six times by tigers, bears, wolves, foxes or a rat. No, I was never troubled in the woods by any animals larger than ticks or mosquitoes ... I must acknowledge, however, that I would like to have rode

a few hundred miles on a wild Elk or a Unicorn — or an Alligator. Alligator!!!!! Who in the known world ever heard of such things?

For nearly a fortnight in the middle of November he failed to make any entries in his journal — an unusual lapse, for which his only excuse was that his 'head could not admit of it'. But on 19 November he recorded that he had twice dined with Jardine (who was then twenty-six), and 'liked him very much'. As winter closed in on the northern city, snow fell and the hours of daylight grew steadily shorter, until he was unable to begin drawing or painting before 9 am. His life assumed a regular pattern: painting or writing for all the hours available, looking in at the exhibition, walking about in search of new contacts, going out to sumptuous lunches and dinners given by his friends, and sitting up into the small hours, scratching away by candle-light at letters and his journal with a quill or metal pen.

His record bulged with accounts of the lavish entertainment he received and the glamorous ladies he met — and yet he was still troubled by insecurity. One woman, clearly of high intelligence, struck terror into him the moment he met her:

> I knew at one glance she had discovered my great inferiority . . . I felt her elevated mind bearing on my feeble intelligence more and more forcibly, the longer I tried to steal a glance at her face. But this was not permitted. She positively riveted me to my blushes, and never before have I felt more stupid.

On 27 November he began to sit, or rather to stand, for his portrait by John Syme. He found the two-hour sessions 'dreadfully long' and 'durance vile', and when the job was finished, he did not think it a very good likeness, although it was 'a fine picture'. The highlight of St Andrew's Day — 30 November — was the Antiquarians' sumptuous dinner held at the Waterloo Hotel:

> It at first consisted entirely of Scotch messes of old fashion, such as marrow-bones, codfish heads stuffed with oatmeal and garlic, black puddings, sheep's heads, tracheas of the same, and I do not know what all. Then a second dinner was served quite à l'Anglaise. I finished with a nice bit of grouse. Then, my Lucy, came the toasts.

When the speakers began to praise Audubon, and he realised he would have to reply, sweat ran down his body, and he thought he was going to faint; but when the moment came, he forced himself to his feet and said:

'Gentlemen, my powers of voice are as humble as those of the birds now hanging on the walls of the Institution. I am truly obliged for your favour. Permit me to say, may God bless you all, and may this Society prosper.'

I felt my hands, and they were positively covered with perspiration. I felt it running down along my legs, and Mr Lizars, seeing how I was, poured out a glass of wine and said, 'Bravo, take this.'

In his exploration of Edinburgh he got the occasional unpleasant surprise: a visit to the anatomical museum proved 'extremely disagreeable,' and the venereal exhibits 'shocking beyond all I ever thought could be'. Later he went to a lecture on anatomy and watched a doctor operate 'on a beautiful dead body of a female, quite fresh'; but afterwards he went to the dissecting rooms, where there was such a 'horrible stench' that he thought he would suffocate.

One night he recorded that he must have 'battered the pavements for twenty miles, and that is equal to forty-five walking through the woods.' His relations with the Lizars continued warm. Again and again the family invited him to spend the evening with them – once to eat a sheep's head, which he found delicious – and he also made friends with William's younger brother Daniel, a bookseller.

One valuable new acquaintance was Captain Basil Hall, formerly of the Royal Navy, who by a strange coincidence had been a midshipman on board the privateer *Leander* in 1806, when the ship attacked and looted the *Polly*, on which the twenty-one-year-old Audubon and his partner Ferdinand Rozier were sailing from France to America. Since then Hall had travelled widely, and he now presented the artist with a copy of his book on South America. As Hill was contemplating a long trip through North America, he asked Audubon numerous questions about where to go and how to proceed. 'Audubon, beware of Irishmen,' was one of his many watchwords.[4]

Altogether, Audubon felt that his position in Edinburgh was 'very extraordinary ... looked upon with respect, receiving the attentions of the most distinguished characters, and supported by all men of science. It is really wonderful, and am I really deserving of this?'

Yet as day after day went by without any communication from Lucy, he became increasingly maudlin and worried. When a letter arrived from America, but not from home, he felt 'quite mad of disappointment,' and another night, after suffering from a headache, he wrote:

> To be ill far from thee would be dreadful. Who would nurse me with thy kind care, kiss me to repose, and do more for me in a day than all the doctors in Christendom can in a twelve month?

By the beginning of December he was worn down by exhaustion, and at 2.30 am one morning wrote, 'What hours I do keep. Am I to lead this life long? If I do, I must receive from my maker a new suit of strength and a better constitution.' He began to believe that Lucy had fallen ill – and then on 10 December, when his head was 'like a hornets' nest' and his body 'wearied beyond calculation':

> I saw thy form move about me in such sickly appearance that I again was almost afraid to remain alone in my room, so distracted was I with the idea that some most shocking accident had befallen thee or one of our dear boys. Oh my God, destroy that suspense – let me know if my sweet Lucy is well – for thy sake amen.

Audubon found it intensely dispiriting not to know how Lucy was, not to know what she was thinking, not even to know whether his letters had been reaching her. At best, in those days, an east-west Atlantic passage took three weeks, so that a letter from England could hardly be delivered in less than a month; and no reply could be expected for at least a month beyond that. To keep track of what he had written, he made, or had made, a copy of every letter – as he himself put it, an arduous task.

On 13 December he at last met Prideaux John Selby, and was relieved

---

4. Hall's book, *Travels in North America*, caused what another author, Fanny Trollope, called 'a sort of moral earthquake' when it came out in 1829, and led her to remark: 'Other nations have been called thin-skinned, but the citizens of the Union have, apparently, no skins at all: they wince if a breeze blows over them, unless it be tempered with adulation.'

to discover that he was 'a gentleman naturalist,' bearing no resemblance to the brutish George Ord, and certainly not 'an hypocritical fool'. He described him as 'well-formed, plain, polite, clever'. Selby spent two hours studying Audubon's pictures, and seemed greatly pleased by them. Afterwards the two dined *chez* Lizars, and the company talked ornithology, Audubon wishing that he possessed as much knowledge 'on the scientific part of that study' as did Selby, who had had a university education.

Like the mercury in the thermometer, his spirits went rapidly up and down. Often at night he was overcome by bitter fits of weeping. On 16 December he received a depressing letter from William Rathbone, saying that his mother had declined to have a bird named after her, and that he himself feared the whole enterprise was going to fail. This naturally made Audubon 'feel dismal,' but he sought to bolster his spirits by observing that

> Since Napoleon became, from the ranks, an emperor, why should Audubon not be able to leave the woods of America a while and publish and sell a book? No, no. I will try by heavens until each and every hair about me will have dropped from my body, dead grey from old age!

One welcome distraction was an invitation to attend a meeting of the Wernerian Society. For this event, Audubon bought a tame pigeon, killed it, packed it up with his wires, hammer and position board, and took a coach to the Society's room. He already knew some of the learned gentlemen present, among them Patrick Neill and Professor Jameson, who made 'quite a eulogy' about Audubon and his work, before the artist demonstrated how he put up his specimens for drawing birds.

This, Audubon reported, 'they thought inconceivably ingenious,' and immediately afterwards Jameson proposed him as an honorary member of the Society. 'Everyone clapped hand and stamped the floor [as a] mark of approbation,' and the professor asked for the normal period of waiting to be waived, so that their guest could be elected at the next meeting. After another round of applause, Audubon promised to read a paper on the habits of the alligator – a subject with more resonances for him than most of his audience can have appreciated. His day was by no means finished. After an elaborate dinner given by Lady Hunter, at which he was asked hundreds of questions about America by all the 'noble folks' present, he returned to his lodgings after midnight 'to commit murder' – that is, to kill two cats which Daniel Lizars had procured for him and asked him to portray. With help from the son of his landlady, Mrs Dickie, he 'hung the poor animals in two minutes each, and I put them up in fighting attitudes, ready for painting when daylight would come.'

On the morrow he spent all the daylight hours painting the cats 'fighting like two devils for a dead squirrel,' and he finished the picture on 18 December, after ten hours' work in all. That evening he went to a meeting of the Royal Academy, of which he hoped to become a member, and whose committee, he trusted, would subscribe to *Birds*. Later, after supper with people called Russell in Abercromby Place, he told Lucy (via his journal) that everything at the party was 'magnificently rich', adding, 'I looked on each tart and wished myself by thy side.'

By then Jardine and Selby were in town, staying as usual at Barry's Hotel in Princes Street. Summoned to breakfast with them, Audubon found they had brought along ducks, hawks and other birds (to be depicted rather than eaten), and after the meal they all went round to his lodgings, where he set up not a bird but a squirrel, for the visitors to draw under his instruction. The lesson lasted till the light failed in the afternoon; at first Selby worked the faster, but Jardine caught up towards the end, and both were delighted, Selby particularly so. That night Audubon recorded, 'It was to me like a dream that I should have come from America to teach men so much my superiors.' The more he saw of Selby, the better he liked him, and soon he decided that he was 'one of those rare characters that come on the earth only at very distant periods, to prove to mankind how good some of our species may still be found.'

A brief but favourable account of Audubon's progress appeared in the *Edinburgh Journal of Science*, whose conductor, or editor, was David Brewster, already a friend. The anonymous author (Brewster himself) gave the first formal notice that publication of the *Birds* was being planned, and declared that 'We have seen two of the engravings … which, for execution, give the greatest promise … We highly applaud Mr Audubon's system, both as works of art and as drawings elucidatory of natural history.'

Phrenology was the order of 20 December. George Combe, the celebrated exponent of the pseudo-science of feeling and assessing heads, had been pursuing Audubon for weeks, and now he cornered him, measuring his skull meticulously and dictating figures to a scribe. The artist was gratified to learn that his skull resembled that of Raphael, but astonished to be told that he was a strong and constant lover, an affectionate father, with a great veneration for high, talented men, that music was not to be compared with painting in his make-up, and that he was extraordinarily generous. All this struck him as true, and he was amazed that it had been discovered so easily.

On 21 December he wrote to Lucy at immense length – nearly 3000 words – analysing his present position and hopes for the future. 'My situation in Edinburgh borders almost on the miraculous,' he began.

> Without education [and with] scarce one of those qualities necessary to render a man able to pass through the throng of the learned here, I am positively looked on by all the professors and many of the principal persons here as a very extraordinary man.

His *Birds* were to be published in Numbers of five prints each, every number costing two guineas (£2 2s – the equivalent of about $10 or $11),[5] the prints 'to be brought up and finished in such superb style as to eclipse all of the kind in existence.' He hoped that the first Number, opening with the splendid Wild Turkey cock, would be complete and on its way to subscribers by the middle of January. If it succeeded in Edinburgh, he thought, it could not fail anywhere – for, as he readily admitted, his immediate objectives were entirely commercial. 'It is not the naturalist that I wish to please,' he wrote. 'It is the wealthy part of the

---

5. To achieve comparison with today's values, the figures must be multiplied by at least 40.

community. The first can only speak well or ill of me, but the latter will fill my pockets.'

As soon as he had the first Number, he proposed to tour England, Ireland, Scotland and continental Europe, showing the prints. But for this he was going to need help. 'In the event of ultimate success,' he wrote, 'I must have either my son or some other person to travel for me, to see about the collection of payments for the work and to procure new subscribers constantly.' Victor, he thought, would be ideal for such a task, which would furnish the boy with an excellent education — better than any he could get in America — and with knowledge of Europe. 'His propensities are such that, attached to me, he would be left at my death possessor of a talent that would be the means of his support for life.'

Would Lucy think of bringing the family over, so that they could all be together? In flowery language Audubon begged her to give the idea serious consideration, and then to write him:

> Cannot we move together and feel and enjoy the natural need of each other? Lucy, my friend, think of all this very seriously. Not a portion of the earth exists but will support us amply, and we may feel happiness anywhere if careful ... Consult thyself, and in a long, plain, explanatory letter give me thy own heart entire.
>
> If I can procure, in the whole of two years, 300 subscribers, we will be rich indeed. God forever bless thee. Remember me kindly to all about thee. Kiss my son and believe me forever,
>
> Thine husband and friend,
> John J. Audubon

As if in answer to his entreaties, next morning's post brought two letters from home, both of which had been four months in transit. 'How I read them!' he exulted.

> Perhaps never in my life were letters so welcome ... Thy being quite well, and anxious that I should be so, was all thy LaForest could wish ... I kissed thy name and a hundred times blessed it ... I felt a new life, and, braced to encounter any difficulties, I rushed out and ran to announce my pleasure to the family Lizars, who take so much interest [in] thee and our dear boys.

Lucy's news included the fact that she had left Mrs Pirrie – which surprised Audubon ('I thought thou wert so attached to her that nothing would make you part') – and that she had sold her piano. She evidently suggested that she might come to England next year, in the summer of 1827. In his reply, Audubon professed himself delighted with the idea, but signalled caution: 'We must not hurry too much – I wish to sound all well and be perfectly assured of the general ultimate success of my work.' He revealed that he had 'come to fine dressing again – silk stockings and pumps; shave every morning; and sometimes dress twice a day. My hairs are now as beautifully long and curly as ever, and, I assure thee, do as much for me as my talent for painting.'

With his reply he enclosed copies of some of the invitations he had been receiving, and a note asking Lucy to forward him acorns and other seeds: 'Send a great quantity, as all the noblemen here are pleased to have some.'

On 23 December his exhibition closed, after bad weather had limited the day's attendance to thirty people, and a meticulous journal entry recorded the takings every day since the show had opened on 14 November. The best day, 16 December, had brought in £8 8s, and altogether in six weeks the exhibition had earned £173 10s 6d, the equivalent of $770 – a satisfactory amount, but a perilously small financial base from which to launch his great enterprise. In gratitude for all the help he had been given, he presented the Royal Institution with his large painting of the Wild Turkeys, lamenting the fact that he could have got £100 for it from a dealer.

Ignoring Christmas – except to buy a brooch as a present for Lucy – he worked at his painting right through 24 and 25 December, with the result that he was overcome by exhaustion, his mind 'agitated by thousands of ideas' about future projects.

Early in January 1827 he began work on a huge oil painting, the largest he had ever done, nine feet by six feet, entitled *Pheasants Attacked by a Fox*, to be exhibited at the Scottish Society of Artists. As always, he struggled with the medium, and he became so bogged-down that he had to refuse an invitation from Jardine, who had asked him to shoot blackcock on his estate near Lockerbie. Writing to apologise, he said, 'You must know that an oil painting when begun is with me like the red hot iron of a smith lying on the anvil – if it is not wrought white hot and at once, the spirit of the moment is lost.' On 12 January, when the picture was nearly finished, he abandoned it temporarily and walked out in disgust at 2 pm, with a good hour of daylight still to come. 'Sometimes I like the picture,' he wrote, 'then a heat rises to my face and I think it a miserable daub ... As to the birds, as far as they are concerned I am quite satisfied, but the ground, the foliage, the sky, the distance are dreadful.'

Pre-eminent among his immediate ambitions was his desire to meet Sir Walter Scott – and his admiration of the great writer was based not merely on appreciation of his novels. He saw the author also as a saviour of the environment, able to describe the wonders of nature in a way few writers could. Often in the wilds of Ohio, he wrote, he had wished Scott would come to America, and he had called on him out loud to

> wrestle with mankind and stop their increasing ravages on Nature, and describe her now for the sake of future ages. Neither this little stream, this swamp, this grand sheet of flowing water, nor these mountains will be seen a century hence as I see them now. Nature will have been robbed of her brilliant charms. The currents will be tormented and turned astray from their primitive courses. The hills will be levelled with the swamp ... Scarce a magnolia will Louisiana possess. The timid deer will exist no more ... Oh, Walter Scott, come, come to America! Set thee hence, look upon her and see her grandeur. Nature still nurses her, cherishes her. But a tear flows in her eye ... Without thee, Walter Scott, she must die, unknown to the world.

His long-awaited meeting finally took place on 22 January 1827. 'I really believe my hat and coat came to me instead of my going to them,' he wrote, so excited was he when Basil Hall arrived to escort him into the presence of 'the Great Unknown'. The celebrated author was struggling to finish his eight-volume life of Napoleon (or 'Nappy', as he called him), and battling against rheumatism in his knee, which burnt 'like a scorpion's bite,' keeping him awake at night. Perhaps it was pain and exhaustion that made his first meeting with the artist rather dry:

> He is an American by naturalisation, a Frenchman by birth,' [Scott recorded in his journal], 'but less of a Frenchman than I have ever seen – no dash or glimmer or shine about him, but great simplicity of manners and behaviour … simplicity is the predominant character.

All the same, for Audubon it was a memorable occasion. He found Scott in his little study, 'wrapped in a quilted morning-gown of light purple silk', and was struck by the author's 'great benevolence' and 'a kindness most prepossessing,' as well as by his long, loose, silvery locks and heavy white eyebrows. He noticed that the manuscript sheets of the life of Napoleon were densely written, the lines 'rather curved as they go from left to right,' with a huge number of words on each page. After a short while Scott sent for his daughter Ann – 'black-haired and black dressed, not handsome but said to be highly accomplished' – and there was much conversation. Audubon took little part, preferring to listen and observe, 'careful if ignorant'.

When the two met again on 24 January, Scott was evidently in better form, having taken delivery of 'a new piece of armour, a knee-cape of Shamoy leather,' which had given him a good night's sleep. Audubon found

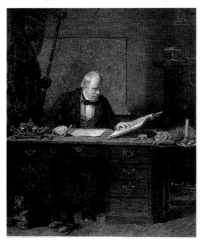

this second visit much more agreeable than the first, and was delighted to discover the novelist 'so willing to level himself with me for a while'. Scott, for his part, thought the drawings 'of the first order, the attitudes the birds of the most animated character and the situations appropriate': privately, he had some reservations about what he saw as a certain stiffness in the pictures, but recognised that 'this extreme correctness is of the utmost consequence to the naturalist'.

24

Sir Walter Scott

One of Audubon's heroes, the great novelist admired the American's bird paintings, even though he found them rather stiff.

In Audubon, 'this sojourner in the desert', he discerned a rare specimen, and he questioned him closely on many subjects, not least the history and habits of Red Indians.

During that winter Audubon burst into print himself, and a scatter of articles in serious journals helped establish his reputation as a naturalist. He had already published two pieces about swallows in America, but his first article in Britain, on the Turkey Buzzard (*Cathartes aura*, also known as *Vultur aura*), appeared in the *Edinburgh New Philosophical Journal* during December. He had written this, in the first instance, as a letter to Jameson, and it set out at length his controversial belief that the birds found their food by sight, rather than by smell. Having described numerous experiments that he had made, he concluded that 'the power of smelling in these birds has been grossly exaggerated, and that, if they can smell objects at any distance, they can see the same objects much farther.'[6]

In the same number of the journal there appeared an extremely generous appraisal of his work, contributed — although the author was not named — by Robert Jameson. This described his pictures as

> admirable in execution, and absolutely marvellous in their representation of the living and intellectual attributes of the species ... We are delighted to learn that these drawings are to be published, and on a scale of magnitude never attempted before in similar works in this country. Already several of the plates, admirably engraved, and beautifully and chastely coloured, have been publicly exhibited.

Audubon followed up in a later edition of the journal with a piece on the natural history of the alligator, which had begun life as a letter to Jardine and Selby, and another on rattlesnakes, originally composed as a letter to Dr Traill and read by the author before the Wernerian Society on 24 February 1827. The *Edinburgh Journal of Science* published his account of the Carrion Crow (*Vultur atratus*), which opened with a

---

6. Modern research has shown that some species of birds do have a well-developed sense of smell. New Zealand Kiwis which feed at night, probe their long bills into wet soil to find worms, which they locate through nostrils at the end of their bills. Pigeons and petrels navigate by smell, and scent does seem to help Turkey Buzzards find food.

characteristically direct sentence: 'The first view of the Carrion Crow is disgusting ... its head and neck resembling in colour that of putrid matter', and also the paper on the Wild or Passenger Pigeon of America (*Columba migratoria*) which he read before the Royal Society of Edinburgh on 19 February.[7]

His writing – as polished by various editors – was more descriptive and anecdotal than scientific, but, because it reported his own experiences, it rang with authenticity; and the pigeon paper must have startled his audience considerably, so extraordinary were the sights he had witnessed when the birds were migrating. He described how 'the light of noonday became dim, as during an eclipse,' from the sheer density of bodies passing overhead, and calculated that he had seen more than one billion birds in a single flock. In the evening

> the pigeons, coming in by millions, alighted everywhere, one on top of the other, until masses of them, resembling hanging swarms of bees as large as hogsheads, were formed on every tree ... The heavy clusters were seen to give way as the supporting branches, breaking down with a crash, came to the ground, killing hundreds of those [birds] which obstructed their fall.

In Audubon's view, such colossal numbers revealed 'the astonishing bounty of the Creator'. Later, Charles Waterton tried to dismiss the entire article as fiction, but this was unwise, for every one of its often grotesque details was clearly a report from the front line – and today it is of still greater interest, because the Passenger Pigeon has become extinct. Extraordinary as it seems – in view of the numbers Audubon reported – the last known survivor of the species died in captivity in 1914.

On 17 March 1827, with only the second Number of the *Birds* in production, Audubon put out his first *Prospectus* for the whole work. (Later versions varied slightly as his plans developed, but the main points remained the same throughout. The details given here are from the 1828 edition.) The document announced publication, 'under the Particular Patronage and Approbation of His Most Gracious Majesty,' of drawings

---

7. Founded in 1783, the Society played an important role in the scientific and literary life of Scotland.

Passenger Pigeon. Male 1. F 2.
Columba Migratoria.

Drawn from Nature & Published by John J. Audubon, F.R.S.E. F.L.S. M.W.S.

Engraved by R. Havell Jun.ʳ Printed & Coloured by R. Havell Sen.ʳ London. 1829.

'made during a residence of twenty-five years in the United States and its territories by John James Audubon, Citizen of the United States.'

The document explained that the 'superiority' of the pictures:

> ... Consists in every specimen being of the full size of life, portrayed with a degree of accuracy as to proportion and outline, the result of peculiar means discovered and employed by the Author, and lately exhibited to a meeting of the Wernerian Society ... The author has not contented himself with single profile views of the originals, but in very many instances he has grouped them, as it were, at their natural avocations, in all sorts of attitudes ... Some are seen pursuing with avidity their prey through the air, or searching diligently their food amongst the fragrant foliage; whilst others of an aquatic nature swim, wade or glide over their allotted element.

The prospectus promised that each Number would contain five plates, including one taken from one of the largest drawings, one from an original of the second size, and three smaller examples. Every bird would be represented at life size. There would be 400 drawings in all, published in three volumes of about 133 plates each. Five Numbers would come out annually, each costing two guineas, payable on delivery. Subscribers were advised to acquire a portfolio in which to keep Numbers, until a volume was completed and bound.

The matter-of-fact language of the prospectus concealed the immense problems with which its author was struggling. Basic arithmetic showed that his project would take many years to complete. Finding far-flung subscribers was only the first hurdle: keeping them up to the mark, delivering Numbers and collecting payments all required a formidable amount of energy and organisation. The cost of a complete set — £175 in England, and $1000 in America — was very high. Audubon must have realised that some of his customers would die, and others would defect, before publication could be completed — and yet, with superhuman determination, he forged ahead.

His optimism seems all the more remarkable in view of the fact that he was apparently worried about Lizars' ability to carry the project through. On 23 February, Basil Hall had written, presumably at his

25 facing page

PASSENGER
PIGEON
Columba migratoria
later *Ectopistes
migratorius*

Male below,
female above.
An exceptionally
beautiful paint-
ing of a species
common in
Audubon's day,
but now extinct.

behest, to the London publisher John Murray, telling him that Audubon was about to set off for London, and asking him 'to introduce engravers, printers and so forth to him, and generally speaking to put him in the way of bringing out his work in an advantageous manner to himself.' Why should he have made such a request, if Audubon had not already expressed doubts about Lizars?

As his departure for London became imminent, several friends strongly advised him to have his hair cut before he descended on the capital. 'Good God!' he wrote on 19 March. 'If Thy works are hated by man, it must be with Thy permission. I sent for a barber, and my hair was mowed off in a trice.' Evidently this was a traumatic event, for on another page of his journal, edged with an inch-thick black line, like a funeral announcement, he wrote:

Edinburgh
March 19th, 1827

This day my hair was sacrificed, and the will of God usurped by the wishes of man. As the barber clipped my locks rapidly, it reminded me of the horrible times of the French Revolution when the same operation was performed upon all the victims murdered at the guillotine. My heart sank low.

John J. Audubon

On 21 March he was considerably put out to find that a set of prints which had just been delivered to Miss Harriet Douglas, a well-to-do visiting American, were 'quite abused and tumbled'. She could treat them how she liked, he wrote – but then, with no mean prescience, he added that he regretted such carelessness 'on her account, that so little care should be taken of a book that in fifty years will be sold at immense prices because of its rarity'. (In spite of his strictures, Miss Douglas – later Mrs Douglas Cruger – became his first American subscriber.)

He left Edinburgh on 5 April 1827, taking with him the first Number of five prints, and his first stop on his circuitous journey south was Twizell House, Prideaux John Selby's home near Belford in Northumberland. The house (now replaced with a later building) stood in a commanding position, looking down over a sloping park towards what was then known as the German Sea, and when their visitor arrived, during the afternoon of 5 April, the whole family, including the squire's wife, Lewis Tabitha Selby, her three daughters and her brother, Captain Robert Mitford, a retired naval officer, were busy planting trees in the grounds.

Audubon immediately felt at home in such down-to-earth, rural surroundings. Next morning he tried to creep out of the house at 5 am, but one of the front doors, which were eleven feet high, made such a noise as he forced it open that he feared he must have been heard all over the building. Once free, he walked, 'or rather ran about, like a bird just escaped from a cage', delighted by the blackbirds, thrushes and larks 'at their morning songs'. For four happy days the Selbys made him one of the family: he drew birds for them and painted a small picture in oil for the eldest daughter, also called Lewis. 'So much at home did we become,' he wrote, 'that the children came about me as freely as if I had long known them.'

Selby, three years younger than Audubon, was another ardent pedestrian, and went on walking expeditions to the wilder parts of the Scottish Highlands – notably the tour of Sutherland which he made in 1834 with Jardine. Later he settled comfortably into the role of country squire, and was content to stay at home, managing his 650 acres, growing fruit (grapes especially), shooting and enjoying his wife's puddings, for which she was renowned. A kind-hearted man, he was once moved to tears by the sight of a hen partridge feigning injury to decoy an intruder away from her chicks; and yet, although easy-going on his own territory, he was a severe magistrate, particularly when sentencing poachers.

Like Audubon, he had been passionately interested in birds since boyhood, even if his methods of study were rather different: he drew entirely from stuffed specimens, of which he had a large collection, those obtained locally being skinned by his butler. Like Audubon, he referred to birds as 'the feathered tribes', and believed that their modes of life had been 'ordained by an all-wise Creator'. Again like Audubon, he had eaten quite a number of species: analysis of his writings suggests that he tried at least sixteen, beyond the normal range of game birds and wildfowl, remarking that Red Godwits were excellent, and that the flavour of bitterns combined the tastes of hare and wildfowl.

A further and more important similarity was that Selby also was engaged on a long-term publishing exercise, and in the middle of issuing his *Illustrations of British Ornithology*, whose aim was to portray all British birds life-size in a series of numbers which were appearing at irregular intervals. He himself etched some of the plates; others were done by his brother-in-law, Robert Mitford, others again by Lizars. Sir William Jardine – another amateur ornithologist, besides being a shooting and fishing companion – was also involved in the production.

The plates were elephant size – about 25½ by 20½ inches (64.7 cm by 52 cm) – and therefore a lot smaller than those which Lizars had started to engrave for Audubon; nevertheless, this was an ambitious project, which eventually included 383 figures in 221 coloured plates, and by the time Audubon came to England, the first volume had been published, along with one volume of text. It is no longer clear exactly who painted or etched what: sixteen of the etchings and fifty-five of the paintings bear Robert Mitford's signature.

For Audubon, Selby's most attractive trait was his generosity of spirit. Far from being poisoned by jealousy of rival artists, he was full of enthusiasm for the American's monumental project, and modest enough about his own abilities to tell a friend in Durham that he had 'derived great advantage' from meeting Audubon, adding that he hoped subscribers to his own work would 'observe an improvement in the future'.

Audubon thought little of Selby's drawings – although of course he did not say so – but he must have discussed publication tactics with his genial host. After fond farewells on both sides, Robert Mitford accompanied the visitor on the next stage of his journey to Mitford Hall, the home of his elder brother Bertram, who was an invalid – 'a pale, emaciated being' too weak to rise from his chair, but 'clever and scientific'. In spite of his poor health, Bertram was an accomplished caricaturist in line-and-wash, and – an artist in his own right – was anxious to see the American's drawings. After looking at nearly a hundred without uttering a word, he suddenly said, 'They are truly beautiful. Our King ought to purchase them. They are too good to belong to a single individual.'

Fired by such extravagant praise, Audubon pressed on to Newcastle-upon-Tyne. There on 13 April he met another of his heroes, Thomas Bewick, the veteran wood engraver, who like Audubon had devoted his life to the study and depiction of natural history.

Bewick was a Northumbrian, born and bred, and his *A General History of Quadrupeds* (1790) and two-volume *History of British Birds* (1797 and 1804) had long since established his pre-eminence as engraver, designer and illustrator; even before meeting him, Audubon called him 'wonderful,' reckoning that 'his work on wood is superior to anything ever attempted in ornithology'.

The two artists' methods were utterly different. Whereas Audubon shot birds by the hundred, Bewick had put away his gun while still a young man, and although he sometimes worked from skins, he had relied mainly on his telescope or the lure of birdseed to get a good view of his subjects. While Audubon insisted on elephantine proportions for his pictures, Bewick wrought in miniature. Most of his wood blocks were no bigger than three inches by two, yet into their tiny spaces he packed a miraculous amount of detail – houses, trees, animals, rain, lowering skies – often spicing his typical country scenes with touches of humour, as when an old woman brandishes her stick at a bull as she goes to cross a stile. He had exceptional powers of observation, and the skill to render what he saw with absolute fidelity. The secret of his ability to produce fine detail was that he pioneered the practice of working on the end grain of wood, rather than on the plank, and some of his blocks were so hard that they have yielded nearly a million prints without becoming worn.

By the time Audubon met him, he was seventy-three, and near the end of his life, but his faculties were unimpaired, and he was still working day in, day out, still sleeping on the floor wrapped in a blanket. The American was immediately enchanted by this 'perfect old Englishman',

The engraver
at work in his
studio, carving a
miniature block
of wood. Audu-
bon, visiting
him at home in
Northumberlan,
delighted in
the old man's
company.

who greeted him wearing a cotton nightcap and showed him the box-
wood block on which he was carving a vignette of 'a dog frightened during
the night by false appearances of men formed by curious roots and
branches of trees, rocks etc'. 'He is tall, stout, has a very large head, and
his eyes are farther apart than those of any man I remember,' Audubon
recorded. 'Now and then he would take off his cotton cap, but the
moment he became animated with the conversation, the cap was on, yet
almost off, for he had stuck it on as if by magic.' After tea and coffee had
been served, Bewick's son Robert produced a set of bagpipes and played
'simple, nice Scottish and English airs with peculiar taste'. The American
afterwards decided that Bewick's eldest daughter 'resembles my kind
friend Hannah Rathbone so much that I frequently felt as if Miss
Hannah, with her black eyes and slender figure, were beside me.'

Audubon cannot have read the old man's delightful, autobiographical
Memoir, for although the book was written by then, it was not published
for another thirty years. But if the two reminisced about their backgrounds, he must have heard how the boy grew up at Cherryburn House,
on the south bank of the Tyne, how he looked after his own small flock

of sheep on the fells, how in spring he 'felt charmed with the music of birds, which strained their little throats to proclaim it' – all his stories laced with the magic of Northumbrian expressions: *sykes* (ditches), *flaid* (frightened), *lonning* (lane or by-road) and many more. Like his visitor, Bewick had been a powerful walker, and half a century earlier had tramped 350 miles into Scotland and back, with three guineas sewn into the waistband of his breeches by his mother, often sleeping out in the heather. Altogether, the pair had much in common.

Next day the whole Bewick family came to see Audubon's paintings, and the old man 'expressed himself as perfectly astounded' at the boldness of the undertaking. On the following morning he invited Audubon to breakfast, and set to work to show him how simple it was to carve wood. 'But cutting wood as he did is no joke,' the American reminded himself afterwards. 'He did it with as much ease as I can feather a bird; he made all his own tools, which are delicate and very beautiful.'

No doubt Audubon was disappointed that the old man did not become a subscriber: Bewick probably realised that he himself would not live long enough to see the *Birds* completed, but he did his best, by putting his own name down on behalf of the Literary and Philosophical Society of Newcastle, which two years earlier had treated itself to a brand-new building. Unfortunately, as Audubon ruefully remarked, the learned body 'did not think [it] proper to ratify the contract.'[8]

Newcastle as a whole gave him a poor return, producing only eight new names. 'How I wish I was in America's dark woods,' he wrote, 'admiring God's works in all their beautiful ways.' Sheer energy kept him going. Waking before dawn one morning, he suddenly thought of how Tobias Smollett had enthused about the view up the Tyne from Isbet Hill. (The notion perhaps resulted from his conversations with Bewick, who positively revered the novelist.) 'If Smollett admired the prospect, I can too,' Audubon thought, and leapt from his bed like a hare started from its form by a huntsman's horn:

---

8. The Society's motto, *Vires adquirit eundo*, 'It gains strength by going [places]' could well have applied to Audubon himself.

I ran downstairs, out of doors and over the Tyne, as if indeed a pack of jack-
als had been after me. Two miles is nothing to me, and I ascended the hill
where poor Isbet, deluded by a wretched woman, for her sake robbed the
mail and afterwards suffered death on a gibbet ... The larks that sprang up
before me, welcoming the sun's rise, animated my thoughts so much that I
felt tears trickling down my cheeks as I gave praise to the God who gave life
to all these in a day.

Another evening *chez* Bewick proved particularly agreeable. Having
greeted his visitor most cordially, the old man said, 'I could not bear the
idea of your going off without telling you, in written words, what I think
of your *Birds of America*,' and handed him a testimonial in an unsealed
envelope. As the two drank to each other's health with hot brandy
toddies, Bewick now and then would start and say, 'Oh that I were young
again! I would go to America too.' When he exclaimed, 'Hey! What a
country it will be!', Audubon gently corrected him, 'Hey! What a country it is already, Mr Bewick!'

By the time Audubon was ready to move on, the friendship had developed into a powerful bond:

As we parted, he held my hand closely and repeated three times, 'God
preserve you.' I looked at him in such a manner that I am sure he understood
I could not speak. I walked slowly down the hilly lane, and thought of the
intrinsic value of this man to the world, and compared him with Sir Walter
Scott. The latter will be forever the most eminent in station ... but Thomas
Bewick is a son of Nature. Nature alone has reared him under her peaceful
care, and he in gratitude of heart has copied one department of her works
that must stand unrivalled forever.

Audubon later named the Bewick's Wren in honour of his old friend – a
bird whose dimensions matched those of the engraver's wood-blocks.

On Sunday 22 April Audubon headed southwards for York, sitting on
top of the coach as usual, even though the weather was cold. Durham
struck him as 'a pretty little town', with its handsome castle and cathedral planted on an elevated peninsula, but York dismayed him: even
though the Minster was magnificent, the streets were 'disgustingly

crooked and narrow, and crossed like the burrows of a rabbit warren.' The landlady of his lodgings in Blake Street looked 'like a round of beef', her husband 'like a farthing candle'. Snow alternated with rain, and the wind blew cold.

York yielded ten subscribers, but Leeds – Audubon's next stop – was much more to his liking. He pronounced the town superior to anything he had seen since Edinburgh. One evening he took a long walk beside the River Aire. As soon as he was out of sight, he undressed and 'took a dive smack across the creek'. The water was so icy that he immediately plunged back across and dressed in a hurry, but not before his flesh had turned 'quite purple'.

On 1 May, the anniversary of his departure from home, he took stock of his position in his journal, addressing his words to Lucy, as usual. Until he reached Edinburgh, he wrote, he despaired of success, but now he felt he was at a turning-point:

> My work is about to be known. I have made a number of valuable and kind friends. I have been received by men of science on friendly terms, and now I have a hope of success if I continue to be honest, industrious and consistent. My pecuniary means are slender, but I hope to keep afloat, for my tastes are simple; if only I can succeed in rendering thee and our sons happy, not a moment of sorrow or discomfort shall I regret.

Back in Manchester, he had difficulty finding lodgings, but was taken in by a friend of a friend, Mr E.W. Sergeant, who not only put him up in his own house, but actively recruited subscribers on his behalf – to such effect that within a week he had eighteen new names. In all, during forty days of campaigning, he secured forty-nine new names – 'a number far above my expectations,' he told Lucy, 'and [one] that astonishes all my friends here'.

On 14 May he returned to Liverpool, where he was delighted to be back among the Rathbone family, 'friends all so dear'. He found them exactly as he had left them, 'full of friendship, benevolence and candour', and he gave them his journal to read. Maybe it was these congenial surroundings that made him unusually cheerful about his prospects when he wrote to Lucy on the 16th. He emphasised the care he was taking not to incur excessive costs. The first fifty copies of the first Number had been engraved, printed and coloured at his own expense and risk; but by then these had been subscribed and paid for, and another fifty had been produced. The main expenses were those of buying and engraving the copper plates (£42 for each Number or set of five), and of hand-colour-ing the prints (£42 10s for 100 sets) The thick paper needed to receive the huge impressions was supplied by two firms, J. Whatman, and J. Whatman / Turkey Mill, both originating from the original company founded by James Whatman in the eighteenth century. The Turkey Mill variety was slightly the lighter, and tended not to hold its whiteness quite so well. Both cost £14 1s 0d per ream, and the printing of every 100 sets amounted to £11 5s. The only further expense (apart from that of travelling) was the £5 for 100 tin cases, in which the prints were for-warded to subscribers. Again, amounts must be multiplied by at least 40 to give modern equivalents.

Encouraged by the fact that he already had 100 subscribers, who paid on delivery, he made some optimistic projections of cash flow:

> When 200 subscribers will be had, the amount [of profit] will be more than double, because the plates are paid for by the first 100 copies sold, and of course the printing, colouring and paper is the only additional expense. Therefore 200 subscribers gives a profit on each Number of £174.18.8, and five times that amount [i.e. on five Numbers] £879.7.4, which makes in dol-lars about 3,902 per annum – enough to maintain us even in this country in a style of elegance and comfort that I hope to see thee enjoy. Should I be so fortunate to reach the number of 500 subscribers, and my health does not impair in consequence of my great exertions, the sum per annum clear of expenses will be £2,821, making in dollars about 10,749!

After a stay of only five days in Liverpool, on 19 May he said adieu to the Rathbones once again 'with a heavy heart', and next morning set out by coach for London.

CHAPTER SIX

LONDON

ON THE SOUTHWARD journey, which took the best part of two days and a night, Audubon was accompanied by his friend the taxidermist William Bentley; they went via Chester and 'the village of Wrexham' to Shrewsbury, where, during an enforced wait, they much enjoyed a walk along the banks of the River Severn. Then, having rattled on through the night, they breakfasted at Birmingham, and proceeded via Stratford-on-Avon, Woodstock and Oxford, reaching the capital at 10 pm.

For years Audubon had longed to see London – St Paul's Cathedral, especially – but no sooner had he arrived than he felt 'a desire beyond words' to be back in his beloved woods. The city, he thought, was 'just like the mouth of an immense monster, guarded by millions of sharp-edged teeth, from which if I escape unhurt it must be called a miracle.' His poor opinion was soon confirmed by Albert Gallatin, the Swiss-born American minister, who, speaking in French, said that he detested the English, and 'spoke in no measured terms of London as the most disagreeable place in Europe'. The minister's opinion of King George IV was no higher: when Audubon suggested that he should seek a royal audience, Gallatin scoffed at the idea, saying: 'the King sees nobody. He has the gout, is peevish, and spends his time playing whist at a shilling a rubber.'

Together with Bentley, Audubon found lodgings at 55 Great Russell Street and spent his first few days walking about like a post-boy to deliver his letters of introduction. The sheer size of the metropolis amazed him. 'Edinburgh is a mere village compared with this vasty capital,' he told Lucy. 'The Duke of Bedford owns several streets himself that would cover Louisville entirely.'

So focused was he on his own affairs that he scarcely ever mentioned matters beyond his immediate sphere of interest. Yet he did acknowledge that in the spring of 1827 the 'critical politique state of affairs here' had certainly deterred many persons of rank from seeing his work. (He was referring to the general economic distress, and the ever-increasing agitation for electoral reform, which led to the Reform Act of 1832.)

Soon Audubon was befriended by John George Children, the naturalist and physicist, who was then secretary of the Royal Society[1] and librarian at the British Museum's department of antiquities. Another of his introductory letters was from Thomas Sully of Philadelphia to Sir Thomas Lawrence, whose status as a portrait painter in London was even more distinguished than that of the American. Lawrence received Audubon civilly and made an appointment to look at his paintings a couple of days later – and when this took place, over breakfast, he appeared to be impressed, several times repeating, 'Very clever, indeed.' Later, however, he seemed ambivalent about the American's work, sometimes praising it, sometimes maintaining an unnerving silence, and for months Audubon remained apprehensive of his reactions.

Lawrence's initial approval naturally encouraged the artist, and he was delighted when, wandering aimlessly about the streets, he came face-to-face with Joseph Kidd, a young landscape painter whom he had met in Edinburgh, and who now joined happily in his exploration of the city, besides coming to paint in his lodgings. Another useful contact was the naturalist Nicholas Vigors, the first secretary of the London Zoological Society, which had been founded a year earlier.

Returning to his rooms one day, Audubon found the new suit of clothes that Basil Hall had insisted he procure for his recruiting drive in the capital. His initial reaction was by no means enthusiastic – 'I looked this remarkable black dress well over, put it on, and thus attired like a

---

1. The oldest scientific academy in existence, founded in 1660.

mournful raven, went to dine at Mr Children's' — but his spirits lifted sharply when he heard that Lord Stanley, whom he considered a real ornithologist, had put his name down for a subscription.

Then, just as things seemed to be going well, dire news arrived from Edinburgh. In the middle of June a long letter from Lizars told Audubon that his colourers had 'struck work', and that 'everything was at a standstill'. The trouble, Lizars wrote, was that the men had become too greedy:

> The high price which they have been in the habit of receiving for Mr Selby's work has poisoned their ideas completely — one of them has gained, at that work, this week, no less than £3.10.0, which is a gross imposition both upon Mr Selby and me, and it must be remedied ... Write me whether you have heard of any others in London and what are their terms, for it is best to be in possession of all the information possible on this matter ... This has been, and continues to be, a most distressing business, and the more so as I cannot yet inform you how it is to turn out.

No wonder Audubon reported, with some restraint, that 'this was quite a shock to my nerves'. Suddenly his whole enterprise was threatened: if he could not fulfil his commitment to produce one new Number of *Birds* every two months, his subscribers would start to desert, and his slender funds would soon be exhausted.

Without any means of quick communication, he could not find out exactly how bad the situation in Edinburgh was, but the last sentence of Lizars' letter was particularly ominous. Audubon's immediate response was to carry on looking for subscribers, and to keep the appointments he had already made; but he evidently sensed that the Scot was unlikely to proceed with *The Birds of America*. Even before the bombshell burst, he had become irritated by Lizars' tardiness, and by his failure to supply subscribers promptly. As he told Lucy, the engraver had 'nearly exhausted' his patience by falling behind schedule — and now he probably realised that Lizars was simply too busy with other work, such as that for Selby and Jardine, to keep his own huge project on schedule.

Having despatched young Kidd post-haste to Edinburgh to obtain twenty-five prints, he immediately set about finding an engraver in London. It is no longer clear who put him in touch with the artist and engraver Robert Havell: Audubon merely reported, 'By chance I entered a print shop, and the owner gave me the name of a man to whom I went, and who has engaged to colour more cheaply than it is done in Edinburgh.' This, it seems, was Robert Havell, whose premises, the Zoological Gallery at 79 Newman Street, sold natural history specimens as well as prints, and lay only a few blocks west of his own lodgings. Spurred by the crisis, Audubon walked round there five times hoping to meet Havell himself, only to find that he was out of town. 'I am full of anxiety and greatly depressed,' he wrote on 19 June. 'Oh! How sick I am of London.'

On 21 June he got another letter from Lizars which did anything but allay his fears. 'I was so struck with the tenor of it,' he wrote, 'that I cannot help thinking now that he does not wish to continue my work.'

Luckily, Havell soon returned – and Audubon's meeting with him proved one of the turning-points of his life. As the bird-man quickly discovered, there were two Robert Havells: the elder, whom he met first, was then fifty-eight, his son thirty-four, members of a large and gifted family of painters, engravers and printers.

The most distinguished was William Havell (a cousin), who was born in 1782 and by the age of twenty-five had established himself as an outstanding water colourist of the new school, a follower of J. M. W. Turner. Unfortunately, his temperament did not match his skill with the brush: he was said to possess 'the egoism of genius without being quite gifted with the ability'; and in 1815, when his painting *Walnut-gathering at Petersham*, which he considered his masterpiece, was rejected by the British Institution, and then failed to find a buyer, he was so chagrined that he went off to China as official artist to Lord Amherst's embassy, thus effectively cutting off his own career when he was at the height of his powers.

The Havells, an ancient family, came from Reading, on the Thames some thirty-five miles west of London, and Robert senior had established his business in London in 1800. Among the firm's successes was a series of twelve *Picturesque Views of the River Thames*, engraved by him and his nephew Daniel. For their *Picturesque Views of Noblemen's Seats*, Robert senior was joined by his son, and during the early 1820s the two collaborated closely, to produce twelve *Views of Public Buildings and Bridges in London*. Father and son had very different characters. Robert senior was described by the naturalist William Swainson (whom Audubon soon met) as 'a complete daudle' – a real slow-mover. Robert junior was lively and adventurous. Tradition holds that early in 1825 the two fell out, and that as a result of the row Robert junior went off for a lengthy sketching tour in South Wales. Whether or not the disagreement was serious, he was back in London by the time Audubon arrived.

27

WILLIAM
SWAINSON

The experienced
and well-known
naturalist offered
Audubon much
moral support,
and accompanied
him on a trip
to Paris.

Another family legend has it that when Audubon made his approach, Robert senior declared he was too old to tackle such a huge project, which he reckoned would take at least a dozen years to complete, but mentioned it to a friendly rival dealer, Paul Colnaghi. When Colnaghi showed him a print done by one of his young engravers, Havell exclaimed 'That's the man for me' – to which Colnaghi replied, 'In that case, send for your son!' Thus reconciled – so the story went – the two Havells formed a partnership and took on *The Birds of America*.

In fact it seems that father and son were already in partnership when Audubon came on the scene, and they agreed to handle the project together: Robert junior would engrave the plates, and his father would colour the 'patterns', as well as supervise the team of colourists, with the artist himself keeping a close eye on proceedings. The terms the Havells offered were 25 per cent lower than Lizars had been charging: £115 for engraving the plates for each Number of five prints.

[125]

As it turned out, the father's involvement lasted little more than a year, for he retired in 1828 and died in 1832; but for Robert junior *The Birds of America* proved the project of a lifetime. For Audubon, it was an extraordinary stroke of luck to find a man so highly skilled, so efficient, so steadfast, so even-tempered, and endowed with endurance at least as great as his own. In due course the two became close friends. Audubon stood godfather to Havell's second child, who was christened Robert Audubon (but lived only two years), and to mark the publication of the second volume of *Birds*, presented a handsome silver loving cup, inscribed 'To Robert Havell from his Friend John James Audubon, 1834.' Havell himself eventually emigrated to the United States.

Experts have expended huge effort and ingenuity in trying to determine the precise history of the early plates. Lizars engraved the first ten, but Audubon had these brought down to London, and most if not all of them were retouched there, probably by Robert senior. His son then took over the remainder of the work. Although the prints in *The Birds of America* bear the legend 'Engraved, Printed and Coloured by R. Havell,' experts believe that they were produced by a combination of etching and aquatint to create the wide variety of textures that the original water-colours demanded.[2]

One mystery remains. How did Havell, in the first place, transfer the image of each painting on to the copper plate? It seems that he may have taken a tracing of the original, damped the tracing paper, laid it face-down on the copper and run plate and paper through the press, so that the pencil lines were left on the metal.

Robert Junior was clearly an artist of exceptional talent, and whenever prints were needed for some particularly important client, Audubon instructed him to prepare them himself. Much excellent work was also

---

2. The term 'aquatinting', a form of etching, comes from the nitric acid (*Aqua fortis*) used to eat into the copper plate. In areas where the artist wishes to produce tone, a porous layer of granulated resin is dropped on to the plate and fused to it by gentle heating. The plate is then placed in an acid bath, which bites into the exposed areas of metal etching lines, and the process can be repeated several times, to produce subtle shadings from pale grey to black.

done by his younger brother, Henry, especially in the later stages of the operation. Yet the Havells alone could not possibly do all the work: as the programme expanded, they took on more and more colourists, until fifty men were working on the project. At times, it is said, they used the broken-off ends of bottles as magnifying glasses to see detail more clearly, and comparison with original paintings shows that they enhanced the prints by adding backgrounds of landscapes or vegetation and by repositioning birds to produce better balance. Audubon often complained about the standard achieved, and sometimes ordered prints to be redone; but on the whole the results were remarkably uniform.

The distribution of prints to subscribers was itself a demanding task. When each Number of five prints was ready, the huge sheets were packed in tin boxes and sent off by coach to their far-flung destinations; and when the first volume of twenty Numbers was complete, copies were issued either as loose sheets, for recipients to have bound to their own specifications, or bound in leather or half-leather at source. Much of this work was carried out by Hering's bindery, a firm at 9 Newman Street run by the three sons of a German immigrant. A leather-bound volume weighed over 40 pounds, and was substantial enough not merely to cover but to crush an elegant coffee-table. At one point Havell warned Audubon that 'every binder I have consulted respecting the open back informs me that it would not do, as the weight of the book is so great that they would soon break out and the binding come undone.'

In the middle of the initial convulsion over Lizars' strike, Audubon heard that Charles Bonaparte was in town. No matter that he had had a

28

TRAVELLING SAFELY

One of the tin boxes, lined with wood, in which loose prints of *The Birds of America* were sent to subscribers.

29

BONAPARTE'S
GULL
Larus bonapartii
now *Larus
philadelphia*

Audubon
painted all three
birds separately,
cut them out and
pasted them on
to one sheet of
paper. Havell
added the
background of
rocks and water.

blazing row with the Frenchman over the way his own drawing of the female Boat-tailed Grackle had been bowdlerised in the first volume of the prince's *American Ornithology*: now he hurried to meet him, and the two shook hands, 'pleased to meet each other on this distant shore.' With his 'fine head ... his musta-chios, his bearded chin, his keen eye,' the prince cut a stylish figure, and he delighted Audubon by at once subscribing for the first Num-bers of *Birds*. Yet his insistence that his own servant should always address him as 'Your Royal Highness' struck the artist as 'ridiculous in the extreme'.

Under the stress of these events, Audubon's journal-writing dwin-dled. On 28 June, after a week's gap, he noted, 'I no longer have the wish to write my days. I am quite wearied of everything in London' – and then, after one more short, lugubrious entry on 2 July ('I am too dull, too mournful'), he gave up altogether for three months, not resuming until 30 September. By then he was back in Leeds, with hot news to be recorded:

> The King!! My dear book! It was presented to him by Sir Walthen Waller, Bart, KCH, at the request of my most excellent friend J.P. Children, of the British Museum. His Majesty was pleased to call it fine, permitted me to publish it under his particular patronage, approbation and protection, became a subscriber on the usual terms, not as kings generally do, but as a gentleman, and my friends all spoke as if a mountain of sovereigns had drummed in an ample purse at once, and for me.[3]

This gushing report glossed over the fact that Audubon's friends in high

---

3. Today a set of all four volumes, in half-leather bindings, is among the jewels of the Royal Library in Windsor Castle.

places had been busy on his behalf. When John Children asked Sir Walthen Waller, the King's oculist, how to obtain this vital subscription, the answer was that Audubon should in effect subvert the monarch by presenting him with *Sauve qui Peut*, the immense oil painting of a fox attacking pheasants, nine feet by six, with which he had struggled over Christmas; but Sir Thomas Lawrence advised against any such attempt at bribery, telling Audubon that the picture would fetch 300 guineas on the open market. When, in the end, Waller prevailed on the King to inspect the prints closely, they made an immediate impression – and Waller also reported that the Duchess of Clarence wished to have her name put on the list.

Audubon's private view of George IV was no more respectful than that of most English citizens, who regarded their dissolute sovereign with contempt. The King and the duchess, Audubon told Lucy, were 'no better in my eye than any other two, but as the world goes it must do me much good'. In fact he maligned the duchess, who became Queen Adelaide when her husband succeeded to the throne as King William IV in 1830, and who took over the former King's subscription.

During the year 1827 Lucy gave up Beechwoods and took the job of governess at Beech Grove, the plantation home of William Garrett Johnson, which was close by, in the same parish. In many of his letters home Audubon besought her to push their sons on to greater efforts

30 below

DISTANT PROMISE

Prospectus for *The Birds of America*, issued by the artist in 1831 when his great project was less than half complete.

UNDER THE SPECIAL PATRONAGE

OF

Her Most Excellent Majesty,

QUEEN ADELAIDE.

THE

BIRDS OF AMERICA,

ENGRAVED FROM

DRAWINGS

MADE IN

THE UNITED STATES AND THEIR TERRITORIES.

BY JOHN JAMES AUDUBON,

F. R. SS. L & E.

FELLOW OF THE LINNEAN AND ZOOLOGICAL SOCIETIES OF LONDON; MEMBER OF THE LYCEUM OF NEW YORK, THE NATURAL HISTORY SOCIETY OF PARIS, THE WERNE-RIAN NATURAL HISTORY SOCIETY OF EDINBURGH; HONORARY MEMBER OF THE SCOTTISH ACADEMY OF PAINTING, SCULPTURE AND ARCHITECTURE, &c.

PUBLISHED BY THE AUTHOR;

AND TO BE SEEN AT

MR R. HAVELL'S JUN. THE ENGRAVER,

77, OXFORD STREET, LONDON.

MDCCCXXXI.

of learning and achievement, particularly John Woodhouse, who was still living at home:

> John may have my gun as his own if he will positively take lessons of music and drawing and improve, but ... he must pledge his word to thee that he will be industrious and a good boy to thee. Branches of trees and flowers – I particularly wish him to do the size of nature and as closely as his talents will permit ... Kiss our dear John for me. Make him put in good whiskey all the beetles he can get ... Urge my son to continue the violin, drawing, everything ... I wish Johnny would attempt to draw for me a male and female Sparrow Hawk, or, if he cannot, have him kill some and send them to me – I mean the skins ... If he could make me a large drawing of a fine cotton plant in blooms and puds [sic], I would be very glad.

The idea developing in Audubon's mind was that if John could turn himself into a sufficiently competent artist, he could contribute substantially to the great work in hand, by drawing many of the birds still missing from the portfolio.

In London Audubon moved house, settling at 95 Great Russell Street, the home of 'a Mrs W., an intelligent widow with eleven children, and but little cash'. He then made what he called a 'sortie' to the north, collecting dues and seeking new subscribers, first at Manchester, where a letter sent by Havell in London reached him in only one day – 'wonderful activity, this, in the post office department'. Having had no luck in Leeds, he went on to York, where everything seemed to go wrong. His agent had done 'almost nothing', and had not even delivered all the Numbers that Lizars had produced. One Number forwarded from Edinburgh turned out to be 'miserably poor, scarcely coloured at all', and Audubon, feeling ashamed of it, sent it straight to Havell for proper treatment.

He was just too late to catch the Duke of Wellington, who had been in York a few days earlier, and when he walked a mile out of town to see if Mr F., a subscriber, had received his first Number, he found to his dismay that nothing had arrived. 'How often I thought during these visits of poor Alexander Wilson,' he wrote on 9 October. 'When travelling as I am now, to procure subscribers, he as well as myself was received with rude coldness, and sometimes with that arrogance which belongs to parvenus.'

In spite of these disappointments, he had set his heart on getting 200 subscribers by the first of May next year, and in a journal note intended for Lucy he wrote:

> Should I succeed, I shall feel well satisfied, and able to have thee and all our sons together. Thou seest that castles are still building on hopeful foundations only; but he who does not try anything cannot obtain his ends.

In Newcastle things looked up. The Marquis of Londonderry immediately took out a subscription, and Audubon's friend Adamson invited him to dine every day that he was free. He looked in on 'old Mr Bewick' and found him in good spirits, working away as usual, and wearing a fur cap in place of the cotton one which had kept threatening to fall off. He also spent two happy days with the Selby family at Twizell House.

If people asked him how he had come to part company with Lizars, he 'felt glad to be able to say that it was at his desire, and that we continue esteemed friends' – and when he reached Edinburgh again, later in October, Lizars was the first person on whom he called. 'He received me well,' Audubon recorded, 'and asked me to dine with him'. Shown the Havell prints for the third Number, the Scottish engraver admired them greatly, summoned his workmen and 'observed to them that the London artists beat them completely'.

Lizars already seemed to regret his decision to give up the job, for he told Audubon that if any further part of the work were entrusted to him, he would see that it was done as well as Havell's, at the same price, and that he would have the plates delivered in London. Audubon paid his account in full, and then, in a shrewd move which may have sprung from his natural friendliness, as much as from guile, he appointed Daniel Lizars, the engraver's bookseller brother, as his agent in Edinburgh.

Audubon had no illusions about the length of the task ahead: 'I am now I consider tied to England for no less than eight years,' he told Lucy, 'and perhaps for ever more if I can make John do what either he or I must do after that time – i.e. to procure more drawings to keep my Grand Work agoing.'

For the rest of 1827 he moved around the north, searching for new subscribers and trying to bolster the resolve of the old. In Scotland alone six of his original names had already deserted, and he wondered uneasily how many would see the project through to its end: 'I find on experiment that the Scotch in Scotland are the same as they are in all parts of the world where they go, tight dealers, and men who with great concern untie their purse.'

As winter came down, travelling grew ever colder and less agreeable. On a journey to Glasgow he shared the inside of the coach with three other passengers, none of whom uttered a single word during the four-hour trip. 'We all sat like so many owls of different species, as if afraid of one another and on the *qui vive*,' he recorded. Later, on the way to York, his companions were 'of the dormouse order: eighty-two miles and no conversation is to me dreadful'. Several times during his peregrinations he was disturbed by the cruelty he witnessed: once the coachman continually lashed his horses, trying to keep up with a superior team ahead, so that the animals became exhausted, 'panting for breath and covered with sweat and the traces of the blows they had received.' Another day, at a small village, the paying passengers were joined by 'three felons and a man to guard them ... bound for Botany Bay'.

> These poor wretches were chained to each other by the legs, had scarcely a rag on, and those they wore so dirty that no one could have helped feeling deep pity for them, case-hardened in vice as they seemed to be. They had some money, for they drank ale and brandy wherever we stopped.

Glasgow fulfilled his worst expectations: in four days he found only one customer. 'One subscriber in a city of 150,000 souls, rich, handsome and with much learning!' he wrote in disgust. Another sweep through York and Manchester was no more productive – but at least in Manchester he collected five letters from Lucy, all at once, and when he returned to Liverpool, on 22 November, he was much more cheerful, especially when welcomed by friends such as William Rathbone and Dr Traill.

On the morning after his arrival he got up before dawn and walked out the three miles to breakfast at Greenbank. When he was half-way there, the sun rose, lighting up the frost on the grass, and he rejoiced at the sound of a blackbird, perched on a fir tree, 'announcing the beauty of this winter morning in his melodious voice'. As he remarked, it was impossible to approach Greenbank in fair weather without enjoying the song of some birds – 'for, Lucy, that sweet place is sacred, and all the feathered tribe in perfect safety.' Breakfast with the Rathbones was pure delight, for he was once again swept into the family's warm heart.

His worst worry, that December, was the campaign of vilification launched by his enemies – principally Ord – in Philadelphia. Word of his progress in London had clearly reached them, and jealousy spurred them into action. Perhaps it was unwise of Audubon to let the editors of learned Scottish journals publish his letters as articles. Those on the Alligator, the Carrion Crow and the Wild Pigeons of America proved relatively uncontroversial; but the one that set tempers raging was 'Notes on the Rattlesnake'.

A letter from Thomas Sully warned the author that he had been 'severely handled' in one of the Philadelphia newspapers, and that the editor had called everything which he had said in his papers 'a pack of lies'. 'Friend Sully is most heartily indignant,' Audubon wrote, 'but with me my motto is: *Le temps découvrira la vérité.*' So it might – but in fact he felt deeply wounded that his professional knowledge, obtained from thousands of hours' study in the woods, should be challenged, and that he should be branded a liar 'by a man who doubtless knows little of the inhabitants of the forests on the Schuylkill, much less of those elsewhere'.

Although he made no public counter-attack, he revealed some of his annoyance in a long letter to Sully, sent from Liverpool on 2 December. He had devoted the 'greatest portion' of his life to the active investigation of nature (he protested), and for more than twenty years he had been in the habit of writing down details of what he had seen on the spot, in special journals kept separately from his main diaries. As a witness of his accuracy, he invoked the name of young Joseph Mason, who had accompanied him for eighteen months on his extended hunting excursion along the Ohio and the Mississippi in 1820 and 1821. 'He drew with me,' Audubon recalled. 'He was my daily companion, and we both rolled ourselves together on buffalo robes at night.'

The papers published in Edinburgh, he said, were merely copies of passages in his journals, tidied up for publication. Why should he have falsified his accounts of any bird or animal behaviour that he witnessed? Pure self-interest would suggest that he stuck rigidly to facts. He had not read any of the Philadelphia papers, but he felt sure that 'the pen that traced them must have been dipped in venom more noxious than that which flows from the jaws of the rattlesnake.'

It was the rattlesnake that nearly proved his undoing. His picture of Mocking Birds defending their nest of eggs against a snake, first shown in London in 1827, remains one of the most striking he ever painted, alive with fear and action; but the point seized on by his enemies is that

31

SNAKE'S TEETH

Detail of Northern Mockingbirds being attacked by a rattlesnake. Jealous rivals claimed that Audubon had depicted the reptile's fangs curving in the wrong direction.

the rattler is up a tree. Snakes, they thought — they knew — could not climb trees, and yet here was Audubon claiming they did, not only in paint, but also in print.

The attack was initiated by Ord, and later taken up by Waterton with such persistence that the controversy smouldered on for years. It was not enough for Audubon's detractors to declare that he had simply made a mistake: they trumpeted that he was a romancer, a fraud and a liar — and their diatribes were given new momentum in 1828 by Dr Thomas P. Jones of Philadelphia, who not only published the rattlesnake article, without permission, in his *Franklin Journal* and *American Mechanics' Magazine*, but then cravenly repudiated it, claiming that it had been printed without his having time to read it. In his lame retraction he damned it, with reckless exaggeration, as 'a tissue of the grossest falsehoods ever attempted to be palmed upon the credulity of mankind,' and claimed that 'the romances of Audubon rival those of Munchhausen'.[4]

Audubon had not deliberately lied about the rattlesnake — and in due course other naturalists rallied to his support, confirming that rattlers do sometimes climb trees. But it seems that for once he had made an unfortunate mistake. In his Edinburgh paper he had written a graphic account of how in 1821, on the Pirrie plantation in Louisiana, he watched a rattler catch a full-grown grey squirrel: the snake climbed trees with ease and swung from one branch to another until its prey was exhausted and dropped to the ground, where the reptile overcame it, coiling itself round the body and suffocating the creature to death before slowly swallowing it whole. It seems almost certain that the killer in question was not a rattler at all, but a blue racer or black snake (*Bascanion constrictor*), which hunts and kills precisely as Audubon described, and vibrates the tip of its tail on the ground. Whether he mistook the species at the time, or became confused when he transcribed his notes, he paid a heavy price.

Lesser controversies broke out over other questions, such as the shape of a rattlesnake's fangs. Waterton sought to ridicule Audubon for

---

4. Baron Karl Friedrich von Munchhausen (1720–97) was celebrated for the tall stories he told of his exploits while serving in the Russian army against the Turks.

asserting that the fangs sometimes turn upwards at their tips, but later observations by the artist and other naturalists showed that here he was right. Yet another dispute ground on for years over whether or not birds, and in particular the Turkey Vulture or buzzard, find their food by scent or by sight. In his paper of 1826 Audubon had set out to show that vultures have a far less well-developed sense of smell than his cotemporaries believed: already he had convinced himself of this with his own experiments, and later he and his friend the Rev. John Bachman conducted more trials designed to settle the question once and for all.

Try as he might, Ord could not discover any incident with which to discredit Audubon, and he fell back on general calumny. 'If I possessed any important information about this man,' he once wrote to Waterton, 'I certainly should give it to you; but all my inquiries have one result, viz. 'that he is a well-meaning sort of man, though a great liar.'

Whether or not the campaign of vilification did have any negative effect, it is impossible to know. But, quite apart from casting doubt on Audubon's intellectual integrity, Ord's attacks obviously posed some practical threat to his publishing enterprise: if the Philadelphian clique, backed up by Waterton in England, managed to cast enough doubt on the accuracy of his paintings, and his ornithological exactitude in general, they might well deter potential customers from subscribing.

As 1827 drew to an end, the artist occasionally let fall a hint that he was starting to feel his age: 'Alas, I am growing old, and although my spirits are as active as ever, my body declines.' Nevertheless, after walking into Liverpool alongside Richard Rathbone, who was on his horse, he recorded, 'I kept by his side all the way, the horse walking.'

> I do not rely as much on my activity as I did twenty years ago, but I still think I could kill any horse in England in twenty days, taking the travel over rough and level grounds. This might be looked upon as a boast by many, but, I am quite satisfied, not by those who have seen me travel at the rate of five miles an hour all day. Once indeed I recollect going from Louisville to Shippingport [about two miles] in fourteen minutes, with as much ease as if I had been on skates.

facing page 32

TURKEY BUZZARD or TURKEY VULTURE
Cathartes atratus now *Cathartes aura*

Controversy raged for years about whether these birds found carrion by smelling it or by seeing it.

PLATE CLI.

Turkey Buzzard.
CATHARTES ATRATUS.
Male 1 Young 2.

Fearing that in his letters he might have cracked up the sophistication of England excessively, he reassured Lucy that his basic allegiance had not changed:

> Now thou must not think me flighty and abandoning my dear America, rough as it is yet, and swelled in thought in favour of all and everything in England ... No – America will always be my land. I never close my eyes without travelling thousands of miles along our noble streams and traversing our noble forests. The voice of the thrush and the rumbling noise of the alligator are still equally agreeable to my sense of recollection.

Wherever he went, whatever setbacks he met, he was always cheered by the sight of birds – whether they were ducks wheeling across a new moon over Regent's Park in London or, in the north, crows that 'flew under the dark sky foretelling winter's approach'. Just as he had been delighted by the tame robin that came in to call through the windows of Greenbank, so he responded to a magnificent Andean eagle, owned by a friend of Selby's.

At the end of 1827 his financial position seemed relatively secure. He had 124 'substantial subscribers', and had made a useful profit. His published work (he told Lucy) was 'looked upon as the first and only one of its kind in existence', and he was developing definite ideas about bringing the family over. He felt sure that he and Lucy could live more comfortably than at any time since they left Henderson, and the pleasure of having John near them, at a good school, would be great. A year later, they might be able to summon Victor, to come and help with the business. The best months for sailing from New York were May and April, so Lucy ought to leave Bayou Sara 'as soon as the waters will admit'. 'Keep up a good heart,' he exhorted her,

> and make all thy preparatory arrangements as soon as possible, but do not take any packages of great weight or incumbrance with thee. Indeed, I would sell off as much as thou canst for cash, as thou wilt be refitted here in much better style.

CHAPTER SEVEN
IN THE SMOKE

AT THE START of 1828 Audubon returned to London, borne up by several New Year resolutions. One was to stop taking snuff, which he realised was 'a useless and not very clean habit, besides being an expensive one', and another was to give up trying to paint in oils. His relative incompetence with oils irritated him intensely. 'My hand does not manage the oil brush properly,' he told Lucy:

> therefore I am very likely to abandon this style for ever. Yet it is with a considerable degree of regret, if it does not amount to sorrow. Man, and particularly thy husband, cannot easily bear to be outdone, and I will think frequently how hard it is for me not to have another life to spend, to acquire a talent that needs a whole life to reach to any moderate degree of perfection.

'I can draw,' he acknowledged in his journal, 'but I shall never paint well', and, rather than waste more time rushing out pot-boilers in oils, he began to go through all his drawings, reworking some of the earlier ones and choosing the twenty-five that he wanted to feature in the Numbers for the coming year.

For the first few days of January his morale was high. He had paid his bills and was well in funds. 'Had I made such regular settlements all my life, I should never have been as poor a man as I have been,' he reflected. 'But on the other hand I should never have published *The Birds of America*.' Then a feverish cough and sore throat undermined his optimism: a 'constant darkness of mood' descended, and on 20 January he wrote:

> Oh! How dull I feel. How long am I to be confined in this immense jail? In London, amidst all the pleasures, I feel unhappy and dull; the days are

heavy, the nights worse. Shall I ever again see and enjoy the vast forests in their calm purity, the beauties of America?

Trying to decide why he disliked London so much, he concluded that one reason was the extreme contrast between rich and poor, which distressed him, and another the sheer press of people. His best, and only, means of countering depression was to work all the daylight hours, either at his own drawing, or supervising Havell, who was himself colouring a special set of prints designed for presentation to Congress. 'While I am not a colourist, and Havell is a very superior one, I know the birds,' Audubon wrote. 'Would to God I was among them.'

On 23 January the receipt of a letter from Lucy put new heart into him. No matter that it was dated 1 November — her 'substantial advices' delighted him; and when he started a new journal, a week later, he inscribed it: 'What I write in you [the book] is for my wife, Lucy Audubon, a matchless woman, and for my two Kentucky lads, whom I do fervently long to press to my heart again.'

He was further pleased by the arrival of his friend Bentley, who came to stay in his spare room, and on 1 February the pair went off to visit the Exeter 'Change, the celebrated menagerie in the Strand, at the invitation of the owner, Edward Cross. They must have heard that less than two years earlier there had been an appalling scene at the 'Change, when Cross's elephant Chunee went berserk and began to smash up its special enclosure, threatening to send not only itself, but also the lions in neighbouring cages, crashing down into the Strand. The great animal had to be gunned down at point-blank range by a squad of hastily assembled riflemen, who fired more than 150 bullets into the poor beast's head, neck and body before it collapsed.

Audubon, in contrast, had the 'honour of riding on a very fine and gentle elephant; I say "honour", because the immense animal was so well trained and so obedient as to be an example to many human beings who are neither.' Dining with Cross, his wife and his keepers, he remarked that his host by no means deserved his name, for he proved a very pleasant man, and a good conversationalist — and although none of the

company was 'very polished', all 'behaved with propriety and good humour'. Later he recorded that Chunee's articulated skeleton had been put up for exhibition at the 'Change, and was for sale at £400.

The new gardens of the London Zoological Society, at the north end of Regent's Park, pleased him less. As he reported, the place was still 'quite in a state of infancy', having been founded less than two years earlier, but he reckoned he had 'seen more curiosities in a swamp in America in one morning than is collected here since eighteen months. All, however, is well planned, clean, and what specimens they have are fine and in good condition.'

Relations with Havell, at this early stage, were not altogether easy. On 17 January Audubon noted, 'It is difficult work for a man like me to see that he is neither cheating nor cheated'; and three weeks later, on 7 February, when the engraver brought the sets which he had produced for 1827, the artist found that 'either through him or Mr Lizars' he had sustained a loss of nearly £100, and had been charged for fifty Numbers more than he could account for. 'This seems strange always to me that people cannot be honest,' he remarked darkly. 'But I must bring myself to believe that many are not, from my own experiences.'

The expense of living in London was 'very great', he told Lucy, and had he not been extremely careful and very industrious, he would have 'run ashore ere now'. A letter he sent her on 6 February showed how, in his mind, he was wrestling with future possibilities. He had bought her a 'good, soft-toned' piano for 40 guineas – and this seems to have been designed to soften the blow which followed. Having thought things over, he had decided not to ask her to come to England straightaway:

> I am really and truly in want not only of a wife, but of a kind and true friend, to consult and to help me by dividing with me a portion of my hard labours. Yet thy entire comfort is the only principle that moves me, and, fearing thou might expect more than I can yet afford, I refrained from doing it for the present.

For the time being, he wrote, he was trying to obtain a post in some public institution, or 'a permanent employment with some lord or others who may be sufficiently wealthy and possessed of taste to pay me well and suffer me to have my own way'. If he did summon her to come over, she should not sell the piano, but pass it on to Victor. Should he be forced to abandon his work 'and return to America with a broken heart', he would bring her another of the highest quality. If, on the other hand, all went well, in the end he and Lucy might eventually return to America together 'and spend our latter days comfortable and happy'.

To keep himself solvent, he reverted to painting in oils, and worked feverishly. A new version of the trapped otter fetched £25, other pot-boilers less. Altogether he sold seven copies of the otter and ten of other subjects. 'I painted all day,' he wrote, 'and sold my work during the dusky hours of the evening as I walked through the Strand and other streets where the Jews reigned: popping in and out of Jew-shops or any others, and never refusing the offers made me for the pictures I carried fresh from the easel.'

The enigmatic Sir Thomas Lawrence, calling frequently at Audubon's

lodgings, began to act as a freelance agent, selling pictures on his behalf
– and although this helped, he only just remained afloat. For weeks, day
in, day out, he was haunted by the spectre of bankruptcy, which could
then be a capital offence, and often resulted in imprisonment:

> I was a bankrupt, when my work had scarcely begun, and in two days more
> I should have seen all my hopes of publication blasted; for Mr Havell had
> already called to say that on Saturday I must pay him £60. I was then not
> only not worth a penny, but had actually borrowed £5 a few days before to
> purchase materials for my pictures. But these pictures which Sir Thomas
> sold for me enabled me to pay my borrowed money, and to appear full-
> handed when Mr Havell called. Thus I passed the Rubicon.

On 10 February 1828 he toiled from seven in the morning until dark,
reworking his picture of a Bald Eagle, which, because it was 'indisputably
the noblest bird of its genus that has yet been discovered in the United
States,' he had renamed it 'The Bird of Washington', 'to honour it with
the name of one yet nobler, who was the saviour of his country'. The
original painting, which he had done on the Mississippi several years
earlier, showed the eagle feasting on a wild goose – and clearly the exercise of recasting it sent his mind ranging out, thousands of miles from
his London gaol, along the mighty river which he knew so well: 'Now I
shall make it [the eagle] breakfast on a cat-fish, the drawing of which is
also with me, with the marks of the talons of another eagle, which I disturbed on the banks of the same river driving him from his prey.' Next
day he again worked right through the span of daylight, and recorded:
'Precisely the same as yesterday, neither cross nor dull, therefore, but perfectly happy.' On the third evening, he was still hard at it, and the objects
on his paper looked 'more like a bird and a fish than a windmill, as they
have done.'

One evening at the Linnean Society[1] a few of his paintings were laid
out on a table alongside some by Selby, and 'very unfair comparisons
were drawn between the two'. With characteristic generosity of spirit,

---

1. The scientific body formed in London in 1788 in memory of the Swedish botanist Carl Linnaeus,
who initiated the modern system of classification.

34

WHITE-
HEADED EAGLE
Falco leucocephalus
now Bald Eagle
*Haliaeetus
leucocephalus*

Dissatisfied with
his first version
of the painting,
Audubon later
changed the rap-
tor's prey from a
goose to a catfish.

Audubon stood up for Selby as best he could, and later wrote:

> I am quite sure that had he had the same opportunities that my curious life
> has granted me, his work would have been far superior to mine ... The fact
> is, I think, that no man has yet done anything in the way of illustrating the
> birds of England comparable to his great work.

By no means all his potential customers were as gentlemanly as the genial
squire of Twizell House:

> Today I called by appointment on the Earl of Kinnoul, a small man, with a
> face like the caricature of an owl; he said he had sent for me to tell me that
> all my birds were alike, and he considered my work a swindle. He may really
> think this – his knowledge is probably small; but it is not the custom to
> send for a gentleman to abuse him in one's own house. I heard his words,
> bowed, and without speaking left the rudest man I have met in this land; but
> he is only thirty, and let us hope may yet learn how to behave to a perfect
> stranger under his roof.[2]

Deciding to visit Cambridge in search of subscriptions, on 3 March
Audubon caught the coach from the White Horse in Fetter Lane, and

2. In spite of his strictures, the Earl took out a subscription only to cancel it later (see page 253).

was chagrined to find that it took a whole hour to get clear of London. 'What a place!' he groaned. 'Yet many persons live there solely because they like it.' The driver, purple in the face, 'held confidences with every grog shop between London and Cambridge,' with the result that the journey took eight and a half hours.

The university town delighted Audubon: he admired its calm, its cleanliness, the spacious deployment of the colleges. He was graciously received by his contacts, and dined sumptuously in hall at Corpus Christi College, where twelve fellows and twenty guests sat at the High Table, and a fine gilt or gold tankard, containing 'a very strong sort of nectar', was handed round. On Sunday, at evensong in the chapel of Trinity College, he had an experience both unnerving and uplifting:

> The charm that had held me all day was augmented many-fold as I entered an immense interior, where were upwards of four hundred collegians in white robes. The small wax tapers, the shadowy distances, the slow footfalls of those still entering, threw my imagination into disorder. A kind of chilliness almost as of fear came to me, my lips quivered, my heart throbbed, I fell on my knees and prayed to be helped and comforted. I shall remember this sensation for ever.

Yet for Audubon Cambridge had two major disadvantages. One was that none of the colleges subscribed to his book, his only successes being with the University Library, the Philosophical Society, the Provost of King's College, the Fitzwilliam Museum, and the undergraduate son of Lord Fitzwilliam — a good-looking youth whose courtesy and refinement impressed him. The other problem was that the scholarly milieu revived his latent sense of inferiority: dining at the Vice-Chancellor's and finding himself among 'men of deep research, learning and knowledge, mild in expressions, kind in attentions,' he fervently wished it has been his lot 'to have received such an education as they possess'. He was dismayed to find that whenever the conversation struck out into water intellectually too deep for him, he had to remain silent until the talk came back closer inshore.

Oxford, which he visited next, was even worse. Not only did none of the twenty-two colleges subscribe: when he went to the Radcliffe Library to inspect the prints of his first Number, he was horrified to find that they were hardly coloured at all, so he rolled them up and took them away, promising to send replacements. His sole success was with the School of Anatomy, where he was befriended by Dr John Kidd, the professor of Chemistry and Medicine, who joined in the search for subscribers: 'He and I ran after each other all day like the Red-headed Woodpeckers in the spring.'

Back in London on 15 March, he was much cheered by the arrival of letters from Lucy, Victor and John. The first was dated 10 November, and had been four months in transit, but John's was relatively fresh, posted only seven weeks earlier. Contact with his family, however tenuous, made him pour out his affection:

> I love thy letters, I adore them. The older I grow, the more I feel thy worth and the more I need thy company. I am sorry to hear of the ravages the Yellow Fever has made about thee. Do not suffer John to be absent long from thee, to lose one of our sons would I fear disturb my brains.

At that moment John Loudon, a publisher and editor in London, was about to launch his new *Magazine of Natural History*, and he asked Audubon to write articles for the journal; but the artist was still smarting so much from the attacks on his earlier papers that he declined, vowing 'I will never write anything to call down upon me a second volley of abuse. I can only write facts, and when I write those, the Philadelphians call me a liar.'

Loudon, however, was undeterred, and on 6 April made another attempt, offering eight guineas for an article. When this also was refused, he had recourse to William Swainson, an experienced zoologist who had made large collections in Malta, Sicily and Brazil, and had contributed sections to several encyclopaedias. When he accepted Loudon's invitation to write a review of Audubon's work for publication in the magazine, the news pleased the artist so much that he changed his mind and himself sent Loudon a paper entitled 'Notes on the Bird of Washington (*Falco washingtoniana*) or Great Sea Eagle' (later believed to have been mistaken for an immature White-headed Eagle), which was published in July 1828.

At that stage Audubon had not met Swainson, but he had an introduction to him from their mutual friend Dr Traill, who had given him a glowing reference. Describing the American as 'a kindred spirit', Traill had written: 'You cannot fail to be pleased with the drawings of Mr Audubon and with his intelligence and manners.' On 9 April the artist sent Swainson a warm letter, directed to his home, Highfield Hall, a farm near the hamlet of Tittenhanger Green in Hertfordshire, some fifteen miles north of London. So began a friendship which, for a while, proved of enormous value to the artist.

In the low days of April he was cheered by the news that he had been elected a fellow of the Linnean Society, but depressed by a visit to Havell's, which made him realise how slowly his 'immense work' was progressing. 'May God grant me life to see it accomplished and finished,' he wrote. 'Then indeed will I have left a landmark of my existence.' Another worry was that some of his drawings had been damaged by damp or atmospheric pollution, and he feared that if the whole lot were somehow ruined, he would never have the energy to recreate them. He decided, if further deterioration set in, 'to remove them to Paris or Edinburgh, where the atmosphere is less dangerous ... I hate it [London], yes, I cordially hate London, and yet cannot escape from it.' Even if he walked out across the fields to the 'pretty village called Hampstead', the pleasure of hearing the birds was spoilt by the knowledge that in another hour he would be back in the 'bustle, filth and smoke'.

By the middle of April his spirits had sunk to their lowest ebb, and he was thinking strongly of returning to America. 'Such a long absence from thee is dreadful,' he told Lucy in his journal. 'I sometimes fear we shall never meet again in this world.' In his mind he was summing up the pros and cons of a transatlantic voyage, and a stay of perhaps twelve months in the United States. Apart from wanting to find new birds, he felt he needed to renew about fifty of his drawings from fresh observations, and to include more interesting backgrounds: 'I am sure that

right & facing
35, 36

GREAT
AMERICAN
HEN OR
WILD TURKEY
Meleagris gallopavo

Audubon began
this painting
(right) of a hen
and her chicks
while floating
down the Missis-
sippi in 1820.

now I could make better compositions, and select better plants than when I drew mainly for amusement.'

Yet he realised that the difficulties were formidable. To leave England for a year would be to take a huge risk. Without his own hand on the tiller, and without any possibility of rapid communication in the event of a crisis, his ship might founder. He needed to find 'a true, devoted friend' who would superintend the work at Havell's, and make sure that Numbers were delivered on time. Somehow he would have to arrange for Havell to be paid regularly. To stiffen his resolve, he fell back on thoughts of the Almighty: 'What reasons have I now to suppose … that the omnipotent God, who gave me a heart to endure and overcome all these difficulties, will abandon me now?'

In May the first number of the *Magazine of Natural History* carried Swainson's article, which commended Audubon's work in embarrass-ingly fulsome terms. To make his own position clear, the author declared: 'I have no personal acquaintance with M. Audubon. I never even saw him

The outlines of the painting engraved in copper (left) is one of the ten plates made by Lizars in Edinburgh and later retouched by the Havells in London.

... but I can appreciate genius, and I shall ever employ my poor abilities to make it known.'

Swainson had seen the first two Numbers of engravings, shown him by a friend, and he wrote that the woodsman seemed to have pursued the study of nature and painting 'with a genius and an ardour of which, in their united effect, there is no parallel.' Describing the prints one by one, he occasionally took off into the empyrean – as in his account of the hen Wild Turkey with her chicks: 'The grouping of these little creatures cannot be surpassed; it would do honour to the pencil of Rubens.'

Occasionally he was more down-to-earth, as when he described the Great-footed [Peregrine] Falcons in the Act of Devouring a Teal [and a Gadwall] as 'a masterful but by no means a pleasing picture', concluding that 'it is a scene of slaughter and butchery'. The general drift of his article, however, was that the prints were marvellous, and ridiculously cheap. 'I can only wonder at the disregard of the author for a remuneration even of his own expenses.'

Would *The Birds of America* be a success? Swainson dropped heavy hints:

> It will depend on the powerful and the wealthy, whether Britain will have the honour of fostering so magnificent an undertaking. It will be a lasting monument not only to the memory of its author, but to those who employ their wealth in patronising genius … There is superabundant wealth (and the liberality to use it, too) in the metropolis alone.

Swainson was then fifty-nine. Himself an excellent draughtsman, he had published a series of 'Zoological Illustrations', but his reputation as a naturalist rested mainly on the fact that, some six years earlier, he had become the chief English advocate of the strange — not to say crackpot — doctrine known as 'the Circular System' or 'Quinarianism', a name derived from the special significance thought to be played by the number five. This held that all organisms 'have been created upon one plan, and this plan is founded on the principle of a series of affinities returning into themselves; which can only be represented by a circle.'

Audubon had no time for such mumbo-jumbo, but he was enchanted by Swainson's praise, and when the author invited him to stay, the two immediately hit it off. For the hard-pressed artist, Highfield Hall proved a haven almost as delicious as Greenbank. Mrs Swainson, he reported, 'plays well on the piano, is amiable and kind; Mr Swainson a superior man indeed, and their children blooming with health and full of spirit.' Stimulated by this new friendship, Audubon talked about publishing a work on the birds of Great Britain, but he evidently realised that he already had more than enough on his hands, and never took the idea any further.

Sometime in June 1828 he shifted his London quarters, taking three rooms in the Havells' house at 79 Newman Street, where he had only to go downstairs to see how work on the plates and prints was progressing. Most mornings he went for an early walk in Regent's Park, and then painted all the daylight hours, using models recruited from far and wide: for his picture of an eagle seizing a lamb, he got Swainson to send him a lamb from Hertfordshire, and obtained a 'superb golden eagle' from Edward Cross of the Exeter 'Change. On 28 July he wrote to Swainson in great excitement:

There is talk of my picture of the eagle and the lamb going to His Majesty. Sir Walthen Waller has written to [me] on the subject, and everything is in train to lead poor I like a lamb to Windsor Castle!

That hope never materialised — and he could not always get what he wanted: 'All my exertions to procure live grouses have been abortive here,' he told Swainson in a letter of 1 July. 'I have written to Scotland to a friend, and perhaps will have some soon.'

In August he received a note from N.A. Vigors, secretary of the London Zoological Society, reminding him that he had promised to contribute a paper to the *Zoological Journal*. After a little flattery — 'We should be much gratified by having your name with us' — Vigors added, 'I believe I have already mentioned that we are in the habit of remunerating those of our correspondents who wish for payment for their labours, at a rate not exceeding £10.10.0 per sheet.' Audubon certainly wished for payment, yet he declined the invitation. 'I have refused him, as all others,' he recorded. 'No money can pay for abuse.'

The artist's spirits remained volatile, up one day, down the next; and they plunged steeply on 13 August, when a letter arrived from Lucy saying that she had abandoned her idea of coming to England indefinitely. On the contrary, she was hoping that Audubon, tired of England, would return to America.

'I am miserable just now,' he complained to Swainson. 'I have laid aside brushes, thoughts of painting, and all except the ties of friendship.' He even hinted that he was becoming suicidal — but then suddenly he went off on a new tack. 'Would you go to Paris with me? I could go with you any day that you would be pleased to mention ... I will go with you to Rome or anywhere where something may be done for either of our advantage.'

Rising swiftly to the bait, Swainson again invited Audubon to Titten-hanger. As the artist was leaving London on a coach, a man begged him to take a carrier pigeon and release it some five miles off. 'The poor bird could have been put in no better hands, I am sure,' Audubon reckoned. 'When I opened the bag and launched it in the air, I wished from my heart I had its powers of flight; I would have ventured across the ocean to Louisiana.'

Tittenhanger again revived his spirits: he and Swainson spent the time shooting, painting, reading, examining specimens and talking endlessly about birds. But the best outcome of his visit was that his host agreed to accompany him on a foray to the Continent, certainly to Paris, and perhaps also to Brussels, Rotterdam and Amsterdam. Swainson had some research to do at the museum in the Jardin des Plantes in Paris; Audubon did not expect to gain many subscriptions from the trip, but was keen to try – and also to escape from London.

On 30 August, when he had already packed his trunk, 'Old Bewick' and his daughters called. 'Good old man!' Audubon wrote that evening. 'How glad I was to see him again. It was, he said, fifty-one years since he had been in London, which is no more congenial to him than to me.' He never saw the engraver again, for Bewick died that November, at the age of seventy-eight.

CHAPTER EIGHT

PARIS

AUDUBON'S OBJECTIVES in going to France were not very clearly defined. He went to search for new subscribers, certainly, and he may have entertained treacherous thoughts of seeing if he could supplant Havell with some cheaper and even better engraver; but probably his main aim was to enlist the support of Baron Georges Chrétien Léopold Frédéric Dagobert Cuvier, the immensely distinguished philosopher, author, theologian, statesman and educational reformer, the doyen of French naturalists. With him went Swainson, his wife and the artist C.R. Parker, whom Audubon had met in Natchez.

The party left London in high spirits on the morning of 1 September 1828, spent one night at Dover and (after a rough Channel crossing) the next at Calais, reaching Paris early on the morning of the 4th. When they went to call on the baron, they were at first told that he was too busy to see them, but after they had sent up their names via a messenger, the great man himself came out. He knew of Swainson and gave him a friendly welcome, and although he had never heard of Audubon, he greeted him politely. The American was evidently struck by Cuvier's appearance, which he described in some detail:

> Age about sixty-five [in fact he was then fifty-nine]; size corpulent, five feet five, English measure; head large; face wrinkled and brownish; eyes grey, brilliant and sparkling; nose aquiline, large and red; mouth large, with good lips; teeth few, blunted by age, excepting one on the lower jaw measuring nearly three-quarters of an inch square.

That first meeting secured an invitation to dinner, and while the visitors

[153]

were waiting for it, they filled in time like any other tourists, visiting the Louvre, the Thèatre Français, the Jardins Royaux. For Audubon, it was a joy to speak his native language, and he relished the food, breakfasts particularly (grapes, figs, sardines, bread and butter, coffee), but he hated walking about, which he found 'disagreeable in the extreme'. Although the streets were paved, he reported, they had scarcely any sidewalks, and a large gutter filled with filthy black water ran down the centre of each. Another naturalist, the young Etienne Geoffroy de St Hilaire, who spoke excellent English, proved exceptionally helpful: having confirmed that Audubon's name was unknown in France, he set about correcting that unfortunate state of affairs by making connections on the visitors' behalf.

Cuvier's dinner party was a success. The guests were met by a servant in livery and received by the baron; sixteen sat down at table, but the meal was relatively unostentatious, going on, as Audubon put it, 'with more simplicity than in London'. Afterwards, the baroness promptly led the whole company into the library, much to the approval of Audubon, who could not bear 'the drinking matches of wine at the English tables'. Later, more guests arrived, until the room was full, but Cuvier and

37

BARON
GEORGES
CUVIER

The doyen of French naturalists was always in a tearing hurry, yet in the end produced a handsome eulogy of Audubon's paintings, scribbling as he walked.

Ambroise Tardieu direxit.

Audubon stuck together until late, talking ornithology. Altogether the American felt well satisfied with this 'introductory step among the *savants Français*'.

Next day he and Parker went to a *fête champêtre* at St Cloud, which he described as 'a handsome town on the Seine, about five miles below Paris', built on hills covered with woods, 'through which villas, cottages and châteaux emerge, and give life to the scene.'[1] After walking the last three miles, they toured the Royal Palace (which was demolished in 1871), and emerged to find such huge crowds assembling that it seemed as if the entire population of the French capital had come out for the day. Audubon was entranced by the music, the jugglers, the equestrian performers, the general gaiety, and he particularly enjoyed the sight of people shooting at a target with a crossbow:

> When the marksman was successful in hitting the centre, a spring was touched, and an inflated silken goldfish, as large as a barrel, rose fifty feet into the air – a pretty sight, I assure thee. The fins of gauze moved with the breeze, he plunged and rose and turned about, almost as a real fish would do in his element.

Nowhere outside France had Audubon seen such happy crowds. After an excellent dinner washed down by a bottle of Chablis, which cost them six francs, he and Parker returned to the showground to find people dancing, fountains playing and the surrounding woods beautifully illuminated. With difficulty they secured two seats in a cart returning to the city, and eventually reached their hotel, tired and dusty, but delighted with what they had witnessed.

Next day, thanks to the advocacy of Baron Cuvier, Audubon showed his portfolio at the Académie Royale des Sciences, where the session opened with 'a tedious lecture on the vision of the mole', but where the bird drawings met with approval. He was well received also at L' Institut de France and by the Prince of Massena, an invalid devoted to the study of natural history who was a friend of Charles Bonaparte; but the prince, although exclaiming, '*Ah! c' est bien beau!*' at the pictures, warned Audubon that very few people in France would be able to afford the work, and that he must not expect more than six or eight names in Paris. (In spite of his reservations, the prince did subscribe.)

An attempt to foist a copy on the king, Charles X, at first met with no success. Audubon called on the royal librarian, Mr van Praet, a small, white-haired man who assured him that it was 'out of the question to subscribe for such a work', and passed him on down a line of contacts.

---

1. St Cloud has been engulfed by the western suburbs of Paris and is now famous chiefly for its racecourse.

Then he was visited by M. Dumesnil, 'a first-rate engraver', who told him copper was more expensive in France than in England, and that good colourers were scarcer – in short, that his book could not be published in Paris and delivered in England as cheaply as if the work were done in London. 'This', wrote Audubon, 'has ended with me all thoughts of ever removing it from Havell's hands, unless he should discontinue the present excellent state of its execution.' Only a few days later he went back on this decision and sought out Constant, another leading engraver. He, according to Audubon, made all the usual noises (*'Oh, mon dieu! Quel ouvrage!*), but proved far too expensive.

An exhibition of his plates, spread over large tables at the Royal Academy of Sciences, was even more disappointing. About a hundred people came to look at them, and on all sides there were exclamations of *'Bien beau! Quel ouvrage!'* but also of *'Quel prix!'* Nobody made a move to subscribe, and when Audubon said he had found thirty subscribers in Manchester, everyone seemed surprised. 'Poor France', the artist lamented:

> Thy fine climate, thy rich vineyards and the wishes of the learned avail nothing; thou art a destitute beggar, and not the powerful friend thou was represented to be ... Had I come first to France, my work never would have had even a beginning: it would have perished like a flower in October.

Meanwhile, as part of his campaign, he had arranged for Parker to paint a portrait of Cuvier, and when the first sitting took place, at the baron's home, he reflected: ' Great men as well as great women have their share of vanity, and I soon discovered that the Baron thinks himself a fine-looking man. His daughter seemed to know this, and remarked ... that the line of his nose was extremely fine. I passed my fingers over mine, and lo!, I thought just the same.' After several more sittings, during which various people read out loud to the baron, the portrait was finished and deemed a success.

New subscribers continued to prove elusive. By 23 September, after almost three weeks in Paris, Audubon had found only two, and remarked dourly, 'Almost as bad as Glasgow.' He was fervently hoping that Cuvier would write a report on his paintings, which he could use as propaganda – but it was not until 22 September that he managed to pin the great man down.

It had been arranged that Audubon would show the baron his whole portfolio at the Institute, at 1.30 pm. Typically Cuvier – in a class of his own as a prevaricator – was an hour late, and when he did arrive, he swept in at great speed, scribbling furiously with a pencil, composing the longed-for report as he walked. For half an hour Audubon shifted the drawings about 'as swift as lightning,' while the baron made notes with equal despatch, until both men were wet with perspiration.

Another week passed before the report was made public – but the wait proved well worthwhile, for Cuvier turned out a handsome 'eulogium,' which praised the paintings in the most extravagant terms and did much to secure Audubon recognition in France. 'The work', said the baron, 'can be characterised briefly by the statement that it is the most magnificent monument which has yet been raised to ornithology.'

A five-year-old letter of introduction led Audubon to a meeting with Pierre Joseph Redouté, the elderly flower-painter, who admired his work so much that he arranged for him to meet the Duc d'Orléans. Here Audubon made a palpable hit. In a most glorious palace he 'passed through a file of bowing domestics' to be greeted by the duke, whose looks bowled him over. 'Kentucky, Tennessee and Alabama have furnished the finest men in the world, as regards physical beauty,' he wrote. 'I have also seen many a noble-looking Osage chief; but I do not recollect a finer-looking man, in form, deportment and manners, than this Duc d'Orléans.' [2]

Even before he had opened the portfolio, his host said he would be delighted to subscribe to the work of an American, since he himself had been so kindly treated in the United States – and when he set eyes on the print of the Baltimore Orioles, he exclaimed, ' This surpasses all I have seen!' Having promised to alert the emperor of Austria, the king of

2. Charles X abdicated and fled to England in August 1830. He was succeeded by the Duc d'Orléans, who came to the throne as Louis-Philippe.

Sweden and other crowned heads, the duke told Audubon to write immediately to the Minister of the Interior and make an appointment, in the hope that the government would order several copies of the book.

Fulsome praise came also from François Gérard, the leading portrait painter – 'a small, well-formed man' who greeted Audubon with the words, 'Welcome, brother in arts,' and then, having studied the pictures of the Parrots and the Mocking Birds, offered his hand, saying, 'Mr Audubon, you are the king of ornithological painters; we are all children in France and Europe. Who would have expected such things from the woods of America?' The artist 'thrilled with pride' at his words:

> Are we not of America men? Have we not the same nerves, sinews and men-tal faculties which other nations possess? By Washington! We have, and may God grant us the peaceable use of them for ever.

Next day found the artist waiting for an audience in the minister's salon, contemplating a picture by Gérard. 'Very different ... from looking up at a large, decaying tree, watching the movements of a woodpecker?' he remarked – and he needed all the patience he could muster, for one official after another fobbed him off with promises of action on the morrow, until he was provoked to write, 'Oh, cursed tomorrow! Do men forget, or do they not know how swiftly time moves on?'

His first visit to the ministry took place on 2 October. By the 20th there had still been no action, and he recorded, 'Nothing to do, and tired of sight-seeing. Four subscriptions in seven weeks ... What precious time I am wasting in Europe.'

At last, on the 26th, came a letter from Baron de la Brouillerie, a senior courtier, saying that the king had, after all, subscribed to *The Birds of America* for his private library. Hardly had Audubon absorbed this good news when the Duc d'Orléans' secretary told him he might now expect subscriptions from most of the French royal family, because none of them liked to be outdone by any of the others.[3] On the same day a letter arrived announcing that the Minister of the Interior would take six

38
CAROLINA
PARROT
*Psittacus
carolinensis*
also known as
the Carolina
Parakeet
*Conuropsis
carolinensis*

Seven birds feed
in a Common
Cocklebur. In
Audubon's day
the species was
abundant, but it
is now extinct.

---

3. This prophecy proved wildly optimistic.

PLATE 26

Carolina Parrot Male 1 2 Young 3

PSITTACUS CAROLINENSIS.

Plant Vitus Cockle Burr

copies for various towns and universities. Thus, suddenly, the hunter's bag was doubled, and by the time he left Paris on 4 November his total of scalps had risen to thirteen — even so a poor reward for two months of travel and intensive diplomacy which had cost him £40. One of his last visitors in Paris was a certain M. Pitois, whom Cuvier had strongly recommended as a possible agent. Audubon concluded a bargain with him, but did not seem altogether confident about his character. 'His manners are plain,' he wrote, 'and I hope he will prove an honest man.'

In the coach for Boulogne he was accompanied by two nuns, who, he thought, 'might as well be struck off the calendar of animated beings. They spoke not, they stirred not, they saw not; they replied neither by word nor gesture to the few remarks I made.' In general, he departed with dismal feelings about the French countryside, its poverty, its beggarly and ignorant peasants who lived in filthy hovels, and he was glad to return to his friends and his work in England.

Back in London, he was delighted to find two letters from Victor, who had been laggardly about writing. In reply, he sent a summary of his commercial and financial situation — 144 subscribers, ten Numbers published, no debts, everything going well. But he also emphasised the scale of the project, and the fact that he could not bring out Numbers any faster: 'The work when finished will contain eighty numbers, therefore I still have seventy to issue, which of course must take fourteen years more.' His main preoccupation was Lucy's refusal to come over until he had acquired 'a great fortune'. This, he realised all too clearly, might take some time. 'How long then I may be without her is quite unknown, and I feel perplexed the oftener I think of it.'

In another letter to Victor, dated 22 December, he reverted to the subject with almost neurotic persistence. He knew, he wrote, that 'your Mamma' was nervous of crossing the Atlantic without a friend — but he would arrange for a friendly captain to look after her. His rooms in London, where he now kept a servant, would afford her perfectly adequate accommodation in 'an excellent part of the west end of the town'. He really needed Lucy, who would be of great comfort to him . . .

Urging Victor to write 'sheets after sheets', 'not so much as to a father as you would do to a friend connected in links of dearest and best conviviality', he for once showed interest in events outside his own avian world:

> Although I am neither a politician nor a churchman I would be glad to know the sentiments of the Americans generally regarding the election of General Jackson. Here, where everything that is Yankee is ridiculed, it appears to make a sensation, but I daresay like everything else in London it will live but one week! [General Andrew Jackson had just been elected president of the United States.]

Only in January 1829 did he at last accept that Lucy would not come to join him. One more letter convinced him she had no intention of moving, and after two restless weeks' internal debate, he decided to go in search of her, on or about 1 April. Although he had long planned a return to America, he had not intended to go so soon; now, he said, his aim was to travel 'with a hope that I can persuade thee to come over here with me and under my care and charge.' He felt confident that one hour's talk, face to face, would win her over more surely than if he wrote a letter 100 pages long.

He was anxious that his departure should remain secret, and proposed to travel under the name of John James:

> Only three or four friends in England will know positively when I have gone. My subscribers and the world will think me on the European Continent after more patronage. This is absolutely necessary for the safe keeping of my present subscribers, most of which would become alarmed and expect the work to fall through.

To increase the chances of his message reaching its destination, he sent two copies of the letter on separate ships, and ten days later wrote again, confirming what he had said earlier. 'I see thee surprised, but it must be so, or we never would meet again, I fear. I want and must talk to thee. Letters are scarcely of use at this great distance, when five months are needed to have an answer.'

Already he had dropped his plan of 'going incog', persuaded out of it by John George Children, who had agreed to act as his agent in London and oversee every facet of his work while he was away. Children would write to him every fortnight to report progress. Robert Havell, who had drawings to work on for a year and a month, would write every Sunday, and would keep in touch with William Rathbone in Liverpool. Enough money had been made available to pay for the engraving, colouring and distribution of Numbers.

So it was that on 1 April 1829 Audubon sailed from Portsmouth in the packet *Columbia*, taking with him £250, $200, a good double-barrelled shotgun, and two copies of his printed Numbers. After an 'agreeable passage' of thirty-five days he reached New York on 10 May. He planned to be away from England as long as he felt sure that publication of *Birds* was proceeding safely without him – certainly for six months, perhaps for twelve. What he did not know was whether or not his wife would consent to accompany him when he returned to London.

CHAPTER NINE
BACK TO THE WOODS

MOST MARRIED MEN, returning to their native land after an absence of nearly three years, would have gone straight home to see their wives. Not Audubon. Having landed at New York, he paused there for a few days to exhibit his drawings at the Lyceum of Natural History, recording that he had been received with great kindness by the 'scientific men' of the city.

He had already made it clear, in a letter from England, that he intended to put work before pleasure or personal gratification. 'It is not my wish to go to Louisiana, if I can help it,' he had told Lucy:

> I wish to go no further south and west than Louisville, Kentucky ... Thou knowest I must draw hard from nature every day that I am in America, for although I am strong and active, I do not expect to make another voyage there except when at last I will retire from Public Life!

Now from New York he wrote again, at length, to set out his stall for Lucy's consideration. He said he wished to devote every moment of his sojourn in America to drawing the birds and plants he needed to complete his great work. His intention was known to no one else, and he wanted it kept secret between them. After a detailed analysis of his financial position, he opened his heart with rare abandon:

> To my Lucy I now offer myself with my stock, wares and chattels, and all the devotedness of heart attached to such an enthusiastic being as I am – to which I proffer to add my industry and humble talents as long as able through health and our God's will, to render her days as comfortable as such means may best afford with caution and prudence. In return for these present offers I wish to receive as true and as frank an answer as I know my Lucy

will give me, saying whether or not the facts and prospects will entice her to
join her husband and go to Europe with him, to enliven his spirits and assist
him with her kind advices. The 'No' or the 'Yes' will stamp my future years.
If a 'No' comes, I never will put the question again, and we probably never
will meet again. If a 'Yes,' a kindly 'Yes,' comes bounding from thy heart, my
heart will bound also, and it seems to me that it will give me nerve for further exertions!

We have been married a good time. Circumstances have caused our
voyage to be very mottled with incidents of very different nature, but our
happy days are the only ones I now remember. The tears that now almost
blind me are the vouchers for my heart's emotions at the recollection of
those happy days.

He did not want her to come under any form of duress, he told her —
only if she really wanted to — and he besought her to meet him in
Philadelphia or Louisville. He claimed that it would be dangerous for
him to go to Louisiana, since there he would not be able to receive
regular news from London.

Away he went into the woods, travelling via Philadelphia to Camden,
New Jersey, where he put up at a boarding house and spent three weeks
shooting and painting. But his pleas evoked only the most lukewarm
responses. Lucy sent two letters which he described as 'full of doubt and
fear' — the exact opposite of what he had hoped for — saying that she
could not travel to meet him because she had no money, and would not
be able to collect any until the fall or winter. Almost worse, she complained of his 'want of affection' and the coolness of his style of writing,
and she took the fact that he would not go to Louisiana as proof of his
indifference.

On 18 July, from Philadelphia, he wrote a puzzled and irritable letter
to Victor, who was then seventeen and working as a clerk in the office of
his uncle William G. Bakewell. 'Where are you?' Audubon asked sharply,
after the boy had failed to answer two earlier missives.

What are you doing? Are you, as your Mother seems to be, quite unwilling
to believe that I am doing all I can for the best for all of us? And in such a
case have you abandoned the idea of ever answering my letters?

Having rehearsed, once again, his motives in coming to America, and his commercial position in general, Audubon instructed his son to tell his mother to settle her debts and, as soon as possible, make her way up to Louisville on a steamboat. Already, he said, he had dropped his idea of returning to England in October, and he had written to Children and Havell saying that he would not sail from New York before the following April or May. He was well aware that people might think him selfish in pursuing birds so single-mindedly, and foresaw 'the numberless critics of my conduct tearing me into peacemeals about it,' but he assured Victor that it was not want of affection that kept him 'east of the mountains'. The thought of meeting his son again, and talking to him, made his heart palpitate and sent blood rushing to his head so fast that he feared his life was 'at an end'.

At the beginning of August he set off by coach for Mauch Chunk, a mining settlement some ninety miles from Philadelphia, taking a minimum of kit in a wooden box, along with his gun and twenty-five pounds of shot. An uncomfortable cart-ride carried him through drenching rain into the Great Pine Swamp in Northampton County, Pennsylvania, where he lodged with an 'excellent woodsman' named Jediah Irish, living largely on bear meat, venison and trout. During the days his host guided him through the country round about, and in the evenings, as his visitor drew, read out favourite poems by Robert Burns.

Audubon remained in the wilds until early October, shooting specimens, drawing intensively, working all-out with an enormous sense of fulfilment, and concentrating mainly on small land birds such as warblers and flycatchers. By the time he returned to civilisation the family frost had started to thaw: Lucy had agreed to come north, and Audubon told Victor that he would be at Louisville to meet her as soon as he heard she was on her way.

Back in Camden on 11 October, he recorded:

I am at work, and have done much, but I wish I had eight pairs of hands, and another body to shoot the specimens. Still I am delighted at what I have accumulated in drawings this season. Forty-four drawings in four months, eleven large, eleven middle size, and twenty-two small, comprising ninety-five birds, from Eagles downwards, with plants, nests, flowers, and sixty kinds of eggs. I live alone, see scarcely any one besides those belonging to the house where I lodge. I rise long before day and work till nightfall, when I take a walk, and to bed.

Back in civilisation, and evidently fired up by the prospect of the family reunion, he shot off one ebullient letter after another to Havell, asking about progress in London, reporting his own – 'I am over head and ears in business' – gossiping about mutual acquaintances and urging the

39
GREEN
BLACK-CAPPED
FLYCATCHER
Muscicapa pusilla
later known as
Wilson's Warbler
Wilsonia pusilla

Painted in New
Jersey during the
autumn of 1829.

engraver on to even greater efforts: 'Keep up a good heart, be industrious, do as if for yourself and all will go well.' In case of difficulties, he wrote, 'only try your best. The time will soon run round, and I will show myself like Napoleon did on his return from Italy!'

Audubon reported that he had sent Children three boxes containing 1300 insects aboard the packet ship *Hannibal*, due to sail on 1 November, and lamented the fact that M. Pitois, whom he had appointed his agent in Paris, had failed to come up with the money he owed. 'I fear Pitois is not the clean thing, as we say in Kentucky, but that also I will see to next summer, as I intend to spend the time in Paris ... Fear nothing. I will be in England in good time if God keeps me alive.' In the middle of October — five months after reaching America — he at last set out for the south to meet his family. From Philadelphia he travelled over the Alleghenies by road to Pittsburgh, finding the roads, coaches, horses, drivers and inns all much improved: nevertheless he complained that 'the slowness of the stages is yet a great bore to a man in a hurry.' Then once again he went down the Ohio on a steamboat: the river was in good order for navigation, and he covered nearly 1000 miles in a week.

At Louisville he found that his sons had grown amazingly: both were taller than him, and Victor had changed so much that at first he did not recognise him. Portraits show that both boys had become extremely handsome, with long, strong faces and their father's luxuriant hair. After a few days in their company, he went on down the Mississippi, and landed at Bayou Sara in the middle of the night. Yellow fever was rampant in the area, and when he went in search of a horse, to ride out to Beech Grove, he found house after house deserted, with windows wide open: the living had fled, and every building was 'the abode of death alone'. Managing at last to borrow a mount, he sent off at a gallop:

> It was so dark that I soon lost my way, but I cared not. I was about to rejoin my wife. I was in the woods, the woods of Louisiana, my heart was bursting with joy. The first glimpse of dawn set me on my road. At six o' clock I was at Mr Johnson's house; a servant took the horse, I went at once to my wife's apartment; her door was ajar, already she was dressed and sitting by her piano, on which a young lady was playing. I pronounced her name gently. She saw me, and the next moment I held her in my arms. Her emotion was so great I feared I had acted rashly, but tears relieved our hearts. Once more we were together.

According to Audubon, Lucy was thin, but in good health, and within twenty-four hours she had agreed to accompany him when he returned to England. 'Although so lately arrived', he wrote to his friend Dr Richard Harlan in Philadelphia:

> I have established the fact that Mrs A. and myself will be on our way towards 'Old England' by the nineteenth of January. We will ascend the

Mississippi and after resting ourselves at Louisville with our sons and other relatives about one month [we will] then proceed with the rapidity of the Wild Pigeon, should God grant our wishes!

Audubon told Harlan that he was hoping to arrange a large shipment of birds, animals and plants to the Zoological Gardens in London: turkeys, alligators, opossums, parakeets, begonias and so on. At the last moment he reopened the letter to add an excited postscript, announcing that he had just killed a

large new falcon, yes positively a new species of hawk, almost black, about twenty-five inches long and four feet broad, tail square, eye yellowish, white legs, feet bare short and strong ... What I have said about the hawk to you must be lawful to Academicians, and you will please announce *Falco Harlanii*

By John J. Audubon,
FLSL

For the rest of 1829 he stayed at Beech Grove, shooting and drawing as usual, while Lucy made plans for her transatlantic excursion. By then Audubon was in such good spirits that he brushed aside an alarmist letter from Havell, who reported that several subscribers and various debtors had defaulted. 'It cannot be helped,' the artist told him. 'There is none of your fault, and I must repair these matters when I reach England again ... Keep up a good heart. We will be in London as soon as possible.'

They set out for New Orleans on 1 January 1830, taking with them, as Audubon put it, 'the only three servants yet belonging to us, namely Cecilia and her two sons, Reuben and Lewis.' Having deposited these retainers with a friend, they took passage on 'the splendid steamer *Philadelphia*' for Louisville. There they stayed for nearly two months with Victor and John, and afterwards, early in March, they went on up the Ohio to Cincinnati. From Wheeling they took the mail coach to Washington, where Audubon met President Andrew Jackson and showed his drawings to the House of Representatives. Until then he had not found a single subscriber in America, but now the House of Representatives took out one subscription as a body, and he got three more in Baltimore.

Perhaps it was just as well that a letter which William Swainson sent in

January from Hertfordshire reached him too late for him to take action about its various requests. Swainson wrote from the depths of an 'uncommonly severe' winter, when snow had been lying for five weeks and was still falling: he hoped that Audubon was not only drawing birds, but also preserving skins, and asked him to procure 'a dozen or two' of the best skins of the Scarlet Ibis. He also sought one further favour: 'Bring me two Grey Squirrels alive, and a cage full of little birds ... The Squirrels would delight the little people [his children] beyond measure, and would prove a never-ending source of entertainment to them.' Luckily no squirrels were to hand – but Audubon had already sent over a shipment of several thousand forest trees, which he intended to present to public institutions, and some of which, he hoped, would act as a memorial to himself.[1]

It was high time Audubon resumed control of his elephant in England. Not only were subscribers defecting or delaying their payments. Worse, word had got about that he did not intend to come back, and people were afraid he would never complete his great project. To scotch such rumours he wrote to Havell: 'All will be well when I return. Tell my friend Children to have an advertisement in the *Times* newspaper to contradict whatever may be said about my not returning to England.'

Before he sailed, he sent Victor instructions for action in the event of his or Lucy's death. In this unofficial will he asked that his son 'should immediately proceed to England and France to take the arrangement of my affairs in those countries.' He was to balance accounts with the various agents, principally Havell, Children and the Rathbones, with whom he had left money.

> Should your Mother survive me, it is my will that you give or pay over to her one entire half of these collections, as well as one full half of whatever other property you may find. The other half I desire you to divide with your dear brother John equally ...

1. It was not until the 1860s that the first grey squirrels were imported to England, where, after a slow start, they established dominance over the native red squirrels and caused incalculable damage to forestry.

Should you feel inclined, with the advice of your dear Mother, to continue the publication of my present work on *The Birds of America*, conjointly with your Mother as administratrix ... you must divide the profits with her and your brother John as expressed above ... Should this not meet your views or those of your Mother, whom I desire you ever to consult and to treat with that attention and respect due to her, make a sale if possible to some one person or persons of the whole on hand and the original drawings. These latter after my death will I think be of value.

The letter, signed 'I am your Father and Friend, John J. Audubon FLSL,' was witnessed and countersigned by W.G. Bakewell and Nicholas Berthoud.

With his affairs thus in order, on 1 April 1830 he and Lucy sailed from New York in the packet ship *Pacific* bound for Liverpool.

CHAPTER TEN
ENTER MACGILLIVRAY

A ROUGH PASSAGE of twenty-five days brought them to Liverpool, where Audubon felt 'glad to be put on this hospitable shore'. While Lucy went to stay with her sister Ann Gordon and met the Rathbones, the artist was delighted to take up the reins of what he called his 'mammoth publication,' and to find that in his absence all had gone well. Havell was making good progress with production of the prints, and not too many subscribers had defected, although many were lagging with their payments. Perhaps the best news was that, a few weeks earlier, he had been elected a Fellow of the Royal Society in London: on 6 May he paid his entrance fee of £50 and took his seat in the Society's Great Hall.

For a while he and Lucy lived in his rooms at 79 Newman Street, where he resorted again to painting pictures for immediate sale; but Lucy did not like London, and when he set off on a new recruiting tour, she went with him — to Manchester, Birmingham, Leeds, York, Hull, Scarborough, Whitby and Newcastle. On their way to Edinburgh they were handsomely entertained by Selby at Twizell House.

One of the worst problems, Audubon discovered in Manchester, was the uneven colouring of the prints, which was putting potential subscribers off. 'Do let me urge you more than ever to pay the strictest attention to the colourers,' he wrote to Havell on 7 June,

> for it is doubtless through their evident carelessness that the work suffers so much at present. I could have had many new names at Manchester, had not the people there seen different sets in different houses almost of different colours for the same plate. I myself saw two sets that I scarcely could believe had been sent from your house.

His visit to Birmingham provoked another critical letter. Complaints, he told Havell, had been pouring in from Manchester and Liverpool.

> Should I find the same complaints as I proceed from one large town to another throughout England, as I am now determined to do, I must candidly tell you that I will abandon the publication and return to my own woods until I leave this world for a better one.

No doubt he was exaggerating, and his morale was improved by a glowing article which appeared in the July issue of *Blackwood's Magazine* by 'Christopher North', the pseudonym of the editor, John Wilson. After ten pages of throat-clearing on the subject of ornithology in general, the author quoted Swainson and Cuvier on Audubon, referred to the artist's 'simple, single-hearted, enthusiastic, enterprising and persevering character', and went on about his magnum opus: 'If ever that of M. Audubon be completed, then it will have to be granted that America, in magnificence of execution, has surpassed the Old World.' In the August issue of the magazine North gave a generous review of the life and work of Alexander Wilson, comparing him with Audubon and concluding that 'they are Two Great American Woodsmen'.

On 22 August, from Manchester, Audubon wrote to Swainson, in the most friendly terms, to apologise for not having had time to procure the squirrels or birds he had asked for. 'I have indeed brought about 150 birds, and some of them good singers and beautiful,' he wrote, 'but all are on Double Elephant paper.'

His letter included many scraps of social and ornithological news. 'I feel as if I had a world of talk for you,' he wrote. He revealed that he had set about assembling a complete collection of skins of the birds of America, and had appointed agents in the United States to find them. His last shipment of 10,000 forest trees had arrived all dead. 'Do you know that the poor woodsman who is now scribbling to you will take his seat at the Royal Society of London tomorrow? The very words make my head whirl, and [how] I will stand it, I do not know. I will indeed be glad when I am seated.'

Among all this chit-chat was one cryptic sentence of great import: 'I

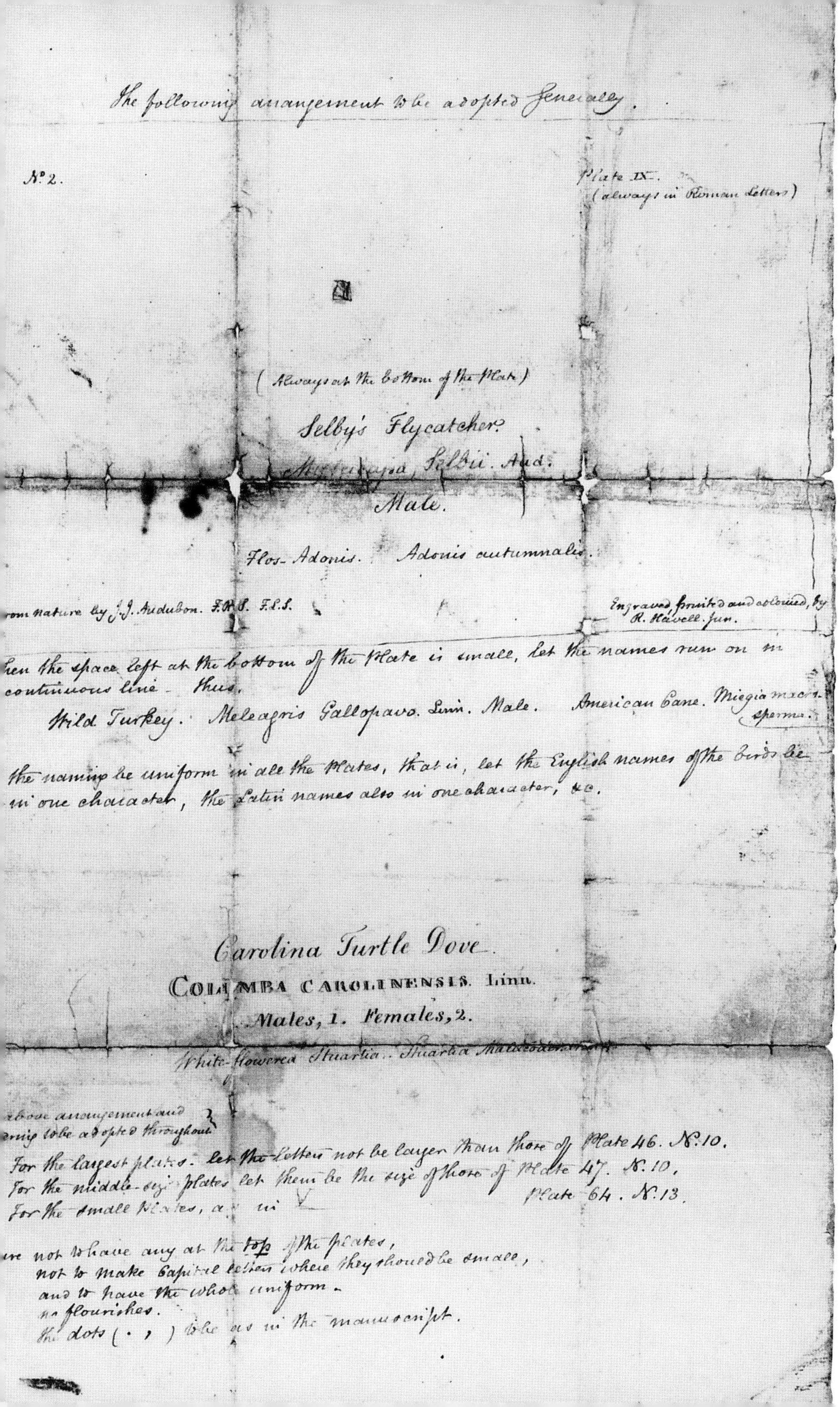

The following arrangement to be adopted Generally.

No 2.

Plate IX.
(always in Roman Letters)

(Always at the bottom of the Plate)

Selby's Flycatcher:

Muscicapa Selbii. Aud.

Male.

Flos-Adonis.   Adonis autumnalis.

from nature by J.J. Audubon. F.R.S. F.L.S.

Engraved, printed and coloured, by R. Havell Jun.

When the space left at the bottom of the Plate is small, let the names run on in continuous line thus.

Wild Turkey. Meleagris Gallopavo. Linn. Male.   American Cane. Miegia macro-sperma.

the naming be uniform in all the Plates, that is, let the English names of the birds be in one character, the Latin names also in one character, &c.

Carolina Turtle Dove.

COLUMBA CAROLINENSIS. Linn.

Males, 1. Females, 2.

White-flowered Stuartia. Stuartia malacodendron.

whose arrangement and naming to be adopted throughout

For the largest plates. let the Letters not be larger than those of Plate 46. No. 10.
For the middle-size plates let them be the size of those of Plate 47. No. 10,
For the small plates, as in V   Plate 64. No. 13.

are not to have any at the top of the plates,
not to make Capital letters where they should be small,
and to have the whole uniform –
no flourishes.
the dots (. ,) to be as in the manuscript.

40

ENGRAVER'S
ORDERS

Letter from
Audubon to
Havell, 1831,
giving a volley
of instructions
for work on the
prints of Selby's
Flycatcher and
the Carolina
Turtle Dove.

am going to write a book!' For several years he had realised that his bird
paintings, magnificent though they were, would seem more authoritative
if backed up by descriptions of the nature and habits of each species.
But Lizars had warned him that if text and pictures were published in
the same volume, the Copyright Act of 1709 would require him to present a copy to each of nine libraries in the United Kingdom – and this he
could ill afford. 'I shall publish the letterpress in a separate book, at the
same time as the illustrations,' he had written in his journal on 24
November 1826, 'and shall accompany the descriptions of the birds with
many anecdotes and accounts of localities connected with the birds
themselves, and with my travels in search of them.'

Yet in the middle of 1830, when publication of the first volume of
prints was becoming imminent, the pictures were accompanied by only
the briefest of captions, and no separate text existed. Rapid action was
needed, and since Audubon was still so unsure of his ability to write
good English, he proposed to enlist the help of Swainson.

Because he had not immediately declared his hand, but only dropped
a hint of what was in it, Swainson answered his letter jovially, starting
off, 'Welcome once more, my good friend, to merry England,' and proceeding to many other matters of mutual interest before saying:

> So you are going to write a book. 'Tis a thing of little moment for one who
> is not known, because they have no reputation to lose, but much will be
> expected from you, and you must therefore, as the saying is, put your best
> leg foremost.

He then revealed that Audubon's enemies from Philadelphia had been
active, particularly Isaac Lea, a member of the firm which once owned
the copyright in Wilson's *American Ornithology*. 'Another friend of yours
has been in England,' he went on, 'Mr Ord, and has been doing all the
good he can. If these are samples of American naturalists, defend me
from ever coming in contact with any of their whole race.'

So far Audubon and Swainson were still in perfect amity. But then in
August, writing from Manchester, Audubon startled his friend with an
extraordinary proposal. Would Swainson have the time and inclination,

he asked, to 'bear a hand' in the writing of his book? The first volume would comprise an introduction and 100 letters or essays referring to the plates of the first volume of illustrations:

> I will enter even on local descriptions of the country — adventures and anecdotes, speak of the trees and the flowers, the reptiles or the fishes or insects as far as I know. I wish if possible to make it a pleasing book as well as an instructive one.

Audubon's plan was that he would furnish the 'ideas and observations', and that Swainson would 'add the science' which he himself lacked. He then floated an even more delicate proposal:

> If it would suit you and Mrs Swainson to take us [himself and Lucy] as boarders for a few months ... being almost always together I could partake of your observations and you of mine. I would like to receive here your ideas on this subject, and if possible what amount you would expect from us as remuneration ... In the event of my living with you we will furnish our own wines, porter or ale.

Swainson's reply was perfectly civil, but it showed that he had not understood what Audubon wanted — which was, in effect, to become his ghost-writer. He first dismissed the idea of the Audubons boarding at Tittenhanger, saying that it would mean too many changes in day-to-day domestic arrangements. Then he went on, apparently welcoming Audubon's plan, but in fact misinterpreting it. Far from agreeing to help shape the artist's prose, he scented a new opportunity to air his own Quinarian views:

> You have to speak of the birds as they are alive, I to speak of their outward form, structure and their place in the great system of their Creator, for the true system, if I have, or anybody else has, discovered is not a human system ... Our parts are totally distinct, and we have no occasion to consult with each other what we should say at every page. Where our views may differ, I shall not of course say anything.
>
> My remarks had better be kept distinct, in the form of Scientific Notes to each letter, and the end, and in this way you will make the work the standard authority on American ornithology, which, without science, it certainly would not be, however interesting or valuable in other respects.

[175]

As to remuneration, Swainson said he would ask the terms he normally received from booksellers: 12 guineas per sheet of sixteen pages, each page averaging 390 words. If he had to revise and correct proofs, he would charge extra. Perhaps the most important point of all came last: 'It would of course be understood that my name stands in the title page as responsible for such portion as concerns me.'

This was not at all what Audubon had in mind, and his next letter from Manchester, written on 29 August, evidently made this clear, for it drew a sharp answer, in which Swainson said he could not imagine that the artist would try to pass off someone else's knowledge as his own:

> I cannot ... suppose that you intended that I should give all the scientific information I have laboured to acquire during twenty years on ornithology, [that you] should conceal my name and transfer my fame to your pages and to your reputation.

Swainson rubbed in his disapproval by adding a brief lecture on the need to name new species of birds properly: 'You may not be aware that a new species, deposited in a museum, is of no authority whatsoever until its name and character are published ... Unless, therefore, this is done, you will, I am fearful, lose the credit of discovering nearly all the new species you possess.'

For once Audubon had seriously misjudged his man, who was far more vain than he had reckoned. His *faux pas* spoiled a rewarding friendship, and although he kept in touch with Swainson, the two were never again on intimate terms. In the end his blunder proved hugely beneficial, for Swainson was a clumsy writer, with little sense of style, and, even if he had agreed to co-operate on the terms originally suggested, the books would probably have been turgid, and rendered unreadable by stupefying Quinarian theory.

By October 1830 Audubon was beginning to feel desperate, goaded by the knowledge that no fewer than three new editions of Wilson's *American Ornithology* were being prepared, one by Jameson, another by Jardine and yet another by 'a Mr Brown'. 'Most people would probably have been discouraged by this information,' he wrote:

but it only had a good effect on me, because since I have been in England, I have studied the character of Englishmen as carefully as I studied the birds in America, and I know full well that in England novelty is always in demand, and that if a thing is well known it will not receive much support. Wilson has had his day, I thought to myself, and now is my time. I will write, and I will hope to be read; and not only so, but I will push my publication with such unremitting vigour that my book shall come before the public before Wilson's can be got out.

Much of his time was being taken up in trying to keep customers up to the mark. In Edinburgh, for example, he found that the wealthy Miss Maria Woodruffe Smith had discontinued her subscription because the prints of Numbers 1–9, which she had received, 'were so bad that she could not think of giving house room to any more such trash, so she called the work. After much talk, and her seeing how beautifully engraved the 19th Number is, and how superfinely coloured, she concluded she would resume it, provided I would take back what she had on hand . . .'.

In his search for a ghost-writer, by another of the amazing strokes of luck which seemed to befall him at critical moments, Audubon almost at once hit upon an ideal collaborator. He and Lucy reached Edinburgh on 13 October, and took lodgings with Mrs Dickie, in whose house he had stayed before. It was Professor James Wilson – a friend from his first visit to the northern capital – who made the vital link. Audubon recorded how he asked him:

> if he knew of any person who would undertake to correct my ungrammatical manuscripts, and to assist me in preparing the more scientific part of the *Biography of Birds*. He gave me a card with the address of Mr W. MacGillivray, spoke well of his talents, and away to Mr MacGillivray I went . . . I made known my business, and a bargain was soon struck. He agreed to assist me and correct my manuscripts for two guineas a sheet of sixteen pages, and I that day began to write the first volume.

Thus baldly did Audubon record one of the greatest strokes of good fortune that ever befell him – for MacGillivray turned out to be almost as vital to his enterprise as Havell, an equally pertinacious supporter, and a close friend. At that time he was thirty-four, a teacher and journalist without a regular job, described by Charles Darwin as having 'not much the appearance and manners of a gentleman'. He was struggling to support his family of six children (in all his wife Marion bore him thirteen, four of whom died in infancy), and he clearly needed the money, modest as it was beside the twelve guineas that Swainson had demanded. Yet no task could have been more congenial to him, for there were a curious number of similarities between his background and that of the American woodsman.

It is hardly surprising that MacGillivray struck Darwin as rather rough and ready, for, like Audubon, he was illegitimate: his parents had not been married, and he hardly knew his mother. He was born in Aberdeen, on the eastern side of Scotland, but brought up by his uncle on a farm at the south-west tip of the Island of Harris, in the Outer Hebrides, away in the far west; and there, as a boy, he shot a Golden Eagle which had been killing lambs — an episode of which he wrote a graphic account.

Like Audubon, he was fascinated by nature from early youth, and although he meant to become a doctor, when he was twenty-one he gave up medicine in favour of the full-time study of zoology. Again like Audubon, he shot birds to dissect and identify them, and despised what he called 'cabinet naturalists', who learned what they knew from stuffed specimens, rather than from pursuing them alive. Yet another similarity was his habit of writing a journal.

41

WILLIAM
MACGILLIVRAY

When it came to writing the *Ornithological Biography*, the scholarly, industrious and equable Scot proved an ideal co-author.

The American ornithologist Elliott Coues gave a crisp character-sketch, recording that he

> was undoubtedly unwise in his frankness; but diplomacy is a stranger to characters ... and MacGillivray's way of handling people whom he disliked or despised often savoured of arrogance. If he never hesitated to differ sharply with anyone, or to express his own views pointedly – if he scarcely disguised his contempt for triflers, blockheads, pedants, compilers and theorisers – if he was also fallible, even as the rest of us, he was nevertheless a lover of nature, an original thinker, a hard student, and finally, an ornithologist of large practical experience, who wrote down what he knew or believed to be true.

MacGillivray was also a formidably active pedestrian, walking hundreds of miles over the northern moors and mountains, as well as along the coast, in search of birds, animals and plants. Even the woodsman would have been pressed to keep up with him on the marathon trek which he made in 1819, at the age of twenty-three, when he decided to walk from Aberdeen to London via various points in the Highlands, often sleeping out in the heather or under hedges as he covered more than 800 miles.

He shared with Audubon a powerful dislike of townspeople, preferring folk who lived healthy lives in the country. He was appalled by the inhabitants of Glasgow – 'the diabolic depravity of the city blackguard, however blended with awkward vulgarity, must excite pure horror and detestation' – but found Manchester even worse:

> Such an abominable dunghill of a town I never before saw. Narrow, irregular, dirty streets, misshapen brick houses daubed over with paint and whitening. Hideous manufactories with their sooty smoke-disgorging chimneys towering amongst the pestilential clouds that rolled over the city – crowds of ill-looking and deformed ragamuffins.

His reaction was extraordinarily like that of Audubon seven years later (page 72) – and so were his powers of walking. He ran out of money, survived on scraps of bread and cheese, cut his thumb to the bone, wore his shoes and stockings to tatters, was repeatedly soaked to the skin, and yet covered the last fifty-eight miles of his journey in a single stretch.

Buoyed up by his achievement in surviving the ordeal, he recorded: 'With a sufficient motive, and an alluring object in view, I would undertake to travel to the uttermost corner of the earth.'

Before he left London he had time to visit the British Museum, and felt that his 'love of natural history was very much increased' by his inspection of the exhibits there, among which nothing impressed him more than the birds stuffed by John Gould. Then, after a few days in the capital, he returned to Aberdeen by sea.

Energy, endurance and intelligence were by no means all of MacGillivray's assets. He also had a lively sense of humour, and was attractively free of the jealousy and self-importance which soured so many contemporary birdmen. Still more important for Audubon, he was a trained anatomist and also an excellent writer. Even though he had been brought up in a remote corner of Scotland, he had been well educated: much as he hated battling with Latin and Greek as a boy, his grounding in the ancient languages stood him in good stead later, being reflected in the clarity and precision of his prose.

facing page 42

THREE SPECIES

Black-throated Green Warbler *Sylvia virens* now *Dendroica virens*; Blackburnian Warbler *Sylvia blackburniae* now *Dentroica fusca*; MacGillivray's Warbler *Sylvia philadelphia* now *Oporornis tolmiei* Audubon was particularly pleased to have painted the female, which no other artist had represented at the time.

Such was the young man with whom fate threw the wandering artist into contact – and such was their immediate rapport that, in the evening of the day they met, Audubon sat down and began to write what became the first volume of his *Ornithological Biography*. There was no subtlety about the book's organisation. It merely followed the order already determined by that of the prints published in the *Birds*, with an essay describing the appearance and habits of each species, starting with the five in the first Number – the Wild Turkey, the Yellow-Billed Cuckoo, the Prothonotary Warbler, the Purple Finch and Bonaparte's Flycatcher. Then, as light relief from what the author himself called 'the mazes of descriptive ornithology', he threw in a general essay about the Ohio and his experiences on the river. After the next five birds – the female Wild Turkey, the Purple Grackle, the White-throated Sparrow, Selby's Flycatcher and the Brown Titlark – came an account of his own wanderings in the Great Pine Swamp.

This simple format proved extremely durable: five birds and an

Drawn from Nature by J. J. Audubon, F.R.S. F.L.S.

Engraved, Printed and Coloured by R. Havell 1837

Black-throated green Warbler.
SYLVIA VIRENS.
1. Male. 2. Female.

Blackburnian. w.
SYLVIA BLACKBURNIÆ.
2. Female.

Mourning Warbler.
SYLVIA PHILADELPHIA.
1. Male. 2. Female.

adventure, five birds and an adventure — the pattern continued right through the first three volumes. Scarcely ever was there much connection between the essays and the birds on either side of them. Nor were auto-biographical episodes restricted to the essays: snatches of the author's experience constantly invaded the bird sections. Suddenly Audubon had found a vehicle for the great mass of incidents that had built up over the years, and out they poured in a flood.

Yet if the arrangement of the text was amateurish, the writing itself, as polished by MacGillivray, was crisp, accurate and easy to read, and it was he who contributed a great many of the scientific and anatomical details. In the words of Elliot Coues, Audubon's 'page is redolent of nature's fragrance; but MacGillivray's are the bone and sinew, the hidden anatomical parts beneath the lovely face.'

Bent over their scratchy pens, the pair worked at prodigious speed. The first volume alone amounted to 500 pages, or nearly 250,000 words, and they completed it in less than three months — which means they were producing at least 2000 words every twenty-four hours. No wonder Audubon recorded:

> Writing now became the order of the day. I sat at it as soon as I awoke in the morning, and continued the whole day long, and so full was my mind of birds and their habits that in my sleep I continually dreamed of birds. I found Mr MacGillivray equally industrious, for although he did not rise so early in the morning as I did, he wrote much later at night (this I am told is a characteristic of all great writers); and so the manuscripts went on increasing in bulk, like the rising of a stream after abundant rains.

Lucy, also, wrote indefatigably, making a copy of each volume for despatch to America, so that copyright could be secured there. In moments of relaxation the two authors must surely have swapped reminiscences about their peregrinations — and perhaps, every now and then, they strode out together to get some air and exercise.

In a wide-ranging introduction to the first volume, Audubon thanked all the people who had helped him produce *The Birds of America*, including Lizars, Havell, Cuvier and Bonaparte. He also paid tribute to the help he had received from his co-author in producing the words. There were persons, he remarked darkly, who sought to suppress any mention of the support they had had. 'This want of candour I cannot endure,' he wrote:

> On the contrary, I feel pleasure in here acknowledging the assistance which I have received from a friend, Mr William MacGillivray, who, being possessed of a liberal education and a strong taste for the study of the Natural Sciences, has aided me, not in drawing the figures of my illustrations, nor in writing the book now in your hand, although fully competent for both tasks, but in completing the scientific details and smoothing down the asperities of my *Ornithological Biographies*.

There was a certain ambiguity about these remarks. If MacGillivray had not helped in writing the book, how had he smoothed down its 'asperities'? Perhaps, if pressed, Audubon would have replied that he alone had drafted the book, and that his assistant had polished his prose. In any event, he also paid tribute to the country in whose womb his elephant had been gestating:

> To Britain I owe nearly all my success. She has furnished the artists through whom my labours were to be presented to the world; she has granted me the highest patronage and honours; in a word, she had thus far supported the prosecution of my illustrations. To Britain, therefore, I shall be ever grateful.

So specialised a work was the *Biography* that at first Audubon could not find a publisher. Then early in 1831 the Edinburgh firm of Adam Black agreed to bring it out, but at the author's expense. The first printing was of 750 copies, and in writing to his agent in the United States about an American edition, the author revealed how keen he was that the text should be exactly the same as in Britain. Type, paper and arrangement should identical – 'a perfect facsimile if possible':

> I perhaps ought not to observe to you that I am anxious that the punctuations should be extremely carefully attended to, but I say [it] because I observe that neither Wilson or Bonaparte have been careful on that head as I wish to be.

The British edition appeared on 31 March 1831, and the American edition came out simultaneously in Philadelphia. In Edinburgh, when copies were ready, Audubon had shipped them down to Havell in London in boxes put aboard various steamers and smacks. Ideally, text and prints should have been sold together, yet the disparity in size and shape between the book and the bound folio made them anything but easy partners: the book compact and solid, the folio huge and sprawling. In Britain the initial price of the book was one guinea (21 shillings) to any-one who had subscribed to the *Birds*, and 25 shillings to everyone else; but later Audubon decreed that subscribers should receive copies of the book free.

The British publication attracted an immediate and highly favourable notice in the *Edinburgh Literary Journal*, whose reviewer had seen the first volume of *Birds*, containing 100 plates, and Volume One of the *Biography*. 'This is the work of an enthusiast in his calling, of a true enthusiast,' he began, 'for the contagion of his feelings extends towards the reader. Never since we read Robinson Crusoe have we felt such a hankering to enact the part of anyone whose adventures we were reading.'

The great charm of the work, the review concluded, lay in the author's 'narratives of the habits of the different birds', and as for the double-elephant folio – there the birds were shown 'with unprecedented fidelity, feeling and intimate knowledge of their habits'. The anonymous reviewer ended with a perceptive remark of wider significance:

> Mr Audubon has done much to silence a set of critics who affect to despise America … Laugh at the young republic, indeed! Where is the state of the old world that can show any results of private and unaided enterprise to stand in competition with what has been effected by three men beyond the Atlantic – Wilson, Charles Bonaparte and Audubon? The giant is awake.

For a modern reader, some of the most haunting passages are those in which the author described the pristine nature of the wilderness along the Ohio when he first knew it, and lamented the destruction which was already taking place:

> When I think of these times, and call back to my mind the grandeur and beauty of those almost uninhabited shores … when I reflect that all this

grand portion of our Union, instead of being in a state of nature, is now ...
covered with villages, farms and towns, where the din of hammers and
machinery is constantly heard: that the woods are fast disappearing under
the axe by day and the fire by night; that hundreds of steam-boats are gliding
to and fro over the whole length of the majestic river, forcing commerce to
take root and to prosper at every spot; when I see the surplus population of
Europe coming to assist in the destruction of the forest, and transplanting
civilisation into its darkest recesses – when I remember that these extraordinary changes have all taken place in the short period of twenty years, I
pause, wonder, and, although I know all to be a fact, can scarcely believe
its reality.

By then the artist was on close terms with his engraver, addressing him as
'My Dear Mr Havell' and signing letters 'Your Friend, John J. Audubon'.
He was also taking an avuncular interest in Havell's well-being:

Push on your work, take early walks and enjoy as much as may be in your
power that nature of which you say I speak with a purpose. Who knows but
what you and yours may not visit the majestic woods of my beloved country? We are quite well, and a happier time have seldom enjoyed since in
Europe than we have experienced in this fairest of cities.[1]

He left Edinburgh on 15 April, heading for London and Paris, and for
part of the way, at Liverpool, 'travelled on that extraordinary road called
the railway, at the rate of twenty-four miles per hour'.[2] Weighing up his
progress so far, he noted that he had balanced accounts with *The Birds of
America*. Fifty of his original subscribers had deserted, leaving him with
only 130. Nevertheless, he thought,

the whole business is really wonderful; 40,000 dollars have passed through
my hands for the completion of the first volume. Who would believe that a
lonely individual, who landed in England without a friend in the whole
country, and with only sufficient pecuniary means to travel through it as a
visitor, could have accomplished such a task as this publication?

On 28 April he demonstrated his generosity of spirit by sending

---

1. Havell had just moved his premises a short distance from Newman Street to 77 Oxford Street.
2. The Liverpool & Manchester Railway had opened in September 1830, and the speed of its trains
caused as much alarm as astonishment.

Swainson — who himself might have had a hand in the writing of the *Ornithological Biography* — a copy of Volume One, together with a note saying that he hoped he would accept the book 'as a small memento of the high regard I have for yourself and your talents'. At the end, as a kind of postscript, he added, 'I never will be ungrateful to anyone who has been kind to me.'

Already he was planning another trip to America and a further search for the birds he was still missing. First, though, he and Lucy spent two months in Paris, rounding up their subscribers in the French capital. In July *Blackwood's Magazine* gave both the *Biography* and the folios of *Birds* a glowing review, predicting that the volumes of letterpress would be 'most delightful reading to everybody', and magnanimously comparing them with the reissue of Wilson's books, then being superintended by Jameson.

On 31 July 1831 Audubon reported to Havell that he and Lucy were 'safe and sound so far and on board the *Columbia* at anchor off Portsmouth harbour'. The wind was fair and the weather beautiful, and they were due to sail for New York on the morrow. How long he would be away, he could not tell — perhaps two or three years, he thought — and again he left Children and Havell in charge of his great project.

CHAPTER ELEVEN
HUNTING AGAIN

THE *Columbia* REACHED New York on 3 September after a passage of thirty-three days, during which Audubon shot and picked up sixteen birds. What the other passengers thought when, during calms, he went off to retrieve the bodies in a small boat rowed by sailors, he did not say (he killed fifty more when the vessel was sailing too fast to stop and collect them). In America he found that the newspapers and scientific journals were 'singing the praises' of his work. 'God willing,' he wrote, 'I may yet come out at the broad end of the horn; at all events, I will either break it or make a spoon!'

On the very day he landed, the *London Literary Gazette* published an obituary entitled 'Wilson the Ornithologist,' observing that the subject had died and been buried 'somewhere in the state of Philadelphia, even while the Edinburgh journals are anticipating his return, laden with scientific treasures'. It never became clear how this gross error was perpetrated; but when, on 8 September, the *Edinburgh Caledonian Mercury* pointed out that Wilson had died in 1823, the *Gazette* explained that they had confused him with Audubon, and then ran his obituary.

This elicited an objection from Captain Thomas Brown, who wrote to the *Mercury* on 2 November, saying, 'I sincerely hope that the announcement . . . of the death of the celebrated Audubon is not correct. Indeed, I cannot believe it to be so.' Brown proceeded to quote from a letter sent by the artist to Joseph B. Kidd from New York on 7 September, showing that he was then 'in good health and spirits', and about to set off into the woods, 'away from white men's tracks and manners'.

Praising Audubon's work enthusiastically, and saluting his 'buoyant spirit' and 'ardent zeal in the cause of physical science', Brown claimed that the death of such a man 'would be an incalculable loss', and ended by hoping that he would be preserved 'to complete a work which never has been, and in all probability never will be equalled'.

'What is the editor of the *Literary Gazette* about?' demanded the editor in a footnote. 'He first resuscitates a man who has been dead eighteen years, only to kill him again, and then, by way of correcting his error, kills another, who is now clearly proved to be alive and well . . .'

Audubon, meanwhile, had gone to Philadelphia, left Lucy there to visit their sons in Louisville, and pressed on to Washington, where he sought the advice of various 'distinguished gentlemen' about his next reconnaissance trip. His plans were grandiose, and, as usual, far exceeded what was practically possible. He aimed first to visit the Florida peninsula and the islands off its east coast, then to explore the country west of the Mississippi, before going on to Mexico, and if possible, continuing as far as California, crossing the Rocky Mountains and following the Columbia river to its mouth. To strengthen his team he recruited two assistants – a young English taxidermist who had crossed the Atlantic with him – and George Lehman, a Swiss landscape painter from Philadelphia.

The party left Washington in the middle of October, and went by steamer to Norfolk and Richmond, Virginia. But it was at their next stop, Charleston, on the coast of South Carolina, that Audubon made another of his invaluable contacts. There he met the Rev. John Bachman, a Lutheran minister of Swiss and German descent, and a passionate amateur naturalist, with whom he struck up an immediate friendship. As Audubon recorded:

> When I first saw this excellent man, he was on horseback, but upon my being named to him, he leaped from the saddle, suffered his horse to stand at liberty, and gave me his hand with a pressure of cordiality that electrified me.

So taken was Bachman with the woodsman that he invited his whole party to stay; they remained in his house for four weeks, and when they

43

VIEW OF
CHARLESTON

The town on the
coast of South
Carolina was the
home of the Rev.
John Bachman,
who became one
of Audubon's
staunchest
supporters.

left, he wrote Lucy this glowing appreciation of her husband:

> The last has been one of the happiest months of my life. I was an enthusi-
> astic admirer of nature from my boyhood, and fond of every branch of nat-
> ural history ... How gratifying was it, then, to become acquainted with a
> man who knew more about birds than any man now living — and who, at the
> same time, was communicative, intelligent and amiable, to an extent seldom
> found associated in the same individual ...
>
> For the short month he remained with my family, we were inseparable
> ... I need not inform you that Mr Audubon was a general favourite in our
> city. His gentlemanly deportment, his travels and experience, his informa-
> tion and general talents, caused him to be sought after by all ... There
> seems quite a blank in our house since he has gone, for we looked on him as
> one of our family.

Even though Bachman had known, liked and worked with Alexander
Wilson in the field, he became one of Audubon's staunchest allies in his
battles against the Philadelphia mafia led by Ord; and a priceless support
he was, for he knew all the naturalists and doctors who had congregated
in Charleston, and brought them all in on Audubon's side.

[189]

For the time being, the woodsman was beyond the reach of any carping critic, once again in his element, at large in the Florida swamps and among the islands. As he himself put it, 'I jumped at once into my wood-hunting habits'.

Every morning the party was up before dawn, and spent the day shooting, skinning and drawing birds. As always, Audubon's insatiable desire to record new species battled with his admiration and love of the 'feathered tribes' — as in this vignette of pelicans, which he spotted 'seated in comfortable harmony' on the branches of some mangrove trees:

> I waded to the shore under cover of the rushes along it, saw the pelicans fast asleep, examined their countenances and deportment well and leisurely, and after all levelled, fired my piece, and dropped two of the finest specimens I ever saw. I really believe I would have shot one hundred of these reverend sirs, had not a mistake taken place in the reloading of my gun. A mistake, however, did take place, and to my utmost disappointment I saw each pelican, young and old, leave his perch and take to wing, soaring off, well pleased, I dare say, at making so good an escape from so dangerous a foe.

It would be easy to condemn Audubon as a heartless murderer, especially when he made remarks like 'I call birds few when I shoot less than one hundred per day'. But in fact it was a lust for knowledge, rather than for blood, that drove him on. He was always searching not only for new species, but for small variations within species — between male and female, between juvenile and mature — and at the same time seeking to defray his own expenses by collecting skins which he could sell to European museums.

That winter in Florida brought him few new birds, but it did furnish him with several episodes for future volumes of the *Ornithological Biography*: alligator-shooting, deer-hunting, and, not least, a stirring account of how the party was forced to spend a night stranded in a small boat in the middle of mud-flats, growing so cold that in the morning they had to revive two of their Negroes, who had become 'as senseless as torpidity ever rendered an alligator'.

In general he was disappointed by Florida, which he had always

facing page 44

BROWN
PELICAN
Pelecanus fuscus
now *Pelecanus
occidentalis*

Audubon probably painted this adult male in breeding plumage in Florida during the spring of 1832.

Brown Pelican
PELECANUS FUSCUS.
Male Adult

imagined to be 'the garden of the United States', and after losing what he thought was a new species of Ibis in a labyrinth of open water and swamps, he was assailed by a strange feeling in an orange grove on an island:

> The oranges were in great profusion on the trees — everything about us was calm and beautiful and motionless, as if it had just come from the hand of the Creator. It would have been a perfect Paradise for a poet, but I was not fit to be in Paradise; the loss of my ibis made me as sour as the oranges that hung about me. I felt unquiet, too, in this singular scene, as if I were almost upon the verge of creation, where realities were tapering off into nothing.

In the spring he and his party explored many islands off the east coast, and whenever he returned to civilisation, he sought out new subscribers. One of his best contacts was William Gaston, a merchant in the port of Savannah, to whom he delivered a letter from the Rathbones. Not only did Gaston become a subscriber himself: he recruited six more, and insisted on acting as the artist's agent, exacting dues and never allowing anyone to lapse. Bachman, meanwhile, was also busy on Audubon's behalf, drumming up support among public institutions in Charleston. Overall, recruitment proved so good that Audubon was able to send Havell $1300 (about £300), but he was seriously disturbed by reports in the New York papers of the civil disorder that was sweeping England in the run-up to the Reform Bill. 'The riots are certainly getting to a frightful pitch, and I fear a revolution there unless the Reform Bill is passed,' he told Lucy in a letter of 4 January 1832. 'Bristol, it seems, has been terribly burnt and some lives lost.'

With the head of the family largely out of touch in the far south, it fell to Lucy and Victor to keep Havell up to the mark, and their strictures about the irregular quality of prints evidently upset the engraver, for in March Lucy felt obliged to apologise, writing, 'I am very sorry any expression of mine should have offended you.' That, she said, had not been her intention: her sole purpose was to maintain high standards. 'We do not doubt your zeal nor good intentions, but we think ourselves at liberty to state any changes we think for our benefit.'

By far the most wounding defections of this difficult period were those of Selby and Jardine, who both cancelled their subscriptions in the spring of 1832. Victor, stung by the news, concluded that 'these gentlemen at least are dissatisfied with their copies'. He was not to know that the two rival ornithologists had taken against Audubon, and, although they were too gentlemanly to join in any public attack on him, they had begun to belittle his achievement in letters to each other.

None of this, of course, reached Audubon for the time being. Yet even though he received much help from government officials and the navy, he never even began planning his trip to the Rockies and the West Coast. Instead, he set his sights on the far north, determined to observe the birds that migrated to Labrador in the summer; but since it was already too late to set up a long-range expedition that year, he contented himself for the time being with a journey up the coast of Maine.

Heading north from Philadelphia with his family early in August, he passed rapidly through New York, where cholera was rife, but stayed for some time in Boston, whose citizens proved exceptionally helpful. In a letter to his friend Edward Harris he wrote of being 'pushed by the season, and the desire I have to fulfil towards my subscribers, the world, and indeed myself, the task allotted me by nature — the completion of my work'. The Audubons then travelled up the coast of Maine, hardly pausing until they reached Eastport, in the far north-eastern corner of the state. From there they explored the surrounding country and went on up the St John's River to Fredericton and Woodstock, before returning via Bangor to Boston.

Much as he loved such research expeditions, Audubon also worried constantly about how things were going in England; and when, during that summer of 1832, he realised that he needed to spend another year in America, collecting birds and subscribers, he decided to appoint Victor as his English agent. The young man — then just twenty-four — sailed for Liverpool on 10 October, while John remained with his father, shooting, drawing and skinning birds. From that point the whole family joined forces in their struggle to complete *The Birds of America*.

Victor took with him a letter from his father to Havell which, if it did not positively threaten the engraver, addressed him in peremptory and patronising terms:

> It is always with sorrow that I find myself forced to remonstrate respecting the faults now and then existing in the publication, and I wish you to listen well to whatever my son tells you on the subject. My own work has now reached the pitch of standing both in America and Europe that calls for the greatest exertion on my part to render quite and entirely true what is said of it ... and you, My Dear Sir, ought to second me in these efforts with all your care and exertion ...
>
> The work connects you with me, and gives you a name that must greatly assist you, even now, in augmenting your general business, and should this immense work fail for want of attention or good finishing in its execution while in your hands, you must become an equal sufferer with me, if not a greater one in a pecuniary point of view.

This must have been one of the most perilous moments in the entire gestation of the elephant. If Havell had been less patient, or less conscientious, he might well have lost his temper under this hail of criticism – much of which was repeated several times over, because Lucy could never be sure whether or not her letters were reaching him. Obviously it was in his own interest to rise above immediate vexations and carry on, but he must have felt severely tempted to throw the whole business over.

A winter in Boston gave Audubon time to draw, to write letters and draft episodes for the next volumes of the *Ornithological Biography*, and to plan his expedition to Labrador. On 24 February 1833 he read aloud to the family a letter sent by Victor from Liverpool, and in reply expressed delight at the boy's progress to date. As always, his communication was packed with advice and encouragement. 'Go on, my Dear Son,' he wrote:

> Keep a strong band of good spirits about your person. It will keep your heart at the right place and I assure [you] all will be well. I must repeat it – suffer not your spirits to droop. Consider your present happy situation in England ... and compare this ... with that of mine when I first visited that country – moneyless, not a friend known, and bearing no nobler name than that of any other forlorn man.

[194]

That day he had bought – for $14.75 – a splendid live Golden Eagle which had been caught in a spring trap set for foxes in the White Mountains of New Hampshire. So determined was he to make the bird live on paper that he worked feverishly at drawing and painting it for fourteen days on end – 'sixty hours of the severest labour' he had experienced since he drew the Wild Turkey. The effort nearly killed him: he was suddenly laid low by what he called a 'spasmodic affection', and although he recovered, he had to seek help from three doctors, and the experience left him shaken.

It seems to have been his emotional relationship with 'the noble bird', as much as sheer artistic concentration, that led to his collapse. In the second volume of the *Ornithological Biography* he wrote a terrible account, haunted and haunting, of how he dealt with his 'prisoner'. So engrained was his habit of depicting birds in particular attitudes that he could not achieve what he wanted by drawing it alive: rather, he had to kill it first.

Having watched the eagle's movements for a whole day, he decided on the attitude in which he would draw the bird, but then was faced with the problem of how to 'take away his life with the least pain to him'. A doctor friend suggested electrification, but came down in favour of suffocation by fumes of burning charcoal – and the scenes that followed might have come from a horror story by Edgar Allan Poe:

> Accordingly the bird was removed in his prison into a very small room, and closely covered with blankets, into which was introduced a pan of lighted charcoal ... I waited, expecting every minute to hear him fall down from his perch, but after listening for hours, I opened the door, raised the blankets and peeped under them amidst a mass of suffocating fumes.
>
> There stood the Eagle on his perch, with his bright unflinching eye turned towards me, and as lively and vigorous as ever! Instantly reclosing every aperture, I resumed my station at the door, and towards midnight, not having heard the least noise, I again took a peep at my victim. He was still uninjured, although the air of the closet was insupportable to my son and myself. I persevered, however, for ten hours in all ...
>
> Early next morning I tried the charcoal anew, adding to it a quantity of sulphur, but we were nearly driven from our home in a few hours by the

stifling vapours, while the noble bird continued to stand erect, and to look defiance at us whenever we approached his post of martyrdom. His fierce demeanour precluded all internal application, and at last I was compelled to resort to a method always used as the last expedient, and a most effectual one. I thrust a long piece of pointed steel through his heart, when my proud prisoner instantly fell dead, without even ruffling a feather

These struggles inspired a dramatic painting, in which the eagle – a female, in spite of the artist's description – is rising into the air among mountain ranges with a white snowshoe hare in its talons. In Audubon's original a man with a gun and a large bird slung on his back is inching his way along a tree that has fallen across a precipitous chasm, chopping off obtruding branches with a small axe as he goes. Some commentators have assumed that this was a self-portrait, intended to show the hunter intrepidly bringing back an eagle in wild surroundings. But for some reason Havell omitted the detail when he engraved the plate, so that it does not appear on the prints: the tree-trunk over the void is still there, but no human figure treads it. Did Audubon instruct him to eliminate the man

right & facing
45, 46

GOLDEN EAGLE
Falco chrysaetos now
Aquila chrysaetos

One of Audubon's most powerful paintings depicts an eagle (far right) climbing above mountains with a snowshoe hare in its talons. The detail (near left) from the original painting shows a hunter, possibly Audubon himself, crossing a ravine on a fallen tree. For some reason Havell erased the figure from the final print.

at the last minute, unsettled by the knowledge that his acquisition of the bird did not match up to the heroic image he had created?

During the spring of 1833 Havell began to ship copies of Volume 1, containing the first twenty Numbers, to New York. Some were full-bound in leather, some half-bound (in leather and board), and some went as loose sheets. These last were the cheapest, at $200; the half-bound copies cost $220, the full-bound $250. On 1 April Audubon sent detailed instructions for further shipments: the brig *Charlotte*, with four copies on board, had gone missing, and the delivery of seven copies in Boston was overdue.

Some of Audubon's remarks to Victor suggest that, in these early days of their working partnership, his son and his engraver were not getting on too well:

> Should you think that Havell does not pay to you all the regard, attention and respect due from his situation towards his employer, let me know of it at once, and I shall settle with him and procure someone else. Do not suffer the least trifle in the finishing of the copper plates to escape ... The work must improve and not fall off in the engraving, when the original drawings are becoming better and more beautiful the more we make of them.
>
> Who engraves at present next to Havell – is it Mr Blake? I liked him very much, and if he is still in the employ of Havell, I would advise you to make some small present now and then, and tell him of the alteration you wish to be done.

By the middle of April Audubon had over fifty American subscribers, and was more anxious than ever that in London high standards of production should be maintained. 'The success of my work depends much on your own exertions in the finishing of the plates as accurately as you are able to do, and in seeing that the colourers do their duty', he told Victor on the 20th.

> Knowing you as I do, I naturally expect all your attention. I might speak otherwise, had I not known you so well as I do. Americans are excellent judges of work, particularly of such as are drawn from their country's soil. They are proud of everything that is connected with America, and feel mortified whenever anything is done that does not come up to their sanguine expectations.

Worry as he might, he was committed to the Labrador expedition. Having packed up ten new drawings, he sent them off to Victor, insured for $2000, and told him:

> The Martins are flying over the city, and tomorrow I shall fly toward the coast of Labrador. If fortunate, I shall bring [back] a load of knowledge of the water birds which spend the winter in our country, and may hope to compete in the study of their habits with any man in the world.

'Fly' was a flight of fancy. Early in May he and John set off by sea from Boston, and the voyage up the coast of Maine took three days. In the north they found snow lying on the ground and the weather 'shockingly cold'. In spite of rain and fog, an expedition into the Bay of Fundy yielded four rare birds, and was enlivened by Audubon's crew having to rescue three local men whose schooner capsized close astern. 'Depend upon it,' Audubon told Lucy, 'the Yankees are the lads for the ocean. They are firm, cool, considerate, human and generous ... Our John behaved like one of them and worked the ropes and sails to my astonishment extremely well.'

The party prepared for the cold of Labrador by acquiring heavier clothes – fishermen's boots with nailed soles, 'pantaloons of Fearnought so coarse that our legs look more like bears' legs than anything else', oiled jackets, overtrousers and round, white wool hats, with pieces of oilcloth dangling from the back, to stop water running down their necks. For nearly three weeks foul weather kept them bottled up in harbour at Eastport, but Audubon reported that he was fast returning to his former rude health on a regime of 'no snuff, no grog and plenty of exercise', and said that during the trip he intended to work 'like a horse' every moment he was awake. John, meanwhile, was fascinated by accounts of vast catches by cod-fishermen and seal-hunters: two men, Audubon reported, had been known to haul in 3600 fish in a single day.

As the day of departure approached – and with it the knowledge that he would be out of communication for the next three months – he became very emotional, begging Victor to look after Lucy, 'should the Author of all things deprive us of our lives', bursting into tears as he wrote to her:

Oh my dearest Lucy! This appears to me one of the most agonising days I
ever felt. May our God grant us the privilege and happiness to meet again!

It was just as well that he did not know what was happening in England.
In the March issue of the *Magazine of Natural History*, Charles Waterton
had loosed off a heavy broadside seeking to sink Audubon's theories
about the scenting powers of turkey buzzards, ending characteristically,
after 4000 words:

> But here I will stop: I have been too long on carrion.
>> *Neque enim tolerare vaporem*
>> *Ulterius potui.*
> Ovid, *Metamorphoses* ii, 301
> ('For I could not endure the smell any longer'.)

Then, in the May issue of the magazine, he followed up with a characteristically unpleasant attack on the *Biography*, in which half-truths and
naked jealousy struggled for supremacy. Describing Audubon as 'the
foreigner' and referring to his 'arrant ignorance', the Squire was at his
least attractive:

> Without leaving behind him in America any public reputation as a natural-
> ist, Mr Audubon comes to England, and he is immediately pointed out to
> us as an ornithological luminary of the first magnitude. Strange it is that he,
> who has been under such a dense cloud of obscurity in his own western lat-
> itude, should have broken out so suddenly into such dazzling radiance, the
> moment he approached our eastern island.
>
> I ask, what production of Mr Audubon's is it that has called forth such
> rapturous applauses . . ? His drawings are out of the question, they being
> solely works of art. Can it be his paper on the habits of the *Vultur aura* . . .?
> No: that production is lamentably faulty at almost every point. Its grammar
> is bad; its composition poor . . .
>
> Then it must be his *Biography of Birds* which has raised the stranger so
> high in the estimation of Mr Bull? No doubt whatever; and were the
> *Biography of Birds* really the work of Mr Audubon's own pen, I should not be
> tardy in praising its literary merit, not withstanding its ornithological
> faults. But, having compared the style of the *Biography of Birds* with that of
> the article on the habits of the *Vultur aura*, I came to the conclusion that
> these two productions could not have been written by the same person . . .

The first is that of a finished scholar; the second that of a very moderately educated man.

One great merit of Loudon's magazine was that it maintained strict editorial independence: rather than support any one writer and his theories, it printed arguments and counter-arguments without comment, allowing everybody his say. Thus, after Waterton had belaboured the point for page after page, claiming to know for a fact that Audubon had approached someone else first for help in preparing the *Biography*, Victor (who was more sensitive to such criticism than his father) was allowed to make a riposte. Whether or not someone helped him with his letter, he soon showed that he was no slouch when it came to sarcastic innuendo. After quoting Swainson as saying that he had no doubt Audubon was the bona fide author of the *Biography,* he went on:

> I shall not notice Mr Waterton further, except to express my thanks for his generous conduct in withholding his attacks on Mr Audubon for two years after the book in question was published, and during the time the author was in England, and bringing these charges forward when my father has returned to the forests of America and is unable to answer himself.

This stung the Squire so sharply that he produced a threatening retort:

> If Mr Audubon, junior, feels alarmed for his father's reputation as a naturalist, at the menacing attitude I have assumed in defence of my own book ... I would recommend to him either to refute my arguments, or send over an express to his father to come back from America without loss of time, and mount guard over his own Biography of Birds, which shall feel the weight of my arm in earnest if the son returns me sarcastic thanks a second time.

So it went on — but another contributor, who styled himself 'R.B. of Hampstead', and was in fact Robert Bakewell, also sprang to Audubon's defence with a general attack on the disparity between the two men's experience:

> Mr Waterton travelled from his own rich plantations in Demarara surrounded with his slaves and attendants. Mr Audubon was a solitary wanderer

in the forests of America, often dependent on his gun for support ... It is much safer to put one's foot in a hornets' nest than to provoke a swarm of naturalists. I could not, however, see what appeared to me a great injustice done to a highly meritorious character, without endeavouring to repel it.

Three thousand miles to the west, after repeated delays, Audubon's party sailed out of Eastport on 6 June 1833 aboard the *Ripley*, a new schooner of 106 tons. To help him, Audubon had recruited, besides John, four other young men, who all proved such 'useful and excellent companions' that he soon felt they were members of the family. Up the east coast of Nova Scotia they went, then westwards through the Strait of Canso, and due north to the Magdalen Islands, on which they landed but found no birds. The celebrated Bird Rock was another matter: from a distance they thought it was covered with several feet of snow, but they all stood 'astounded and amazed' when they realised that what they could see was a mass of nesting gannets. Even when thousands rose into the air, the top of the rock remained white. This one sight, they all felt, made the whole trip across the Gulf worthwhile.

After they had passed the end of Anticosti Island, twenty miles off on their port bow at just over 49° North, they saw what they thought were white sails on the horizon ahead, but these, they soon found, were snow fields on the Labrador mountains. They breakfasted on fresh-caught cod, and Audubon reckoned he 'never relished a breakfast more'. As they approached the coast, he was astonished by the profusion of sea-birds:

> The air was now filled with Velvet Ducks; millions of these birds were flying from the northwest towards the southeast. The Foolish Guillemots and the Alca torda (Razor-billed Auks) were in immense numbers, flying in long files a few yards above the water, with rather undulating motions, and passing within good gunshot of the vessel.

On 18 June they landed at the mouth of the Natashquan River. At first the landscape of dark-red granite, swampy moss and dwarf vegetation struck Audubon as 'delightfully curious', but when they tried to walk across country, they found it very fatiguing. 'A poor, rugged, miserable country,' he decided, 'the trees like so many mops of wiry composition, and where the soil is not rocky it is boggy up to a man's waist.'

Disappointed by the lack of land birds, they pushed on up the coast for some 300 miles, visiting scores of inland lakes and several hundred islands, on which sea-birds were breeding by the thousand. The farther north they went, the wilder and colder their surroundings became: snow lay deep in the sunless valleys, and they constantly had to light fires to warm themselves — yet the mosquitoes and black flies tormented them as fiercely as they had in the swamps of Florida.

Moved by the grandeur and ferocity of the landscape, Audubon responded by working feverishly, rising at 3 am (when the short northern night was already breaking) and drawing for up to seventeen hours a day, on what he called the 'great table' set beneath the open deck-hatch; but on 6 July — not for the first time — he was shaken by intimations of his mortality. By 5.30 pm his fingers could no longer hold his pencil, and he was forced to go ashore for some exercise. 'The fact is that I am growing old too fast,' he wrote. 'Alas, I feel it — and yet work I will, and may God grant me life to see the last plate of my mammoth work finished.'

On 10 August he suffered unprecedented physical exhaustion: in response to the demands of his body, he began to lie in his berth for longer in the mornings, and to retire earlier in the evenings. Yet whatever the privations — rough seas, rain, fog or cold — he filled his journal with such vivid and copious entries that his record of the voyage stretched to more than 40,000 words — a book in itself.

By the end of August the party was back in Halifax, where Audubon prevailed upon a barber — taking a day off work on Sunday — to shave off the long beard which he had grown during the trip. On the 28th he witnessed the famous phenomenon of the Bay of Fundy, where the tide rose sixty-five feet, 'accumulating with a rapidity I cannot describe'. By placing three-foot sticks in a steep bank, one above the other, his party established that the water came up three feet every ten minutes, or eighteen feet in an hour.

On 7 September he was once again in New York. The expedition had yielded eight new birds, including a finch which Audubon named *Fringilla*

47 overleaf

NORTHERN GANNET
Sula bassanus now *Morus bassanus*

Painted in the Gulf of St Lawrence during Audubon's visit to the Gannet Rock in 1833.

lincolni, after one of his young men, Thomas Lincoln, who came from Maine. The artist returned with twenty-five drawings, including two large plates, one showing a covey of Willow Grouse and the other male and female Labrador Falcons. Writing to Victor on 9 September 1833, he reported that the voyage had cost $2000, but that he was glad to have made it, as it would give him 'a decided superiority' over any other account of America's birds.

Awaiting him in New York were Numbers 32 and 33 of the *Birds*. These thrilled him. 'I look on these ten plates as the best I ever saw, ' he wrote to Victor:

> They do Havell and yourself my beloved son great credit. Everything is better – the birds are the facsimile of my drawings, soft and beautiful. The colouring is clear, transparent and true to nature. The plates are seriously better. I am delighted ... If Havell goes on in this present style and principle, I will be bound that neither I or you will have a word of complaint about his works.

Nevertheless, he continued to send volleys of instruction and exhortation eastwards across the Atlantic. 'The black-capped Titmouse is not dark enough on the back, and in my drawing there must be a white spot at the lower end of the black cap next to the shoulders ... You must stick a cricket or a grasshopper on a thorn before the bill of the male Shrike on the wing,' he told Havell. 'Have the edges of the little Grouse (young) softened in the engraving ... Tell my friend Children that I will send him some insects this autumn without fail.'

Belatedly acknowledging that the sheer size of the prints was a handicap when it came to selling them, he at last began to propose a second, smaller edition, with the letterpress attached to the paintings. 'The price of our great work is such that besides public institutions and men of great wealth, few copies only can we expect to sell,' he told Victor. 'A reduced edition would be within almost every person's compass.' The smaller plates of *Birds*, he thought, could be used as they were, but the paintings of the larger species would have to be redone, and new plates cut. He returned to the idea in several later letters, calling it the 'Little' or

'Petite' edition, and was obviously thinking hard about possible ways of proceeding: 'The drawings would have to be very correctly diminished and exactly copied in their details.' But, he added, no word of any such project must get out until the main one was complete. As for the immediate future:

> If you can possibly do without me in England for another year, acquaint me immediately – do the same should the case prove vice versa … I should like much, very much to remain on this side the waters one more year, after which I could go to London full-headed and full-handed - I mean that I would by that time have drawings finished and knowledge enough to enable us to complete the work without recrossing the sea.

Victor, for the time being, was on the Continent, travelling through France and Germany in search of new subscribers, but with little success. When Audubon learnt that his son had not been able to recruit a single name in Germany, he came to the conclusion that America must after all be their best market. The Continent – apart from Russia – was too poor, and little more could be expected from England, where the people were 'agog on emancipation, reform etc. etc'. In America, by contrast, 'all works well. Every industrious man makes and saves money. The taste for science improves daily. Youth is educated with much care, and books of every useful kind are sought for more than ever.'

Once back in London, Victor again took advantage of *Loudon's Magazine* to give Waterton a taste of his own medicine, writing from 121 Great Portland Street on 19 September 1833 with a withering comment on the Squire's own book, *Wanderings in South America*:

> Ignorant of the science of natural history myself, I have enquired among the eminent scientific naturalists of the metropolis what Mr Waterton has done to entitle him to assume the office of censor general; but the answers I have received are somewhat unsatisfactory. He has written, it seems, an amusing book, but whether of facts of or fables is differently believed …
>
> Finally, Mr Waterton, professing to be learned in the ornithology of America, very complacently tells us … that 'Azara is totally unknown' to him. This, for an American ornithologist, is like an astronomer asking who was Sir Isaac Newton? Mr Waterton, by this single admission, proclaims his

own degree of intelligence: even I can inform this 'learned Theban' that Azara, for several years, explored the forests of South America, published four volumes, which have gone through three editions, on their natural history, described the habits and manners of the birds ... and is, in short, the very first authority on these matters.

Meanwhile in New York Audubon had sorted out five Numbers of water birds, for the start of Volume Three of *Birds*, and he arranged for them to be sent off to England separately from a batch of land-bird drawings, 'to divide the chances of loss at sea'. He then set off for Charleston, where the hospitable John Bachman had invited him, Lucy and John to spend the winter.

John proceeded directly to the south, but Audubon's journey was packed with incident. In Philadelphia he was arrested for an outstanding debt, but escaped gaol when a friend offered bail, and he himself paid

48
BACHMAN'S
WARBLER
Sylvia bachmanii
or *Vermivora
bachmanii*

Audubon never
saw this species
alive, but painted
it from skins
kept by his friend
the Rev. John
Bachman, who
discovered it.

the necessary amount – an incident which did nothing to soften his dislike of the city. He then went on via Baltimore, Washington, Richmond, Virginia and Columbia, South Carolina, collecting subscriptions along the way.

In Charleston he filled every waking hour with shooting, drawing, painting, writing about and discussing birds. His mind dwelt constantly on the progress of his great work, and on 24 November he asked Havell:

> Can we not push the work still faster? Can you not publish the second volume … at the rate of ten Numbers per annum? It would be a great satisfaction to me, as I conceive myself growing old very fast. So much travelling, exposure and fatigue do I undergo that the machine methinks is wearing out; and it would indeed be a pleasure for me to see the last of the present publication.

Havell responded by taking on an extra engraver, and told Audubon that, provided all the paintings came to hand in time, he could complete the entire project in five or even four years. This news galvanised the artist. He might complain, 'I will have to work harder than ever, and God knows if I shall be able to stand it', but by the end of the year he had finished nearly a hundred more paintings of water species, and on 18 January 1834 he sent off five Numbers to New York, insured for $4000, for onward shipment to London.

He and his genial host also found time to conduct further experiments designed to settle the controversy, stirred up by Ord and Waterton, about whether or not vultures, or turkey buzzards, found their food by sight or by smell. Already, in an earlier trial, he had stuffed the skin of a deer with dried grass, let it cure until it was hard as leather, taken it to the middle of a large field and laid it on its back with its legs in the air. Buzzards had attacked the eyes, which were solid globes of painted clay – and this had convinced Audubon that they were hunting by sight alone.

Now, when they set out a coarse painting of a sheep, skinned and cut open, vultures quickly spotted it, landed close by, hopped over and began to tug hopefully at the canvas, before retiring baffled – and they repeated their manoeuvres more than fifty times as the painting was moved to new sites. When the decoy was put down within two feet of a concealed pile of offal, the birds reacted as usual and pecked at the painting but failed to notice the food. Finally the researchers put out small pieces of beef, no more than an inch square, on a canvas cloth, under which was hidden some high, stinking offal. The vultures ate the beef but failed to detect the putrescent remains right under their beaks: only when a small rent was made in the canvas did they at last start to devour the offal.

Armed with this evidence, which had been witnessed and ratified by six professors and lecturers from the Medical College of South Carolina, Bachman wrote an article for *Loudon's Magazine* which was read to the Boston Society of Natural History on 5 February, and which, in Audubon's view, would 'astound Mr Waterton and his fraternity'. Loudon, meanwhile, had already published Victor's defence of his father, and another by Swainson, on the same lines. 'The copy of your reply to Monsieur Waterton is excellent,' Audubon told Victor.

> That from Swainson ought to prove a death-blow to the Demerara gent! [Waterton]. I hope that these letters are now before the world, for my mortification has been great enough respecting the blackguardism of G. Ord and others, and yet I am heartily glad that I never paid (personally) any attention to them through the press or otherwise ... The moment is at hand when these scoundrels will be glad to find some hiding place to resort to, and to wait for time to obliterate their obvious jealousy and falsehoods.

When he finally sent Victor an account of his latest experiments, on 1 January 1834, he described it as 'a plain paper, no nonsense, no fudge, but so full of plain truth that I hope the armour of Waterton will fall to the earth and leave the man a poor, worthless carcass fit (if fresh) for the very buzzards which he has so deeply abused.' Remarking that, instead of travelling thousands of miles at enormous expense, he could 'with tenfold ease' settle himself in some corner of London and write 'all such fables' as came into his head, and 'publish these without caring a jot about the consequences', he declared himself happy with what he had done:

I feel greatly proud of our work. I feel greatly proud that I am the happy possessor of a most excellent wife and two sons, whom I can view as my dearest and best attached friends. I am greatly proud that I possess the knowledge that every word I have published or shall publish is truth, and nothing but the result of my own observations in fields and forests ...

There is another thing of which I am equally proud – that is, that I have firmly attached to me, both in Europe and in our country, a large set of excellent and learned friends. I have received unprecedented privileges at the hands of our Government, as well as from that of England. I see our work progress well and steadily. In a word I feel happy within my heart. This is the palm I have always searched for, and it is the truest blessing on Earth!

For much of that winter Audubon was planning what he called his 'last journey' – another foray to Florida; and it was a measure of his standing in Washington that the Secretary of the Treasury issued an order to all commanders of Revenue cutters south of Delaware Bay, instructing them to convey him and his associates to any part of the coast within their cruising grounds. Further, General Lewis Cass, the Secretary of War, promised that if a government expedition was formed to explore the Rocky Mountains, Audubon could go with it.

Writing to Victor on Christmas Eve, 1833, he emphasised how anxious he was to finish all his work in America – finding both birds and sub-scribers – before he crossed the Atlantic again, and he spoke of needing a year or fifteen months to accomplish everything. When he did go to England, he said, he would have to remain there for several years, 'if not until the completion of the engraving'.

Yet early in March 1834 he suddenly decided not to attempt either of the ambitious journeys he had been considering. Instead, after a com-plete change of mind and plans, he headed north for Washington, Baltimore and New York, whence he and Lucy sailed for Liverpool on 16 April aboard the 'superb packet' *North America*.

The reasons for his premature return are not clear; Victor had urged him to come back as soon as possible, but he knew that he had not recorded by any means all America's birds, and that he needed more time to seek out those which had eluded him so far. He seems to have been driven back to Europe partly by his feeling of time running out. He was still only forty-nine, and yet, echoing what he had written to Havell, he told Victor:

> I am growing old very fast. In three or four years my career as a traveller will be ended, and should I be obliged to renew my field labours, it is doubtful if my constitution could bear it. One year now is equal to three, three years hence.

By then John had improved so much as an artist that his father spoke of leaving the depiction of new birds to him. 'John has drawn a few birds as good as any I ever made,' Audubon recorded, 'and ere a few months I hope to give this department of my duty altogether to him.' The news which did not appear in any letter was that during the winter John had fallen in love with Maria, the Bachmans' eldest daughter.

Chapter Twelve
FAMILY FIRM

A GOOD PASSAGE of nineteen days returned the Audubons to Liverpool, where they received the warmest of receptions from the Rathbones and their other friends. After a short stay on Merseyside they went down to London, to find business 'going on prosperously' and Victor in fine health and spirits. 'The very sight of him was a restoration of life to me,' Audubon recalled, 'and our happiness was as complete as it may ever be expected on this earth.' The family found good rooms at 73 Margaret Street, only a short walk from Havell's premises in Oxford Street; Lucy would have preferred to be farther from 'all this crowd and noise of London', but the central location suited Audubon ideally, and he sent Bachman a fond if not altogether flattering description of their domestic bliss:

> My Old Friend [Lucy] mends our socks, makes our shirts, reads to us at times, but drinks no brandy nowadays. She has cast off her purchased sham curls [and] wears her own dear grey locks, and looks all the better.

Among the letters of introduction that he had brought from America was one to Baron Rothschild. The name alone promised riches, but when Audubon called at the recipient's private office, he was received less cordially than he hoped. Having glanced at the letter, the fat, red-faced banker (who had come into the room hitching up his trousers) made a reply that struck Audubon as offensively arrogant: 'I never sign my name to any subscription list, but you may send your work and I will pay for a copy of it. Gentlemen, I am busy. I wish you good morning.'

A few days later the artist, still smarting, sent round a half-bound copy of the first volume of *The Birds of America*, and followed it with new Numbers as they came out. After eight or ten months John made out an account, which Havell took to Rothschild's bank. As Audubon recorded in disgust:

> The baron looked at it with amazement and cried out, 'What! A hundred pounds for birds! Why, sir, I will give you five pounds, and not a farthing more!' Representations were made to him of the magnificence and expense of the work, and how pleased his baroness and wealthy children would be to have a copy; but the great financier was unrelenting. The copy of the work was actually sent back to Mr Havell's shop, and as I found that instituting legal proceedings against him would cost more than it would come to, I kept the work, and afterwards sold it to a man with less money but a nobler heart.[1]

Paintings apart, Audubon had brought back with him from America hundreds of bird-skins, and during the summer he sold two lots, worth £77 in all, to the British Museum. Of greater significance were the drafts of many episodes for the second volume of his *Ornithological Biography*. He had composed these during the winter at Charleston, and Lucy had 'transcribed' them for him, no doubt improving the English. Yet he still needed his ghost-writer to polish them, and to work up the science in his descriptions of birds.

Since he and MacGillivray had last worked together, the Scot had been extremely busy. Indeed, his productivity was astonishing. During the decade 1830–40, quite apart from the five volumes of the *Ornithological Biography* and its concluding *Synopsis*, he wrote thirteen books of his own, as well as twenty-seven scientific papers and the new catalogue for the Edinburgh Royal College of Surgeons' Museum, of which he was appointed Conservator in 1831. One of his first tasks there was to move the establishment's entire collection into a new building and rearrange it;

---

1. Audubon's list of original subscribers included N. M. Rothschild (the 1st Baron Rothschild), but it seems that the volumes of *Birds* entered in his name went to the man with less money but a nobler heart. Later, the 2nd Baron Rothschild did buy a set, which is now in the Natural History Museum in London.

and when in the summer of 1833 the curators of the museum asked him to draw up a new catalogue, he travelled widely to other museums in search of information and ideas, visiting Glasgow, Liverpool, Dublin, Bristol and London.

Luckily his job left him time for outside assignments, and when Audubon wrote to him from London in June 1834, inquiring after his well-being and asking for his help once again, he promptly agreed to resume work, and added these jaunty paragraphs:

> You ask if I draw birds yet with a view to publish. My answer is that I dissect, describe and draw birds, quadrupeds, whales, reptiles and fishes, with a view of astonishing the world, and bettering my condition. I have about a hundred drawings, all the size of life, excepting two dolphins. But I have determined nothing as yet respecting publication.
>
> Some time ago a friend of mine called on Mr Havell with a letter in which I desired that person to engrave for me a few of my drawings, for the purpose of being exhibited at a meeting of naturalists. I had no answer, and so Mr Havell can go to Jericho, or elsewhere, as he likes; but further your correspondent saith not.

MacGillivray suggested that, besides the *Ornithological Biography*, Audubon might bring out 'other various works which could not fail to be popular; for example, a biography of yourself ...' He clearly thought this a real possibility, for he was never sycophantic, and on 9 July, when he had revised the first eighteen articles for the new book, he reported:

> You wish to know my opinion as to the improvement of your style. It seems to me to be much the same as before, but the information which you give is more diversified and more satisfactory.

Nor did MacGillivray shrink from giving the author literary and commercial advice. Several times he urged Audubon to reduce the size of the book and to include some illustrations, perhaps woodcuts. If he did that, he wrote,

> It would spread over the land like a flock of migratory pigeons. Even without embellishments it would fly, but were you to give it those additional wings, it would sweep along in beautiful curves, like the nighthawk or the purple-breasted swallow.

For Audubon, the idea of an autobiography clearly had some appeal, for in a letter to Bachman dated 25 August 1834 he said, 'This coming winter I will spend at writing my own biography, to be published as soon as possible' – and he did start work on a book called *Myself*, cast in the form of a letter to Victor and John. The manuscript, which ran to about 10,000 words, described his early life, and was characteristically slapdash[2]; but the fact was that the *Ornithological Biography* absorbed so much of his writing energy, and so many of his own experiences, that he never went any farther with his own story.

Audubon was so strongly encouraged by Havell's progress that in June 1834 he published an announcement, saying that production of the *Birds* was running ahead of schedule, and trying to bluff would-be subscribers into taking early action:

> It is now certain that *The Birds of America* will be a very scarce work; and the author cannot bind himself to furnish copies to those who may neglect to order them before the work is finished. He will, therefore, consider it a favour of those persons desirous of possessing it, if they will forward their orders, as soon as convenient, to J.J. Audubon, or to Mr Robert Havell, Zoological Gallery, 77 Oxford Street, opposite the Pantheon.

That same month, Waterton returned to the attack with another venomous blast in *Loudon's Magazine*, firing grape-shot at everything which displeased him – the scenting powers of Turkey Buzzards (yet again), Audubon's claim to be the author of the *Biography*, his account of his meeting with Alexander Wilson at Louisville in 1810, his description of Passenger Pigeons. At the end of his tirade the Squire once more betrayed his jingoistic jealousy of the American intruder and his supporters: 'I now leave ... [all these matters] to the consideration of those British naturalists who have volunteered to support a foreigner in his exertions to teach Mr Bull ornithology in the nineteenth century.'

Yet again Audubon ignored him. During the summer of 1834 he stayed in London, sending material up to Scotland for MacGillivray to work

---

2. It was printed in his granddaughter Maria R. Audubon's *Audubon and His Journals*.

on; and in the autumn, when he himself moved to Edinburgh, the two men worked away together at least as fast as before. By the time Audubon wrote the introduction to Volume Two of the *Biography* on 1 December, they had completed a tome even larger than Volume One — 580 printed pages, or nearly 300,000 words.

"BIRDS OF AMERICA."

J. J. AUDUBON has returned from the UNITED STATES, and begs to inform his Patrons, that since his arrival, he has made arrangements with Mr. R. HAVELL, his Engraver, that will enable him to complete his Work on the BIRDS OF AMERICA in Four Years, although originally contemplated to require Eight Years from this period.

The Third Volume, now in progress, will consist of WATER BIRDS, and the Fourth, which will be the last, will contain what remain unpublished, of both the Land and Water Birds.

The Water Birds and the remainder of the Land Birds will be found to be equal, if not to surpass, the Two First Volumes, in interest, beauty, and execution.

The Second Volume of Letter-press will soon be published.

It is now certain that the "BIRDS OF AMERICA" will be a very scarce Work; and the Author cannot bind himself to furnish copies to those who may neglect to order them before the Work is finished. He will, therefore, consider it a favor of those persons desirous of possessing it, if they will forward their Orders, as soon as convenient, to *J. J. Audubon*, or to *Mr. Robert Havell, Zoological Gallery*, 77, *Oxford Street, opposite the Pantheon, London.*

London, June 1834.

49

LOOKING AHEAD

Touting for subscribers on his return from America in 1834, Audubon accurately predicted that his *magnum opus* would in time become very scarce.

The author was not at his best in the introduction – a twenty-three-page canter through his own career, laced with over-effusive tributes to various people who had helped him. Starting with his father and proceeding through J. G. Children, the Prince of Musignano, Sir Thomas Lawrence, 'my friend Swainson', 'my friend Bachman', Professor Jameson, 'my eldest son Victor Gifford, the younger John Woodhouse' and dozens more, he hit a rather self-satisfied note, which would have been acceptable in his journal, but seemed less attractive in print. Towards the end he thanked Havell for his work, but only with the faintly patronising remark that he had 'improved greatly in the execution of the plates' – and he made no mention of his most recent and efficient assistant, MacGillivray.

The format of Volume Two was the same as that of its predecessor – five birds and an essay – and Audubon, while announcing that he had adopted Bonaparte's system of nomenclature, openly admitted that the order in which the plates had been published precluded the possibility of arranging the species in a systematic manner. He was thus able to avoid any discussion of 'affinity and grouping' – an area on which he knew he was very weak, and Volume Two, having kicked off with the Raven, went on with the Blue Jay (another corvid), but then switched to the Canada Flycatcher, the Chipping Sparrow and the Red-bellied Nuthatch.

The author's strength lay in his own direct knowledge of his subjects. No one could challenge him when he wrote that the flesh of the raven 'is tough and unfit for food … When wounded, it bites severely, and scratches with its claws as fiercely as a hawk.' Squeamish readers sometimes got more than they fancied. Describing how he had once examined the stomach of a Snowy Owl, Audubon wrote that he had found

> the whole of a large house-rat, in pieces of considerable size, the head and the tail almost entire. This bird was very fat, and its intestines, which were thin, and so small as not to exceed a fourth of an inch in diameter, measured 4½ feet in length.

Such owls, he added, were 'not indelicate eating'.

Many of the interlarded essays had nothing to do with ornithology –

facing page 50

Snowy Owl
Strix nyctea now
Nyctea scandiaca

Original examples of this magnificent print of owls under a night sky now fetch over $100,000 apiece.

yet the author had some cracking good tales to tell, and set them out with relish. The first in Volume Two, 'The Runaway', told how, late on a sultry afternoon in the Louisiana swamps, he had come across a runaway Negro slave, who led him back to his secret hideaway in the middle of a cane-brake. There he spent the night, in the company of the man's wife and three young children, melted by the story of how the family had been dispersed when its members were sold at auction, and of how the father had escaped from his master, found the rest of his brood, and reunited them.

Even if there is a saccharine taste in Audubon's telling of the saga, it is easy enough to believe that he was deeply moved by it:

> The runaways, after disclosing their secret to me, both rose from their seat with eyes full of tears. 'Good master, for God's sake do something for us and our children,' they sobbed forth with one accord. Their little ones lay sound asleep in the fearlessness of their innocence. Who could have heard such a tale without emotion? I promised them my most cordial assistance.

In the morning, he shepherded them out to the plantation of their original master, whom he knew, and persuaded the man to take them back: 'Ere an hour had elapsed, the Runaway and his family were looked upon as his own.'

Another gripping episode described an earthquake in Kentucky. The author had been riding through the area known as the Barrens when he noticed 'a sudden and strange darkness rising from the western horizon'. Next came a loud rumbling, like that of a tornado, but when Audubon tried to spur his horse on towards shelter, it gradually slowed to a halt and stood with its feet spread apart, groaning so piteously that he thought it was about to die. Before he could dismount, the earth started to shake, the ground 'rose and fell in successive furrows', and the shrubs and trees 'began to move from their very roots', After a few minutes the convulsions subsided, the sky cleared, the horse recovered its composure and galloped off 'as if loose and frolicking without a rider' ; but the author's brief attack of terror – that the earth would split open and swallow him – came over with an immediacy that no reader would forget.

So Audubon's stories poured forth, with a vigour and authenticity that no rival ornithologist could match. Even without its mass of ornithological information, Volume Two would have been a good read: the lumberers on the Maine rivers, moose-hunting, the turtle-turners of the Tortugas Islands off Florida, the amazing tides in the Bay of Fundy – all the narratives were spiced with the excitement of wild, faraway settings.

Audubon ordered 750 copies of the book for England, and the same for America, where it was published in Boston by Hillard Gray & Co. During December 1834, while it was being printed, MacGillivray signed on to work on Volumes Three and Four, at the same rate of two guineas per sheet, as well as on 'any other work which you may intend to publish'.

In a generous review of Volume Two, the *Athenaeum* remarked:

> He has told us what he has seen and undergone, not perhaps in the smooth, nicely balanced periods of a drawing-room writer … but with unstudied freedom, rising at times to eloquence, nor been ashamed to utter the thousand affectionate and benevolent feelings which a close and enthusiastic communion with nature must nourish. The work is full of the man.

By then MacGillivray had launched out on a major project of his own – his *History of British Birds*, which eventually ran to five volumes – and he sent Audubon a collection of his bird drawings, asking for comments and criticisms. The American replied in rather stilted, formal terms, but summed up: 'In short, I think them decidedly the best representations of birds I have ever seen.'

The two continued their collaboration in close harmony and became firm friends. Nevertheless, the strain of their work sometimes produced minor explosions. In one of his notebooks MacGillivray wrote a semi-humorous sketch, evidently to ease his own feelings:

> *A large room, in which are a heap of birds' skins and a long table with others arranged in lines. Mr Audubon seated, and transcribing references to authors. Mr MacGillivray enters with a portfolio.*
>
> AUDUBON, *pretending to be very busy, and not looking up.* How are you?
> MacG. Pretty well.
> AUD. I will be done presently.

MACG. *stands until he is done.*

AUD. Well, what do you think of the Buntings now? Have we none in America?

MACG. I don't care about Buntings. I have given up thinking about them ... I wish, if you please, to begin at the other end of the series, and take the Icterines ...

AUD (*cross*) That I think is a very bad plan. It is strange to begin with the Icterines, at the wrong end ...

They argue with increasing irritation, until Audubon says:

It is impossible to bear this. It is really awful.

MACG. Well, I will give up the plan, and take up whatever group you please ...

AUD. God bless me! This will never do. If we cannot get on with it, let it alone.

MACG. Very well. What is the use of squabbling in this way? You say it is all nonsense, mere child's play. If you think so, let it alone.

Rises and throws the paper on the table.

AUD. I'll have nothing more to do with it. I would not be plagued in this way for anything.

MACG. *Goes off without speaking.*

AUD. Goodbye to you. I am done with you.

The exchanges end with the pair making things up next morning, when Audubon apologises for losing his temper, 'he having been so vexed and irritated by various recurrences, disappointments relative to money, and the hurry of arranging for departure.' Although the sketch is basically good-humoured, the mere fact that MacGillivray wrote it reveals the underlying tension brought on by the intensity of composition.

The essential warmth of the relationship between the two was made manifest in several ways. MacGillivray christened one of his sons Audubon Felix, and the woodsman in turn named two American birds after his invaluable Scottish assistant, besides arranging to have him elected a member of the Natural History Society of Philadelphia, the Lyceum of New York and the Philosophical Society of South Carolina. MacGillivray dedicated his first ornithological book, *Descriptions of the Rapacious Birds of Great Britain*, to Audubon 'in admiration of his talents as an ornithologist, and in gratitude for many acts of friendship.' Never-theless, several commentators felt that the Scot never received the credit due to him, and in the 1880s Elliott Coues wrote that he was 'the source of inspiration in all that pertains to the technic' of Audubon's work:

> Not to put too fine a point on it, he furnished nearly all the 'ornithology' of Audubon's work ... Audubon was primarily and chiefly an animal painter, and he finally acquired no little familiarity with bird life; but he began to paint without the slightest idea of ornithology, and never attained even mediocrity as a strict scientist.

He loved warmth, colour, action: he liked to exaggerate and 'embroider', and make his pages glow like a humming bird's throat, or like one of his own marvellous pictures; he had no genius for accuracy, no taste for dull, dry detail, no care for a specimen after he had drawn it. MacGillivray supplied what was necessary to make his work a contribution to science as well as to art. In fact he wrote a great deal of Audubon's book.

ORNITHOLOGICAL BIOGRAPHY,

OR AN ACCOUNT OF THE HABITS OF THE

BIRDS OF THE UNITED STATES OF AMERICA;

ACCOMPANIED BY DESCRIPTIONS OF THE OBJECTS REPRESENTED
IN THE WORK ENTITLED

THE BIRDS OF AMERICA,

AND INTERSPERSED WITH DELINEATIONS OF AMERICAN
SCENERY AND MANNERS.

BY JOHN JAMES AUDUBON, F.R.SS.L. & E.

FELLOW OF THE LINNEAN AND ZOOLOGICAL SOCIETIES OF LONDON ; MEMBER OF THE LYCEUM
AND LINNEAN SOCIETY OF NEW YORK, OF THE NATURAL HISTORY SOCIETY OF PARIS, THE
WERNERIAN NATURAL HISTORY SOCIETY OF EDINBURGH; HONORARY MEMBER OF THE
SOCIETY OF NATURAL HISTORY OF MANCHESTER, AND OF THE SCOTTISH ACADEMY OF
PAINTING, ARCHITECTURE, AND SCULPTURE, &c.

EDINBURGH:

ADAM BLACK, 55. NORTH BRIDGE, EDINBURGH ;

R. HAVELL JUN., ENGRAVER, 77. OXFORD STREET, AND LONGMAN, REES,
BROWN, & GREEN, LONDON ; GEORGE SMITH, TITHEBARR STREET,
LIVERPOOL ; T. SOWLER, MANCHESTER ; MRS ROBINSON, LEEDS ;
E. CHARNLEY, NEWCASTLE ; POOL & BOOTH, CHESTER ; AND BEILBY,
KNOTT, & BEILBY, BIRMINGHAM.

MDCCCXXXI.

Title page of the first volume of the *Ornithological Biography* published in 1831: a 500-page volume written with scratchy pens at the rate of 2000 words a day.

CHAPTER THIRTEEN

WRITERS AT WORK

WHEN AUDUBON and Lucy moved down to London for the winter of 1834–35, writing was again the order of the day. As usual, the artist went at the task all-out, informing Bachman:

> I am almost mad with the desire of publishing my third volume [of the *Ornithological Biography*] this year – I am growing old fast and must work at a double quick time now ...
>
> I am at work generally about 5 o'clock of the morning and work, if not sadly interrupted, twelve hours. After this I dine, take a walk, chat with my dear old friend [Lucy] and my sons, go to bed early, and repeat the dose from one year's end to the next. May God grant me a few more years of this happy life of pleasurable activity.

He completed a quarter of the material for Volume Three within a month, but the effort left him severely short of breath and without appetite. His remedy was a change of work:

> I took to drawing! And what do you think? I have positively finished thirty-three drawings of American birds in England. This has enabled me to swell my third volume of illustrations with fifty-seven species not given by Alexander Wilson and therefore forestalling my friend Charles Bonaparte.

Crow as he might, the artist was running short of material for his narrative sketches, and asked Bachman to send him 'some good stories for *Episodes*. Send quickly and often.' He was also feeling harassed by the general air of instability which had come over England, and on 28 April he wrote to Edward Harris:

> I thought [it] better to push my publication, on account of the woeful

dulling of the times in this country, where political strife engrosses the mind of every person so much that arts and sciences are, as it were, put on the shelves ... The Reformers are struggling against the Tories, and vice-versa. The Churchmen are aghast at the prospect of the future, and all this puts a complete stoppage to business.

In the nine months after he returned to England, he found only two or three new subscribers, and lost between one and two dozen. Whether or not any of these defections were caused by the sniping of his critics, it is impossible to tell – but Waterton kept up his attacks, launching four in 1835 alone. Audubon continued to maintain his silence, and to affect indifference, remarking to Bachman, 'As to the rage of Mr Waterton ... I really care not a fig. All such stuffs will soon evaporate, being mere smoke from a dung hill.'

A much greater threat, in his view, was an incipient change of fashion, which he described to Edward Harris:

We receive no new subscribers in Europe. The taste is passing for birds like a flitting shadow. Insects, reptiles and fishes are now the rage, and these fly, swim or crawl on pages innumerable in every bookseller's window.

The same theme came out in a letter to Bachman:

The world is all agog – for what? For bugs the size of water melons. There is in fact a bug now in Havell's shop for which the owner asked – how much? Once, twice, thrice? You give up? No less than fifty pounds sterling. Two hundred and fifty dollars for a beetle – as large as my fist, it is true, but nought but a beetle after all. Thirty guineas have been offered and refused. I almost wish I could be turned into a beetle myself!

Audubon was also disconcerted by the growing fame of his English competitor John Gould, whose own great project, *Birds of Europe*, was now in full production. Like Audubon, Gould tended to portray himself as a child of nature, but he came from an entirely different background. Son of the foreman in the gardens of Windsor Castle, he was born in 1804, and had only a sketchy education; but he learnt some botany work-ing with his father, and became such a proficient taxidermist that in his teens he began selling stuffed birds to boys at Eton College, across the river. In 1824 he set himself up as a taxidermist in Windsor, and in 1827 he became the first Curator and Preserver for the new Zoological Society of London's museum in Bruton Street. During the next three years he stuffed numerous specimens for King George IV, among them a thick-kneed bustard, two mouse deer, an ostrich and (most famously) a giraffe.

Industrious, cunning, equipped with a good business sense, if not entirely straightforward, Gould was neither a talented draughtsman nor a dedicated naturalist; but he was fascinated by birds, and had such a feeling for them that, even when clumsily drawing from skins or stuffed specimens, he was somehow able to capture their characteristics; and when he married Elizabeth Coxen, an artist of high ability who also came from a bird-minded family, he forged a powerful partnership. It was Elizabeth who, for the next decade, worked up most of the 3000 illustrations that he published.

His first book — *A Century of Birds Hitherto Unfigured from the Himalaya Mountains* — came out in several parts in 1830 and 1831, and found almost 300 subscribers — more than double the number recruited by Audubon in England. 'Mr Gould has been very successful in his *Birds*, which has caused him to think not a little of himself,' Havell remarked sourly; and Audubon was naturally scornful of his rival's efforts, for Gould had never travelled in distant lands, but had derived his information from a collection of skins brought back from the east by someone else.

Lack of field experience, however, was no deterrent to somebody so ambitious, and in 1832 he began work on *Birds of Europe*, which appeared in successive volumes over the next five years, produced by the process known as lithography, in which the picture is drawn on a block of lime-stone with a waxy or greasy crayon, and printed from that. Of the 448 plates included in the work, sixty-two were drawn by the highly talented young Edward Lear, who had already begun publishing work of his own, in the form of *Illustrations of the Family of Psittacidae or Parrots*, which started coming out in 1831, when he was only nineteen. It seems likely that Gould, who did not like competition, brought Lear into his team in an attempt to slow down the progress of an active rival.

[227]

Goaded by all this activity, Audubon found his patience with rival ornithologists wearing thin, and in letters to Bachman and Edward Harris he let fly, particularly at Selby and Jardine, who, he knew, had made critical remarks about his own work:

> I have read Selby's and Temminck's works, but they are, I am sorry to say, not from nature. Not a word could I find in them but what was compilation … Sir Wam [sic] Jardine is published [sic] an enormous quantity of trash, all compilation, and takes the undue liberty of giving figures from my work and those of all others who may best suit his views. Mr Gould is publishing the *Birds of England, of Europe*, etc., etc., etc. in all sorts of ways. Swainson has seventeen volumes in his head and on papers half-finished.
>
> Works on the birds of all the world are innumerable – cheap as dirt and more dirty than dirt. Sir William Jardine will encumber the whole of God's creation with stuff as little like the objects of the Creator's formations as the moon is unto cheese.

Audubon envied Gould his position as curator at the Museum, which gave him free use of the Zoo's facilities, and enabled him to maintain contact with the scientific gentry such as Jardine and Selby. Nevertheless, he and Gould agreed to exchange copies of their respective works.

Waterton's implacable hatred of Audubon and his supporters seethed on, surfacing most noxiously in the Squire's letters to Ord, and in a spectacularly rude fourteen-page diatribe against Jameson, who had stood up for Audubon in the arguments over the rattlesnake: 'Pray, Sir, where were your brains … when you received, and approved of, a narrative at once so preposterous and so palpably fictitious?' he demanded in a letter dated 27 January 1835. No matter that the Squire was referring to a dispute already eight years old: so avid was he for publicity that he had copies of his letters privately printed and distributed at his own expense, fifty in London, twenty-five in Edinburgh. His main target was Audubon, but he also sought to savage Jameson along the way:

> Through Audubon you have aimed a blow at me; through Audubon I will level a shaft at you in my turn, with aim so just and true that it will be out of your power to ward it off. It is a matter of perfect indifference to me whether you praise or condemn Mr Audubon … If, however, my opinion

were asked, I should say that I do not consider you qualified to review a book on ornithology ... I may yet consider it necessary to show to the public that you are no better qualified to review a work on birds than you are to lecture on the poisonous fangs of snakes ...

If the contents of this letter should sting you, pray reflect, sir, that you deserve to smart a little for your wanton imprudence in holding up to public animadversion the conduct of a gentleman who has never used you unkindly either by word or deed.

Three days later Waterton wrote to Ord:

Professor Jameson ... very fortunately for me, but very unfortunately for himself, has stood forward the avowed champion of Audubon and commenced an attack upon me. This is just what I wanted. I shall now have an opportunity of exposing his lamentable ignorance, and of defending myself. As for Audubon, of course, he will catch it to his heart's content ... Now, my dear friend, if you can procure authentic information relative to Audubon before he first came to England ... pray lose no time in doing so. I care nothing about his ornithology ... But what I want particularly to know, and to be quite certain of, is this. In what towns did he keep shop after his marriage, and how many years did he remain in those towns? You see my drift.

Even though Ord failed to dig up new dirt, Waterton returned to the attack in another bilious missive directed at Swainson on 10 March. Stung by the fact that Swainson had referred to him as an amateur, he resorted to bald abuse: 'Believe me, Sir, you have a vast deal to learn before you become an adept in ornithology.'

'Depend upon it,' he told Ord in another letter, 'that quack [Audubon] never pretended to be a naturalist till he came over to this country and found how easy it was to gull John Bull ... Let me request you most earnestly to write a critique on Audubon's work. That ornithological impostor ought to be exposed.' It may be that the Squire's enmity did have some effect, for he was a crony of the Duke of Northumberland, and consistently sought to belittle the *Birds* – with the result that Audubon had to make repeated attempts over nearly ten years, from 1826 to 1836, to persuade the duke to take out a subscription.

[229]

Fulminate as Waterton might, in March 1835 *Loudon's Magazine* gave Volume Two of the *Ornithological Biography* a glowing notice. The anonymous reviewer, signing himself only 'B', greatly enjoyed the Episodes between the more technical sections, and concluded that the work as a whole would be 'perused with delight by every lover of natural history'. He also quoted some of Baron Cuvier's remarks about *The Birds of America*, made to the Royal Academy of Sciences in Paris, calling it, among other things, 'the most magnificent monument that has yet been raised to ornithology'.

In *Blackwood's Magazine* another ally, Christopher North, praised Volume Two no less lavishly, and described how the woodsman, 'fresh from the Floridas and breathing of the pure air of far-off Labrador', had called on him at two o'clock one morning, 'muffled up in a cloak and furred like a Russ'. After pages of scorn directed at the blockheads and 'hornythologists' who were fouling the waters of zoology, the review concluded that the volume teemed 'with interest and amusement'.

Such praise clearly infuriated Waterton, who hit back in *Loudon's* April issue with an article that attempted to show that Audubon could not have done all his drawings in the time he claimed. Even when writing about other subjects — like the tawny owl, on which he held forth in June — the Squire could not refrain from side-swipes, referring irrelevantly to 'Mr Ord (the elegant and scientific biographer of poor Wilson)'.

In mid-summer 1835 the object of these attacks returned to Edinburgh, still labouring away on Volume Three, and his letters portrayed the whole family industriously at work. John was earning good money as a portrait painter, tackling five sitters a day, Victor was turning out landscapes, and Lucy was knitting socks for them all.

Every few days Audubon wrote to Havell, enthusing over the latest prints, exhorting him to keep up his standards and urging him to proceed ever faster, even though by then the engraver was producing new Numbers of the *Birds* at the rate of one a month, and the costs of running his shop had risen to the unprecedented height of £100 a week. In the autumn Audubon's letters to Bachman became no less demanding, for he urgently needed information missing from his own records: could his friend discover anything more about the Black-winged Hawk (*Falco dispar*) – its eggs and young – the Red-bellied Woodpecker, the Bank Swallow, various Woodpeckers and Warblers, and many others? Could he find a nest of the American Bittern, and could Doctor Strobell, if in Florida, procure eggs of numerous species, among them the Flamingo and the Scarlet Ibis?

Often in writing to Bachman (by now his closest friend and confidant) he hit a more ebullient note than in his other correspondence – as when the Irish reformer Daniel O'Connell visited Edinburgh in mid-September:

> A fine fat jolly man he is I assure you – a perfect ladies' man I take him to be. God bless us what a fellow at scraping and bowing and dodging he is, especially when the whole rabble of Auld Reekie is at his heels! Such hurrahs, such banners sending forth their voices towards the empty air – such speeches, such toasts, such answers. But alas, alas! The devil of a drop of drink at the O'Connell's dinner, not a shillaly admitted, nay although it poured rain not an umbrella was admitted to enter the vaults where the alligator alias agitator partook of the sumptuous repast. Now mind me, for I was not there – not I. Who would dine with an Irish beggar, I should like to ask of you? A man who after draining his constituents of something like £14,000 per annum sings fol-de-rols to them and sends them to our shore to be thereafter hung and d—d! Such a farce you never saw, and I hope I never will.

While at dinner on 26 September, Audubon received the prints of Number 54 of *Birds*, and pronounced them 'quite beautiful'. 'You have exceeded anything previously done,' he told Havell, 'and you may now challenge the world of ornithological engravers without any fear!' Once again he urged him to press ahead, as he had wind of some sinister development: 'I know something is coming forth from another quarter, with no good feelings towards myself or yourself.'

By the middle of October, with Volume Three of the *Biography* completed, his thoughts were again turning to America and a final research trip; but he had also developed a sudden, intense interest in anatomy, and he sent Bachman detailed instructions for pickling any

PLATE CXI.

Pileated Woodpecker.

PICUS PILEATUS, *Linn.*

Adult Male, 1. Adult Female, 2. Young Male, 3, 4.

birds he shot in whisky or rum. Precise anatomical description – he seems to have decided – would enable him to crack the problem of accurately classifying birds in families, and would be his secret weapon in the final volumes of the *Biography*: by producing information unknown to other specialists, he would finally blow the opposition out of the water. 'The internal structure of our birds is extremely instructive,' he told Bachman. 'Nothing has been done in it, and whatever you and I do must be kept a secret from all the world until published!'

Calling on the priest for assistance as he would 'on a brother', he asked not only that Bachman himself should procure specimens, but that he should prevail on others – for instance 'the captain who runs our Revenue cutters to Key West' – to do the same. His anxiety was almost comical: 'Delay not one single opportunity, I beg of you, and see that the jars (earthen) or kegs or barrels are good and sound and so closed when filled as not to leak at all.'

Havell, meanwhile, was also receiving peculiar instructions. At the beginning of November Audubon told him to go to a poulterer in Davies Street, in the West End of London, and buy a Great Horned Owl, which was to be put in a box and shipped up to Leith, the port east of Edinburgh, as soon as possible. 'See that one wing at least is complete.'

Volume Three of the *Ornithological Biography* was published by Adam and Charles Black on 1 December 1835 . At 639 pages, not counting the introduction, it was even bulkier than its predecessors, and followed the same pattern of bird-descriptions and Episodes interspersed. Audubon was immensely relieved to have it off his hands, for while writing it he had been nagged by the thought that every statement he made would be pored over by critics. He admitted to Bachman that the Episodes were 'very so-so indeed', but boasted that 'the information connected with the birds is 'pretty fair', and revealed that he had included a surprise:

> I have at last given to the world my long kept secret on the formation of the toes and claws of our maritime birds, by which species may be at once distinguished and separated.

This information came in the form of a short, four-page section at the

52 facing page

PILEATED
WOODPECKER
Dryocopus pileatus

A female (top), a male and two juveniles search a dead tree for insects.

end of the text, illustrated — a striking departure, this — by nine wood-cuts of toes and claws. 'By this means,' Audubon reckoned, 'the young of *Ardea rufescens* (Peale's Egret) is clearly proved to be the "Reddish Egret" of Buffon, Latham, Brison and a dozen other authors. Thus again can the Fresh Water Marsh Hen be known from the Salt Water Marsh Hen, *Grus canadensis* [to be the same as] the young of *Grus americana, Larus argentatoides* to be the same as L. argentatus etc. etc. etc.'

At the end of Volume Two Audubon had published the names of sub-scribers to *The Birds of America* obtained since the publication of Volume One. That list contained more than sixty entries, mainly American, but a few English. A similar list at the end of Volume Three was only six names long — and yet the author did not seem worried. On the contrary, when he wrote to Havell on 12 December, predicting his imminent return to London, he told him: 'We are all in excellent plight and have been frol-icking these past few days at a most furious rate.'

The family travelled south in two parties, the boys going by steamer from Leith, the parents by coach via Newcastle and Liverpool. In London they lodged with Lucy's sister, before renting a house of their own at No. 4 Wimpole Street. On 22 January 1836 Audubon became tremen-dously excited when Havell told him that, barring accidents, the 'enor-mous work' would be completed in twenty-two months. The idea sent him into a frenzy of speculation, and made him redouble his efforts to obtain 'all imaginable assistance from all and every one' with whom he was acquainted. Every possible discovery had to be made within the next twenty-two months; once that time was up, it would be too late: 'all exer-tions will be useless'.

Bachman, of course, was foremost on his list of potential helpers, and received a volley of orders:

> Take to your gun at all your leisure hours, go to the woods and go to the shores, or if you cannot go at all, send some worthy one on whom you can and I also can depend. Note down every insignificant incident brought forth to your eye ... Measure the depths, the diametrical width, of every nest you meet with this coming spring ... Whatever yunglings [sic] you

meet with, do describe, or put them in plain whisky or common rum . . .

Write a circular to each of our friends, request of them to go 'a-shoot-ing' twice or thrice. Nay if you please put a general advertisement in the newspapers of Charleston . . . and request every man to send you specimens in. Have barrels or jars or gallipots prepared of all sorts and sizes, and in these place the specimens and then have them covered to the brim.

So he went on, direly frustrated that he himself could not be in the Charleston woods during the breeding season. He had hoped to sail again for America on 1 April, but after a fire in a New York warehouse had destroyed his books, bedding, drawing implements and guns, he felt obliged to postpone his departure until new guns could be made. Mean-while, he sent Victor and John off on a tour of the Continent, which he hoped would 'improve both of them pretty considerably'. From Mar-seilles they travelled to Florence, Rome and Sicily, reporting favourably on the grandeur of the landscapes through which they passed.

Tedious as the delay was to Audubon, it must have been even more irksome to John, who had corresponded continuously with Maria Bach-man for the past two years, and was longing to see her again. Once he was back in England, he and his father left Lucy and Victor to hold the reins of the business, and took passage on the *Gladiator*, which sailed from Liverpool for New York on 1 August. With them went an amazing var-iety of effects, including three pointer dogs (one sent by the Earl of Derby as a present to Bachman), two tail-less cats and 265 birds, all but fifteen of which died during the thirty-three-day voyage.

PLATE CCXLII.

Drawn from Nature by J. J. Audubon. F.R.S. F.L.S.

Engraved, Printed, & Coloured by R. Havell, London, 1835.

Snowy Heron, or White Egret.
ARDEA CANDIDISSIMA, Gm.
Male adult Spring plumage.
Rice Plantation — South Carolina.

CHAPTER FOURTEEN
DEEP SOUTH

THE *Gladiator* REACHED New York after dark on the evening of 7 September 1836. Rockets were fired to attract a pilot, and when one came alongside, and an American sailor leaped on board, Audubon 'cried like a child', falling on his knees to thank God for delivering him and Victor safe to shore.

He did not immediately head for Charleston – partly because cholera was raging there, but mainly because he heard that the Academy of Natural Sciences in Philadelphia had acquired a collection of rare birds from the Rocky Mountains and the West Coast – the very area on which he had set his own sights several times before. In the past his relations with the Academy had been by no means friendly, and he was not sure how he would be received; but in the event he 'had a great treat in looking over and handling the rare collection', made by the naturalists Thomas Nuttall and Dr John Kirk Townsend. 'It contains about forty new species of birds,' he reported, 'and its value cannot be described.' Naturally he wanted to buy the whole lot, but because the expedition to the west had been sponsored by the Academy, the collection was not for sale – not even when Edward Harris offered to buy it outright for $500.

Disappointed for the time being, Audubon set off to seek subscribers in Boston. Since his last visit, on his way back from Labrador, transport arrangements had been revolutionised. Now, for a fare of seven dollars, which included supper and breakfast, he took the steamer *Massachusetts* up to Providence, and from there went on by train 'at the rate of fifteen miles per hour'.

53 facing page

SNOWY HERON
OR WHITE
EGRET
Ardea candidissima
now Snowy
Egret *Egretta thula*

In the background marsh and water stretch away to a Carolina rice plantation.

[237]

From Thomas Brewer, a keen young ornithologist, he received seven eggs of species which he lacked; but a still more valuable contact was Thomas Nuttall, who had just returned from California. A Yorkshireman of exactly Audubon's age, Nuttall had been apprenticed as a printer in England, but had emigrated to the United States at the age of twenty-one, and had made a name for himself as a botanical explorer. His *Manual of the Ornithology of the United States and Canada* had been published in 1833 and 1834, and for twelve years he had been Professor of Natural History at Harvard University, as well as curator of the Botanical Gardens there. Now he generously promised Audubon duplicates of all the birds he had brought back from the far west.

Brisk recruiting in Boston and New York produced a clutch of new subscribers — eighteen in a single week in New York City; but Audubon was burning to return to the collection at the Academy in Philadelphia, which he reached in the middle of October. Again, there were difficulties: Townsend was still on the Columbia River, in the far west, and Nuttall had not returned from Boston. Audubon reported testily:

> Loud murmurs were uttered by the *soi-disant* friends of science, who objected to my seeing, much less portraying and describing, those valuable relics of birds, many of which had not yet been introduced into our fauna.

After some negotiation it was agreed that he might buy duplicates, provided the specific names which he and Nuttall agreed on were published in Townsend's name. He therefore purchased ninety-odd skins, and told Brewer in a letter that, together with other recent acquisitions, these would swell the number of birds in his great work to 475. The deal was an amazing stroke of luck — a godsend — for it put into his hands a rich haul of material that he never would have managed to collect in the field, and enabled him to make the final volume of his *Birds* that much more comprehensive. No wonder he wrote exultantly to Bachman:

> Now good friend, open your eyes! Aye, open them tight! Nay, place specks on your proboscis if you choose. Read aloud! Quite aloud! I have purchased ninety-three bird skins! Yes, ninety-three bird skins! Well, what are they? Why, nought less than ninety-three bird skins sent from the Rocky

Mountains and the Columbia River by Nuttall and Townsend! Cheap as dirt, too — only 184 dollars for the whole of these, and hang me if you do not echo my saying so when you see them!! Such beauties! Such rarities! Such novelties! Ah my worthy friend, how we will laugh and talk over them!

When he came to describe the acquisition in the introduction to Volume Four of the *Biography*, he claimed that the idea of acknowledging Dr Townsend as the discoverer of the birds was 'perfectly congenial' to his feelings, and disingenuously pretended that he had 'seldom cared much about priority in the naming of species'. But he also let fly a rocket at the officials who had obstructed him:

> Let me assure you, Reader, that seldom, if ever in my life, have I felt more disgusted with the conduct of any opponents of mine than I was with the unfriendly boasters of their zeal for the advancement of ornithological science, who at that time existed in the fair city of Philadephia.

Long gone were the days when he had insisted on drawing only freshly killed specimens, set up on his special frame while the colours were at their brightest. Now the pressure of competition, and the fact that he was running out of time, forced him to use bought skins as his models, and to scrounge about for new species, rather than hunt them himself. The result was that his paintings of the western birds were less successful than many of his earlier pictures: lacking first-hand information about the habits and habitats of the species new to him, he could not achieve quite the same authenticity.

He was still hell-bent on a final trip to Florida, even though the Seminole Indians were on the rampage there, plundering and burning plantations while government forces tried to suppress them. Audubon was advised that the west coast of the peninsula should be safe enough, and he proposed to go on from there to Mexico. First, though, he visited Washington, where his friend Colonel John Abert, head of the Topographical Bureau, secured him support at the highest level by taking him to meet the president, Andrew Jackson. The president, who himself had fought the Seminoles and been governor of Florida, was pessimistic about Audubon's chances, but said he would do all in his power to help,

and invited the naturalist to an informal dinner at the White House, at which the *pièce de résistance* was a fine young turkey shot within twenty miles of the capital.

Declining the offer of a passage down the coast to Charleston on the 55-ton Government gun-boat *Campbell*, because he tended to be sea-sick, Audubon travelled southwards for six days on 'the most extraordinary railroads in the world', and spent the winter with the Bachmans. As he waited week after week for the *Campbell* to arrive and pick them up, he drew all the new birds he had got in the Nuttall-Townsend collection. In the end, tired of hanging around, he and John and Edward Harris set off on their own for New Orleans, first by coach, then down the Alabama River to Mobile. After some preliminary bird-hunting forays in that area, they went on to New Orleans, where the *Campbell* picked them up on 29 March 1837. In an ebullient letter to Bachman, Audubon described how they had been hunting alligators, and could not resist a reference to their mutual *bête noire*:

> We took Harris on an alligator hunt on a fine bayou. We killed about twenty of these beautiful creatures and brought only seven on board. Harris killed several. He had never seen any before. He likes their flesh, too, but not so Johnny. Excepting the latter, our mess made a grand dinner out of the tail end of one, and, after all, alligator's flesh is far from being bad. God preserve us from ever 'riding' a live one.

Two days later they were joined by the 12-ton Revenue schooner *Crusader*, whose black paintwork made her look like a pirate vessel, and for the next three weeks they explored the coastline from the Mississippi to the Bay of Galveston. Vexed though he was by the lack of edible oysters, and by the swarms of insects, Audubon rejoiced at being among birds that

N°. 30.

55

NIGHT HAWK
*Caprimulgus
virginiana*
now Common
Nighthawk
Chordeiles minor

The birds are
shown pursuing
insects in and
around a white
oak.

56 overleaf

ROSEATE
SPOONBILL
Platalea ajaja
now *Ajaia ajaja*

In his original
painting
Audubon left
the background
nearly blank, and
the water and
wooded islands
were filled in by
Havell.

worked the shore and the sugar plantations inland. Snipe, Gallinules,
Curlews, Herons abounded; Mocking Birds sang in the evenings, and
Nightjars fluttered out as dusk came down. The hunters skinned the
birds they shot and pickled the bodies in rum. On 18 April he reported
cheerfully to MacGillivray:

> It is now four weeks since a razor came in contact with my chin. All my
> companions are equally hircine; or, if you please, hirsute. As to our cloth-
> ing, were you to see us at this moment, you would be ready to exclaim,

'What vagabonds these fellows are!' Coats and trousers plastered with mire,
shirts no longer white, guns exhibiting the appearance of being in constant
use, and all sorts of accoutrements that pertain to determined hunters complete our tout ensemble.

The weather was cooler than they had expected, but such was the exer-
tion of struggling across mud flats that Audubon shed 12 pounds. On 24
April they reached Galveston, where the fort returned the *Campbell's* 26-
gun salute, and where they were soon met by the secretary of the Navy
from the brand-new Republic of Texas, which had just declared its independence. After three weeks exploring Galveston Island and its environs,
they set off through torrential rain for the embryonic capital, Houston,
some 75 miles to the north-west, at the invitation of the president, Sam
Houston, who had wrested the country from the Mexicans.

Audubon's description of the place made it sound like the set of some
third-rate amateur stage production. The president's home was a small
log-house of only two rooms, one of which was awash with mud. The
Capitol, or parliament building, had as yet no roof, and the floors,
benches and tables had been soaked by the recent downpours. The settlement was crowded with hundreds of Indians, 'only a few of whom were
sober': the majority were 'hallooing and stumbling about in the mud in
every direction', and their 'howlings and gesticulations were by no means
pleasing'. The first time the visitors set eyes on the President, he came
walking out of one of the grog-shops, 'where he had been to prevent the
sale of ardent spirits' – a tall, bulky figure, sporting a large, grey, coarse
hat; but by the time he greeted them in his primitive house, he was wearing a fancy velvet coat and trousers trimmed with broad gold lace.

> He received us kindly … and offered us every facility within his power …
> We were severally introduced by him to the different members of his cabi-
> net and staff, and at once asked to drink grog with him, which we did, wish-
> ing success to his new republic. Our talk was short, but the impression which
> was made on my mind at the time by himself, his officers and his place of
> abode, can never be forgotten.

The expedition was over; but it took Audubon more than three weeks to return via New Orleans to Charleston. Even though the arduous journey had yielded no new species of bird, he was pleased with the results: he had collected numerous eggs and gathered a rich store of knowledge, especially about migration and breeding habits. He felt, at any rate, that he now had enough to complete his *magnum opus*, and once more he set his sights on England.

For him the great event of June 1837 at Charleston was his son John's marriage to Maria Bachman, on whom Audubon doted. Delighted as he was to have her as his daughter-in-law, he missed no opportunity of praising her looks and character. Towards the end of June the newly augmented family started north, travelling by steamer to Norfolk and subsequently on to Washington, where Audubon thanked the various government officials who had been of assistance to him, and presented a letter to the new president, Martin van Buren, who had been elected in his absence.

57

JOHN WOODHOUSE AUDUBON

A likeness of the artist's second son, painted in watercolour on ivory, *c.*1845.

From Philadelphia the young couple went on for two weeks' honeymoon at Niagara Falls, while Audubon saw to his affairs in New York. The city, like most of the country, was in the grip of a deep financial depression: as he told Havell, 'the times here are hard past reckoning'. There was no money about, and therefore no subscribers, but he was able to buy £1100 worth of gold in the form of half-eagles and sovereigns at an advantageous rate, and so equipped himself with a large enough sum (he hoped) to finish the task in England. Even after this large withdrawal, he managed to leave $8000 in the care of his brother-in-law Nicholas Berthoud.

On 17 July the family sailed for Liverpool in the packet *England*, along with only twenty other passengers. The captain — Benjamin Waite, a friend from an earlier voyage — allocated John and Maria a spacious cabin of their own; Audubon had a state room amidships, and was confident they would all be 'as comfortable as can be wished while thus caged on the waves', especially as the ship carried ice for the whole voyage, a fine bath house and a 'very decent library'. Waite thought that Audubon looked rather thin when he arrived on the dock, but reckoned that 'with turtle soups, good wines and agreeable company' he would render him fit to meet his wife and friends in England.

Chapter Fifteen
FINAL PUSH

On this, Audubon's final voyage to England, the passage proved a fast one: passengers and crew sighted Ireland only fifteen days after leaving New York, and three days later, on 4 August 1837, the ship docked at Liverpool. As soon as their baggage had been cleared by customs, the artist's party set off for London, speeding to Birmingham by train (ninety-six miles in four and a half hours), and then, after an overnight stop, proceeding by coach to London. 'At eight of the evening I was in the arms of my Lucy,' Audubon told Bachman:

> Dear Old Friend, she was not very well. Our arrival produced a great revolution of her nervous system, but after a while all was gaiety and happiness at our house in Wimpole Street . . . Our dearest Maria, with a mind and eyes filled with wonders, was not at all fatigued, and ever since then she has been enjoying the sights of this as it were new world to her.

In Audubon's absence, Victor and Havell had made good progress. Number 76 of the *Birds* was out, and the engraver promised that the entire work would be finished by 1 January 1838. This date soon proved optimistic, but even though several subscribers were still defaulting on their payments, the promising state of his affairs put Audubon into high good humour. Telling Bachman that 'the arrival of JJA, his son and his daughter has been proclaimed throughout these realms etc. etc. etc.', he reported:

> London is just as I left it, a vast artificial area, as well covered with humbug as are our pine lands and old fields with broom grass. Swainson is publishing his incomprehensible works. Gould has just finished his *Birds of Europe*,

and will now go on with those of Australia. [William] Yarrell is publishing the *British Birds* quarto size, and about one thousand other niny tiny works are in progress to assist in the mass confusion already scattered over the world.

MacGillivray, also, had burst into print again with the first volume of his *History of British Birds*, and Audubon was delighted to find that some carping reviewer had announced: 'The writing appears to us an affected attempt to imitate the styles of Isaac Walton and of Audubon, which, being extremely peculiar, can only be relished in the originals.'

Yet another ornithologist produced a major work that year: John Gould published Volume 1 of *Birds of Europe*, with an introduction whose generosity should have made Audubon smart. 'By far the greater number of the plates of this work ... have been drawn and lithographed by Mrs Gould from sketches and designs by myself taken always from nature,' he wrote. 'The remainder of the drawings have been made by Mr Lear, whose abilities as an artist are so generally acknowledged that any

comments of my own are un-necessary.' Gifted though Lear was, his work at that stage did not bear comparison with Audubon's. The two Golden Eagles which he painted for Gould in 1833 are woodenly unrealistic when set beside the sharply climbing predator in *The Birds of America*.

Audubon's high spirits per-sisted for weeks, even though he was exceedingly busy, work-ing 'like a Trojan' towards his self-imposed deadline. Already, while still in New York, he had sent Bachman a list of almost

PLATE CCCCX

1. Profile view of Bill at its greatest extension
2. Superior front view of upper Mandible
3. Interior front view of upper Mandible
4. Inferior front view of lower Mandible

American Flamingo
PHOENICOPTERUS RUBER, *Linn.*
Old Male

6. Profile view of Tongue
7. Superior front view of Tongue
8. Interior front view of Tongue
9. Perpendicular front view of the feet fully expanded

50 species headed 'Wanted! Wanted!! Wanted!!!' Another target for requests was young Thomas Brewer in Boston — 'I hope you will have a pair of Pied Ducks (*Fuligula labradora*) for me.' Edward Harris, also, was under bombardment: 'Stir, work hard, be prompt in everything. My work must soon be finished, and unless everything is received here by the month of May next, why, I shall have to abandon to others what I myself might have accomplished.'

As the weeks went by, Audubon kept raising further questions. Did flamingos sit on their nests with their legs dangling down outside, or what? Could Bachman procure a Wood Ibis in rum, and a pair of Freshwater Marsh Hens? Was the cottony substance attached to the breast and rump of Herons capable of becoming luminous during dark nights, to help them find prey?

One only moderately welcome visitor to Wimpole Street was Charles Bonaparte, who was continuing the work of Alexander Wilson by publishing the *Birds of Mexico*. Audubon described him as 'a most amiable good man', and 'a mild, pleasant-speaking personage, not at all of the Prince about him while with us at least, but so very fond of praise that I doubt of his sincerity.' He wanted to believe that Bonaparte was a true friend; yet he became increasingly irritated when the Frenchman came sponging off his family, calling in at their house to shave and dress, seeking help in his search for private lodgings, and generally soaking up information about birds. 'Methinks he is over anxious to pump me,' Audubon wrote — and in any case, now that *The Birds of America* was almost complete, what was the use of Bonaparte's latest venture?

> I cannot well imagine why he should continue Wilson's *Ornithology* after my work is finished, unless it is merely to arrange our fauna in squares, circles or triangles, in the manner of Swainson and all the other crazed naturalists of the closet.

When the prince departed for France, Audubon reported: 'Bonaparte is gone at last, and I am much relieved, for the days are very short and I have a great deal to do.' His worst suspicions were confirmed in January 1838, when the Frenchman published his *A Geographical and Comparative*

List of the Birds of Europe and North America, which included twenty species more than he himself had managed to assemble:

> Charles Bonaparte has treated me most shockingly. He has published the whole of our secrets, which I foolishly communicated to him after his giving me his word of honour that he would not do so, and now I have cut him, and he never will have from me the remaining unpublished Numbers of my work.

Meanwhile, other helpers continued to contribute the missing pieces of his colossal jigsaw puzzle; by the last days of October 1837 Audubon reckoned that he had 459 'positively good' species, and hoped that his ultimate total would be 470. By Christmas 400 plates had been published, and the end of the marathon was in sight. So many candidates were demanding inclusion in the final volume of prints that he abandoned his plan, which he had nursed for years, of publishing paintings of eggs — and towards the close he was obliged to crowd the birds themselves together, as many as six species to each page, purely to fit them in.

For much of the winter Lucy was ill, or at any rate under the weather, confined to her room if not to her bed. For the first half of 1838 Audubon remained in London, hard at work on his remaining drawings, and by the middle of April he had completed a hundred new ones. For English people, the great event of the summer was the coronation of the young Queen Victoria, which took place on 28 June; and the artist's family had double cause to celebrate, for on 20 June Havell took a print from the final plate of *Birds* — No. 435, which portrayed two stocky little American Dippers.

Only one letter survives to indicate the relief Audubon felt when his

60

AMERICAN
DIPPER
Cinclus mexicanus

These two chunky little water birds formed the final plate, No. 435, in *The Birds of America.*

mighty work came to an end. 'An immense weight from my shoulders,' he told his friend Dr Samuel Norton in Philadelphia, 'and a great relief to my ever fidgety anxious mind respecting the immense undertaking.'

For twelve years it had occupied his every waking moment; for twelve years, in the face of problems that would have crushed lesser men, he had toiled heroically to reach his goal. Harassed by unscrupulous rivals, deserted by many subscribers, stressed by long separations from his loved ones, he had shown astonishing stamina in battling through. As he himself frequently remarked, the struggle had made him old: his energy and powers of concentration — once superhuman — had diminished; his hair had turned grey, and many of his teeth had fallen out, giving his mouth a collapsed appearance; yet he had created an immortal work of art.

The final stages of its production were by no means easy. As Havell battled to fulfil orders for the last few Numbers of *Birds*, slovenly workmen in his print-shop packed and despatched so carelessly that a dozen Numbers were returned by irate subscribers, who found that instead of five different prints, they had received several copies of the same one. The infuriated Earl of Kinnoul had cancelled his subscription after finding pieces of beef wedged between the prints. Such setbacks naturally drew savage condemnation from Audubon, who told Havell that 'the idle rascals who did the like of this deserve the severest punishment'.

The root cause of the trouble was surely that Havell no longer had his mind entirely on the job. Influenced by his long connection with Audubon, and encouraged by him to make a move, he had decided to close down his business in London and emigrate to America, taking his family with him. He was then forty-five, and thought that he would find better opportunities to exercise his skills in the United States. But the faults were not entirely his. Audubon, short of funds in England, prevaricated over settling final accounts, and asked Havell if he would mind waiting for payment until he reached America.

The engraver's decision to leave London meant that he had to dispose of all his own stock, as well as that belonging to Audubon — which included copper plates engraved for *The Birds of America*, numerous prints

61

HAIRY
WOODPECKER
Picoides villosus

THREE-TOED
WOODPECKER
Picoides tridactylus

Audubon thought he had included five species in this print, but in fact there are only two: the Three-toed Woodpeckers are the second pair from the top, and the rest are Hairy Woodpeckers.

(some coloured, some black-and-white), and copies of the *Biographies*. Audubon was inevitably anxious about the future of his effects, and he kept sending Havell instructions, among them one to insure the plates for £5000 and forward them either to Victor or to Nicholas Berthoud in New York.

His own urgent need, now, was to complete the *Ornithological Biography*. Once again he depended on the help of his 'good friend' MacGillivray, so at the end of June he went up to Edinburgh, and was there on coronation day — only to find the celebrations 'poor beyond description'. Although there was scarcely anything to be seen (he told John), 'the whole population was on foot the entire day, and nearly the whole night, gazing at each other like lost sheep.' He and MacGillivray went to see the fireworks at the castle, but soon returned disgusted.

On 13 July 1838, Maria gave birth to a daughter, another Lucy, in Wimpole Street, and on 8 August the family moved to Edinburgh, settling comfortably at No. 6 Alva Street. By then Audubon had resumed work with his good-natured Scottish partner. At once, he reported, he and MacGillivray were 'up to the elbows among the birds which I had brought in spirits with me from America, I acting as secretary, he as prime minister.' He himself rose at 4 am or earlier, MacGillivray not until 10 am; but whereas Audubon went to bed at 11 pm, the Scotsman stayed up until 2 am. At first he was reluctant to dissect the pickled intestines — not out of squeamishness, but because Audubon's final tomes were going to appear before his own second volume, and he feared his own information might appear second-hand. Yet when he learnt that Audubon had already credited him with the 'anatomical structure', 'he was much pleased and began on the instant'.

Work progressed so well that at the start of September the whole party, including the infant Lucy, broke off for a brief holiday in the Highlands, with MacGillivray acting as guide and recommending hostelries at which they should stay. Deposited by steamer at Stirling, they walked round the ramparts of the castle, perched on its vertically sided rock, before going on to Doune and Callander, where they spent the night. Next day they 'marched in a body to the Falls of Bracklin, guided by a rosy-cheeked Highland lassie', and Audubon rejoiced in the wild scenery — the hills purple with heather in bloom, a cataract plunging into a ravine, lichen-encrusted rocks, blood-red berries of mountain ash hanging in clusters, and of course the birds — Magpies, Tits and Dippers. In that primitive setting he felt he was among the 'Celts of the olden times ... enjoying the pleasure of living in the wilds, and then bethought me of the many similar spots yet belonging to our own sons of the forest.'

On they pressed, sometimes on ponies, sometimes on foot, Audubon in such good fettle that he went rolling and frolicking in the heather. He was disappointed by the Trossachs and the scrubby trees that grew on them, but enchanted by Loch Katrine, with its jutting headlands that receded, one beyond the other, into hazy distance. After a night at the inn on Loch Arklet, they walked over the pass and came down to Loch Lomond, where they found a few small stone cabins on the rocky shore, 'some fat bairns, abundance of ale and a sufficiency of capital whisky'. As they waited for a steamer, they ate, drank and talked about Rob Roy — and had time to scramble up to a triangular opening giving access to a cave in a great cairn of fallen rocks, in which the outlaw was said to have taken refuge.

Refreshed by the trip, Audubon went back to his writing. His initial aim had been to produce one final volume, but his manuscript had grown to such proportions that he realised he must divide it in two. 'The book has now increased to 512 pages,' he told Bachman on 29 September. 'Seven sheets more will finish the first part of the Fourth Volume, for I now find that one volume of 1,200 pages would not do.'

Volume Four was finished in October 1838 and published in November, sections having been sent to the printer as they were completed. Another huge tome, over 600 pages long, it consisted of separate essays, one for each bird, enhanced (if that is the word) by thirty-nine anatomical drawings, mainly of digestive organs. In his Introduction the author explained that he had been obliged to exclude the Episodes which had graced earlier volumes 'in order to make room for anatomical notices, of more interest to the scientific reader.' It is true that many of the essays were lightened by passages describing the author's own experiences in the field, but for anyone except a dedicated student or specialist, the illustrations of stomachs, oviducts and cloacae were hardly edifying, and much of the text was intolerably technical — as in its description of the Black Skimmer:

> The posterior aperture of the nares is 1⁵/₁₂ inch long, with a transverse line of papillae at the middle on each side, and another behind. The tongue is sagittiform, 6½ twelfths long, with two conical papillae at the base, soft, fleshy, flat above, horny beneath. Aperture of the glottis 4½ twelfths long ...

Audubon sought to justify this overpoweringly scientific approach by claiming that mere observation of birds was becoming out of date. The time was fast approaching, he said, when students would 'go forth not only to observe the habits and haunts of animals, but to procure speci-mens of them to be carefully dissected.'

Volume Five came out in May 1839. Even without any Episodes, the text outran all its predecessors, extending to nearly 700 pages; the second half consisted of a huge appendix, 'comprising additional observations on the habits, geographical distribution and anatomical structure of the birds described in this work, together with corrections of errors relative to the species.'

The opening pages of the Introduction were deceptively lyrical. In prose tinged with purple the author recalled the wild dreams that at var-ious times had assailed him — of sickness and poverty, of attacks by Red Indians, snakes, vultures and sharks. He then portrayed himself as a weary traveller reaching home after mighty wanderings:

> In health and in sickness, in adversity and prosperity, in summer and winter, amidst the cheers of friends and the scowls of foes, I have depicted the Birds of America and studied their habits as they roamed at large in their peculiar haunts ...
>
> Now, Reader, you may well imagine how happy I am at this moment, when, like the traveller alluded to, I find my journeys all finished, my

anxieties vanished, my mission accomplished ... I have pleasure in saying that my enemies have been few, and my friends numerous. May the God who granted me life, industry and perseverance to accomplish my task, forgive the former and for ever bless the latter!

There followed an agreeable but essentially irrelevant account of the author's Highland tour, and his usual thanks to people who had helped him in his long quest. Lulled by this soft opening, readers may well have hoped for easy entertainment — and indeed at the beginning of the first bird section, on the Red-and-White Winged Troopial (*Icterus tricolor*), Audubon cleverly slipped in an imagined description of 'those enthusiastic naturalists, my friends Nuttall and Townsend', traversing the ridges of the Rocky Mountains in 'grand and impressive scenery'. By this sleight of the pen he was able to create the impression that he himself had once again been tramping the wilderness, and at the same time gave prominence to two of his most useful contributors.

Yet after this brief glimpse of the great outdoors, the text became leaden, as the author once again crammed in a mass of unreadable anatomical detail in the hope that it would leave competitors floundering. After earlier friction, he was now very generous in distributing praise and thanks: he repeatedly cracked up Nuttall and Townsend, and dedicated one of the new birds found by them on the banks of the Columbia River — a pretty little Warbler — 'to my excellent friend William MacGillivray, Esq.,' naming it *Sylvia macgillivrayi*.

The authors' final task was to compile *A Synopsis of the Birds of America*, yet another volume, published almost immediately: a methodical catalogue of the 491 species described in the pictures and text.

The fifth volume of the *Ornithological Biography* concluded with a list of subscribers for *The Birds of America*, of whom there were only eighty-two in America and seventy-nine in Europe — 161 in all, a paltry total, far short of that for which the artist had hoped. One name is conspicuously absent from the European list: Rathbone. But its absence is easily explained: the family had no need to buy a copy, because Audubon gave them one.

CHAPTER SIXTEEN
PASTURES NEW

EVEN THOUGH his greatest work was finished, Audubon's creative life was by no means over. Late in the summer of 1839 he settled his affairs in Edinburgh and London, and crossed the Atlantic for the twelfth and final time.

Back in New York, he bought a house at 84 White Street, in the uptown district of the city, which served as both home and office, and quickly launched into two new projects which he had long been planning: the miniature or octavo edition of *Birds*, and a major survey of the *Quadrupeds of North America*. For both he engaged the services of a lithographer, J.T. Bowen of Philadelphia, and for the new version of *Birds*, John set to work reducing the huge folio prints with his camera lucida.

The first Number of the octavo *Birds* came out in December the same year, and proved an immediate success. Three hundred copies were printed, but these ran out almost at once; in January 1840 another 300 were needed, and a year later 1475 copies had been produced. For once Audubon was in funds. Yet modest commercial success was marred by domestic difficulties and disasters.

In the autumn of 1839 John's wife Maria gave birth to a second daughter, Harriet – a sister for little Lucy – but then fell ill with tuberculosis, and went home to Charleston, hoping to recover in the warmth of the south. When Audubon went to see her, she was obviously dying, and he was so distressed by her decline that he sought solace in whisky, thereby grievously offending her father, who hated intemperance above all things. Maria died on 23 September 1840, aged only twenty-three.

62 facing page

ARCTIC TERN
Sterna arctica now
Sterna paradisaea

Drawn during
Audubon's voyage
to Labrador in
June 1833.

[259]

Victor, meanwhile, had fallen in love with and subsequently married Eliza, the Bachmans' second daughter, known in the family as 'Rosy'; but she had been in poor health even before the wedding, and she too went down with tuberculosis. A winter in the tropical climate of Cuba could not save her, and she died in New York on 25 May 1841, a year younger than her sister had been.[1] Perhaps shared grief helped Audubon and Bachman bury their brief disagreements: soon they were once again as close as ever.

Audubon's spirits were lifted by new friendships, principally one with a young naturalist called Spencer Fullerton Baird, then only eighteen, who wrote from Carlisle, Pennsylvania, to say he thought he had discovered a new species of flycatcher. Audubon replied promptly, and the correspondence which followed established a life-long bond.[2] At the

63

THE HUDSON
RIVER

Oil painting on canvas (*c.* 1840–5) by Victor Audubon of the area where his father bought 25 acres of land in 1841. Audubon is sitting on a rock in the foreground.

1. Both sons found new wives. On 2 October 1841 John married Caroline Hall, with whom he had seven further children. Victor married (2 March 1843) an Englishwoman, Georgiana Richards Mallory, with whom he had five girls and one boy.
2. Baird (1823–87) became one of America's most distinguished naturalists, a pillar of the Smithsonian Institution in Washington and author of numerous books on zoology and archaeology.

outset he lost no time in calling for help with specimens: 'Please to collect all the shrews, mice (field and wood), rats, bats, squirrels etc and put them in a jar in common rum, not whiskey, brandy or alcohol. All of the latter spirits are sure to injure the subjects.' Later, Victor weighed in

64

MINNIE'S LAND

The house built by Audubon above the Hudson River. He embellished the surroundings with fruit trees and a menagerie of birds and animals.

with a more esoteric request: 'Should you procure a black fox, be sure to forward him uncut to our office.' Another stimulating contact was William Yarrell, the English naturalist and shooting man, who was then bringing out his three-volume *A History of British Birds*.

Working feverishly at his *Quadrupeds*, drawing for up to fourteen hours a day, soliciting skins and pickled corpses from far and wide, the artist became disenchanted with New York. He had always hated urban surroundings, and in 1841 he bought twenty-five acres of land on the Hudson River in Carmansville (later Washington Heights), which was then in open country north of the city. There, in a grove of chestnuts, oaks and evergreens, on a site commanding fine views of the river, he built a comfortable, flat-roofed wooden house, raised on pillars to keep it clear of floods, and with a high verandah. He decorated the walls of his studio with antlers and spread a panther's skin on the floor. He made the place over, legally, to Lucy, and called it Minnie's Land, using the Scottish version of her name. The family moved in during April 1842, and built up a menagerie of poultry, horses, cattle, deer, elk, bears, foxes and wolves.

The author Parke Godwin, who went to the house in the first summer of their occupation, left a vivid written glimpse of its owner, who was then fifty-seven:

A tall, thin man, with a high arched and serene forehead, and a bright penetrating grey eye; his white locks fell in clusters upon his shoulders, but were the only signs of age, for his form was erect, and his step as light as that of a deer. The expression of his face was sharp, but noble and commanding, and there was something ... partly derived from the aquiline nose and partly from the shutting of the mouth, which made you think of the imperial eagle.

The family enhanced their grounds by planting over 200 young trees, including pears, apples, quinces, apricots, nectarines and plums. They could fish with a seine net in the river whenever they liked – for the property included 300 yards of the bank – and that first summer they caught an eight-foot sturgeon weighing over 300 lbs.

Audubon's family thought him too old to strike out on any more long journeys; yet, like Tennyson's Ulysses, he could not rest from travel, and he had scarcely moved into his new home before he began planning a major excursion – the trip to the far west that had been in his mind for years. He was now in search of mammals, rather than birds, but the wilderness called him no less powerfully.

First, however, he went on what he called 'a tramp to the Canadas', canvassing subscriptions for *Quadrupeds* and the small *Birds*. In a month, starting on 12 September, he covered 1500 miles, visiting St Johns, Montreal and Quebec City. At the outset of the journey, as his steamer went down the Hudson, he passed Minnie's Land and saw his sons sailing on the river; he hailed them, and the sight moved him to tears.

Canada proved most fruitful. In Quebec he sold a double-elephant set of *Birds* to the Earl of Caledon (then a captain in the Coldstream Guards), along with a subscription to *Quadrupeds*. In Montreal he found takers for several copies of the small *Birds*, and 'several good names' for *Quadrupeds*. In Kingston he sold copies of the original *Birds* to both Houses of Parliament, and procured two more subscriptions to the mammal books. All the while he was collecting 'most valuable specimens of rare quadrupeds, and a fund of information that can never be met with unless on the ground of action.'

Home again, he did all he could to persuade Spencer Baird to join him on his western expedition. If he came, he told him, he would need a 'strong mosquito-bar' made of beaver-grass cloth. 'It would be a pleasure to my whole family to know that you are my companion,' he wrote on 2 January 1843, describing the expedition as 'this last and grand journey I plan to make as a naturalist'. When he sensed that 'that rascally article cash is the cause which prevents you from going along with me to the Yellowstone River', he offered to pay half the young man's costs, then all of them. For various reasons, mainly pressure from his mother, Baird declined to accept his overtures, and in the end the team consisted of Audubon himself, his old friend Edward Harris, the artist Isaac Sprague, a taxidermist (John G. Bell), and young Lewis Squires, who acted as helper and secretary.

Together with Victor, Audubon left New York on 11 March 1843 for Philadelphia, where they met the rest of the party. Victor then went home, and the others carried on by train, coach and steamer to Baltimore, Cumberland, Wheeling, Cincinnati and their jumping-off point, St Louis. Throughout the seven-month trip that followed, Audubon kept a journal: his entries were no longer shaped like letters to Lucy, but gave a lively, straightforward vivid account of the wilderness and its creatures, written on sheets of linen paper that he could roll up and carry in his pocket.

From St Louis they set out up the Missouri on 25 April aboard the *Omega*, a small, wood-burning steamer that carried 'a hundred and one [fur] trappers of all descriptions and nearly a dozen different nationalities' – French Canadians, Creoles and Indians – many hung-over and some still drunk. As they moved slowly up-river, often grounding and sometimes being forced backwards by the ferocity of the current, Audubon observed the animals with intense interest, shooting specimens that he needed; but he could draw only at night, by candlelight, when the ship tied up and her engine ceased vibrating, or when she stopped to refuel.

From the start grey squirrels and marmots were abundant. Later the party shot rabbits and pouched rats, or gophers, and numerous species of bird. But it was the big animals – the wolves, the antelope, the deer and above all the buffalo – that gripped Audubon's imagination. He began to see buffalo when they reached South Dakota, and at first he hunted the great beasts enthusiastically; but when the party started up the Yellowstone River, he became horrified by the numbers of skulls that dotted the prairies – evidence of the hunters' habit of killing the animals, cutting out their tongues, and leaving the bodies to rot – and by the flotillas of corpses that came bobbing downriver. He saw that if the slaughter continued on that scale, compounded by deaths from natural disasters, like floods, the mighty herds would dwindle and vanish:

> One can hardly conceive how it happens, notwithstanding these many deaths and the immense numbers that are murdered almost daily on these boundless wastes called prairies, besides the hosts that are drowned in the freshets, and the hundreds of young calves who die in the spring, [that] so many are yet to be found ... But this cannot last; even now there is a perceptible difference in the size of the herds, and before many years the buffalo, like the great auk, will have disappeared.

Often his journal captured the sounds and sights with memorable clarity. 'Wolves howling and bulls roaring, just like the continued roll of a hundred drums,' he wrote on 19 August; and then, two days later: 'Buffaloes all over the bars and prairies, and many swimming; the roaring can be heard for miles.'

Impressed as he was by the animals, he felt nothing but disgust for the Indians. Earlier in his life he had seen them as noble savages, but now he was revolted by the way they ate the rotting flesh of drowned buffaloes, and he described them as 'miserably poor, filthy beyond description', with their black faces and foul-smelling buffalo robes making them 'appear to be like so many devils'.

At Fort Union the members of the party built themselves a barge, which they named the *Union*, and on this they floated back down the Missouri to St Louis, arriving there in mid-October. On his way home to New York, aboard a canal boat from Pittsburgh to Philadelphia, Audubon made an indelible impression on another traveller who saw him, the young Charles Winterfield.

The artist was lying on a bench, wrapped in a great green coat with a fur collar, and when he sat up, 'A patriarchal beard fell white and wavy down his breast; a pair of hawk-like eyes glanced sharply out of a fuzzy shroud of cap and collar.' Still in his wilderness clothes, Audubon was 'hale and erect, with sixty winters upon his shoulders, and like one of his old eagles, feathered to the heel.' The accuracy of that description is strikingly borne out by the picture which John painted of his father

65

John Woodhouse Audubon's striking oil portrait of his father at fifty-eight, when he returned unshaven from his expedition to the Yellowstone River in 1843.

when the old man reached home: so taken were the family with his wild appearance that they persuaded him to sit for a portrait before he went to the barber.

That November Audubon wrote to Spencer Baird, saying how much he would have enjoyed the journey, and reporting:

> Abundance of large game was killed, and much more could have been procured had we wished for it; but when a fat buffalo weighing some 1500 lbs or upwards … is roasting by large, juicy pieces, who would have the heart to kill more for the sake of the tongue, or for that of the wolves?

The expedition yielded fifteen new birds, of which eleven species were included in the seventh and last volume of the royal octavo *Birds*, published in 1844. This added seventeen species to Audubon's previous total, and brought his protracted ornithological labours to an end. Thereafter he devoted what remained of his creative energy to the animal drawings, of which the large folios had been appearing as Numbers of five plates each since 1842. Two volumes of *The Viviparous Quadrupeds of North America*, containing altogether 150 coloured lithographic plates, but no text, were published in imperial folio (22 inches by 15 inches), in 1845 and 1846.

Bachman, meanwhile, was labouring on the letterpress on the same subject, and three volumes, with the same title, came out in royal octavo format (10 inches by 6 ¼ inches), the first in 1846, the second in 1851, and the third (after Audubon's death) in 1854.

By the summer of 1846 the artist's eyesight had begun to fail. Although he never went blind, his close vision deteriorated so badly that he could no longer paint accurately, and although he remained quite fit physically,

66

FAILING
PATRIARCH

Daguerrotype
of Audubon by
Mathew Brady
in about 1848,
showing how the
loss of his teeth
had made his
cheeks collapse
and the corners
of his mouth
turn down.

his mind gradually gave way as he lapsed inexorably into senility. When Bachman visited Minnie's Land in May 1848, he was sadly distressed by the state of his long-time colleague and confidant. 'Alas, my poor friend Audubon,' he wrote, 'the outlines of his countenance & his general robust form are there, but his mind is all in ruins … [He resembles] a crabbed restless uncontrollable child – worrying & bothering everyone. He thinks of nothing but eating – scarcely sits down two minutes at a time, hides hens' eggs – rings the bell every five minutes calling the people to dinner.'

For his last few years the family kept him secure in their bosom. Lucy – still in excellent health – Victor, John and eight grandchildren surrounded him with love. 'My dear old father is apparently comfortable, and enjoys his little notions,' Victor told Bachman early in 1849, 'but requires constant care and attendance.' It was just as well that he did not understand what John was doing in February when he went off to revive the family fortunes by joining the California gold rush – an expedition that ended in heavy financial loss. In December 1849 Lucy sent a pathetic note to Mrs Benjamin Phillips, the wife of her doctor in London:

Alas, I have only the material part of my old friend, all mind being gone. It is melancholy to me to see him, and I am obliged to reflect from whom these trials come, and believe he at least feels no pain, to be at all reconciled to such a sad change.

Audubon died on 27 January 1851, aged only sixty-five, and it is hard not to believe that his prodigious exertions, both physical and mental, had burnt him out, contributing to his early demise. As his granddaughter Maria wrote, 'He had never done anything by halves; he had played and worked, enjoyed and sorrowed, been depressed and elated, each and all with his highly strung nature at fever heat.' High-flown tributes were published on both sides of the Atlantic, but none was more lyrical than that which appeared in *The Gallery of Illustrious Americans*:

> From every deep grove the birds of America will sing his name. The wren will pipe it in our windows – the oriole carol it from the meadow grass – the turtledove roll it through the secret forests – the many-voiced mocking bird pour it along the evening air – and the bird of Washington, from his craggy home far up the rocky mountains, will scream it to the tempests and the stars.

During the next two years both of Audubon's sons built houses of their own close by Minnie's Land, and in 1856 Victor brought out another octavo edition of *Birds*; but soon after that he was crippled by a severe fall – either from a train, or into the basement well of his house – and he died at home in 1860. Undaunted, John conceived the idea of recreating the *Birds* in their original size and glory by bringing out a double-elephant folio edition printed from lithographic plates. The first volume, of 106 prints, was published by Julius Bien of Broadway in 1860, but the project was brought to an abrupt end by the outbreak of the Civil War, and the stone plates were smashed when a warehouse in New Orleans was shelled.

In 1857, when she was seventy, Lucy went back to teaching, and set up a small school in Victor's house (her own having been let). There she instructed her grandchildren and a few others, with the gift for imparting knowledge that she had shown as a young woman. But her husband's

After her hus-
band's death
she resumed her
teaching, and
outlived him
by more than
twenty years.

financial improvidence seemed to dog her, and in 1863 she was obliged to sell 464 sheets of his original paintings (430 of them from *The Birds of America*) to the New York Historical Society. She lived to be eighty-six, and died, with her wits fully intact, in 1874.

The good-natured William MacGillivray never achieved the success that his talents seemed to deserve. The first three volumes of his master-work, *A History of British Birds*, were so harshly criticised that he never recovered his former ebullience. In 1841 he became Regius Professor of Civil and Natural History at Marischal College – one of the two universities then existing in Aberdeen. For the next nine years he continued to pour out books and articles, including an eight-part work on domestic cattle, and in the autumn of 1850 he set out to describe the natural history and geology of Deeside, where he spent six weeks ferreting about the hills, and where Lochnagar became his favourite mountain.

There is no record of whether or not he learnt of Audubon's death in January 1851; but by then his own health was failing, and although he managed to complete the two final volumes of *A History of British Birds*, he died on 8 September 1852, aged fifty-six. Several of his remarks in the preface to the final volume might equally have been written by Audubon – especially this: 'I have been honest and sincere in my endeavours to promote the truth.'

Charles Waterton died in 1865 at the age of eighty-three. Having survived many earlier, more serious accidents, he came to an ignominious end when he tripped over a bramble in his own park and fell heavily on to a log, apparently rupturing his spleen. Although he managed to walk away from the scene, he expired two days later. Several authors have written biographies, but his own work has long since gone out of print.

George Ord outlived him by a year, dying in 1866. The nine volumes of Alexander Wilson's *American Ornithology*, which he edited and completed, have become collectors' items.

William Swainson turned against Audubon at the end, damning him, with some justice, as only a field naturalist, rather than a scientific one. He emigrated to New Zealand in 1837 and died there in 1855. His final remarks on Audubon appeared in *The Cabinet Cyclopædia*, published in 1840.

Robert Havell, together with his wife and daughter, emigrated to America in September 1839 and for a while were guests of the Audubons, before settling in Brooklyn. Havell painted and engraved views of New York, Boston, the Niagara Falls and Hartford, Connecticut. He then bought some land at Sing-Sing (today's Ossining) and built a house which he called Rocky Mount. There he became a leading member of the Hudson River school of artists, and later moved five miles downstream to Tarrytown, continuing to paint for the rest of his life. He died on 11 November 1878, aged eighty-five.

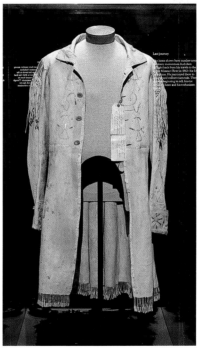

68

SKIN COAT

The garment was made for Audubon by the Mandan Indians, or a related tribe, and acquired by him during his expedition on the Upper Missouri River in 1843.

PLATE CCXXVI

Whooping Crane. GRUS AMERICANA. Adult Male.

CHAPTER SEVENTEEN
THE LEGACY

AUDUBON's magisterial biographer Francis Hobart Herrick, writing in 1917, described the creation of *The Birds of America* as:

> one of the most remarkable and interesting undertakings in the history of literature and science in the nineteenth century. Unique as it was in every detail of its workmanship, it will remain for centuries a shining example of the triumph of human endeavour and of the spirit and will of man.

That verdict holds good to this day. Audubon made numerous mistakes. He missed many species, his science was faulty, and he was occasionally economical with the truth. Yet the splendour of his paintings, as reproduced by Lizars and the Havells, remains stunning: the big birds in particular – the Wild Turkey, the Whooping Crane, the Golden Eagle – take one's breath away. Just as Chapman's translation of Homer inspired Keats, so Audubon's pictures speak out loud and bold, proclaiming the immense energy and confidence of their creator. Had he known Latin, he might justifiably have quoted Horace: '*Exegi monumentum aere perennius* – I have created a monument longer lasting than bronze.'

Nobody knows exactly how many complete copies of the double-elephant folio were produced, but the best estimate is between 175 and 200. There were also at least 120 incomplete sets, whose owners defaulted on their subscriptions in mid-course; but over the years the scarcity of entire copies has forced their value ceaselessly upwards.

After the First World War several were offered at auction by British universities and other institutions in need of funds for the restoration of damaged buildings. Other sets were broken up by their owners, who found

69 facing

WHOOPING CRANE
Grus americana

The bird is about to devour a baby alligator. Painted near New Orleans in 1821. The species almost went extinct, but is being rescued by intensive conservation efforts in Florida.

that they could get more by selling individual prints than they could from disposing of their copies whole. No complete copies were sold in the United States between 1942 and 1963, but in May 1966 a set went for $60,000 at the Parke-Bernet Galleries in New York.

Thereafter the amounts paid began to rise astronomically – to $1,540,000 in 1984, to $3,096,000 in 1989, and $4,070,000 in 1993. Research by the specialist author Susanne M. Low suggested that at the end of the millennium the total of intact copies was 119. Then came a surprise which electrified all Audubon enthusiasts: in 2000 the Marquis of Bute offered for sale a copy which had belonged to his family for the best part of a century. This turned out to be the one originally ordered in 1834 by George Lane Fox, the Yorkshire squire and Member of Parliament, which had been sold in 1909 for $1850, and thereafter had disappeared from the records. Ninety-one years later, on 10 March 2000, it came up as Lot No. 39 at Christie's premises on Rockefeller Plaza in New York. The pre-sale estimate was $3–4 million, but it went for the amazing figure of $8,802,500. In contrast, a good set of Alexander Wilson's *American Ornithology* fetches between $12,000 and $14,000.

The 435 copper plates engraved by Lizars and the Havells were shipped to New York in the summer of 1839. A persistent legend claimed that the ship carrying them sank in New York harbour, and that

70

GOLD MINE

The set of *The Birds of America*, subscribed by George Lane Fox and later the property of the Marquis of Bute, which was sold for $8.8 million at Christie's, New York, in 2002.

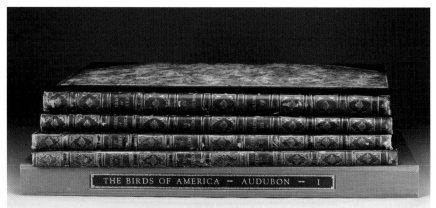

the plates spent months immersed in salt water before being salvaged. Audubon himself, however, never mentioned any such accident. A letter to Victor, dated 1842, shows that by then the plates were stored in a warehouse in New York; but when a large area of the city was devastated by fire on 19 July 1845, some of them were badly damaged.

In 1852, a year after Audubon's death, when his sons both built themselves houses on Lucy's estate, John erected a separate small building, which became known as 'The Cave', specially to hold the 350 plates which had been rescued. By 1869, however, Lucy was so short of money that she put the whole lot up for sale, and they were bought – extraordinary as it seems – not for their artistic value, but for scrap, no public institution having been prepared to bid for them. At the Ansonia Brass & Copper Company in Ansonia, Connecticut, a man had started loading them into the furnace, to be melted down into copper bars, when a fourteen-year-old boy called Charles Cowles noticed a representation of a bird's foot on one of them, realised what it was, and made such a fuss that the rest were spared. Later the president of the company, William E. Dodge, presented a few to the American Museum of Natural History in New York, the Metropolitan Museum of Art, the Smithsonian Institution in Washington, DC, and Princeton University. In all, seventy-eight plates are thought to have survived.

In 1985, to mark the 200th anniversary of the artist's birth, six of the plates owned by the American Museum of Natural History were flown to London, where the firm Alecto Historical Editions painstakingly restored their surfaces and brought out a limited edition of new prints, using a process called '*la poupeé*', in which the copper was inked with colour applied with a pad of fine rag (*poupeé*) rather than with black only, thereby much improving definition and reducing the amount of hand-colouring required later. The outstanding quality achieved by the latter-day printers – even better, experts agreed, than that of Havell – ensured that the 125 portfolios were quickly snapped up by institutions and private buyers at prices up to $50,000.

Today the artist's name is huge throughout America. The National

Audubon Society, founded in 1905, has over 600,000 members, 500 chapters, and assets of more than $200 million. In its early days it was concerned solely with the welfare of birds, but now it is active in every form of conservation, working to protect wildlife and the environment, sponsoring scientific research projects and promoting education. The Society owns and manages many reserves, the largest being the 26,000-acre Paul J. Rainey sanctuary in Louisiana.

The John James Audubon State Park at Henderson, Kentucky extends to 692 acres, including a 325-acre nature reserve and a 28-acre lake. The museum has a large collection of memorabilia, drawings and paintings. Minnie's Land, the family home in New York, was demolished during the 1930s, but Mill Grove, where the artist first settled in America, has been preserved as a visitor centre within the 175-acre Audubon Wildlife Sanctuary in Lower Providence Township, Pennsylvania.

In England, Rathbones still exists as a family firm – though now it is a leading investment management company, with offices in London and Liverpool – and Liverpool is dotted with memorials to the clan which did so much for the city. The little watercolour of a robin perched on a mossy stone, which Audubon lovingly painted for dark-eyed Hannah Mary, now belongs to the University of Liverpool Art Gallery, which owns many of his pictures, including the self-portrait in profile.

Greenbank – in a way the cradle of Audubon's whole enterprise – remained the family home until 1940, when it was requisitioned by the Admiralty for war use. In 1944 the Rathbones gave the house to Liverpool University, and in 1963 it became a club for staff and students, known locally as 'The Pub in the Park'. Today, alas, the building stands empty, although future roles for it are planned. Liverpool has long since expanded eastwards to engulf it, and the University's red-brick halls of residence crowd in on what remains of its grounds. Nevertheless, the place retains an aura of calm and style that belongs to another age.

The Gothic front of the house – scarcely changed since Audubon knew it – still looks down over the smooth, sloping lawn where he saw the ladies practising their archery. Opposite, beyond the ornamental water, another lawn sweeps up in symmetry. The two-storey, wrought-iron verandah still graces one side of the building. Fine beeches stand guard. All this the Kentucky woodsman would recognise in an instant. Any latter-day visitor interested in him and his great book must feel his spirit hovering over this enchanted spot, and imagine him striding up to the porch with a portfolio of drawings slung from his shoulder to greet his foster family — the wanderer from the New World who found salvation in the Old.

71 below

AUDUBON
THE NATURLIST

Oil-on-canvas portrait painted by his sons Victor and John.

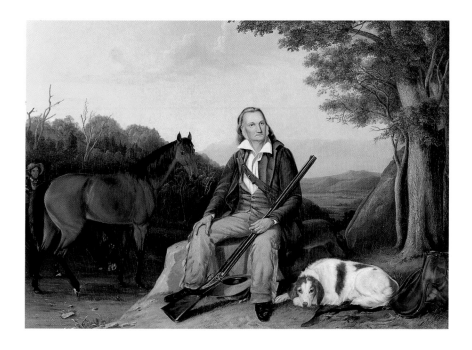

LIST OF PLATES & ACKNOWLEDGEMENTS

All bird plates are engravings from the original subscribers' sets of the four volumes of the double-elephant broadsheets of John James Audubon's *The Birds of America*, unless otherwise stated. Every effort has been made to ensure that the information provided in the captions, credit lines, list of plates and acknowledgements is accurate. Errors brought to the attention of the publisher and verified to our satisfaction will be corrected in future editions.

The following abbreviations have been used to indicate sources: [NHM] The Natural History Museum, London, UK; [BAL] The Bridgeman Art Library; [MEPL] Mary Evans Picture Library; [BL] British Library, London, UK; [NYHS] New York Historical Society, New York, USA; [AMNH] American Museum of Natural History Library, New York, USA; [NPG] National Portrait Gallery, London; [ULAG] University of Liverpool Art Gallery & Collections, UK; [ULL] The University of Liverpool Library.

Front cover: [Detail] John James Audubon (1758–1851) *Self-portrait* 1826; inscribed: 'Audubon at Green Bank/<u>Almost</u> Happy!!/Sepr 1826. Drawn by himself', pencil and black chalk, 5⅝ x 4¼ in; Ref. No. RPXXV.8.30. By courtesy of [ULL].
[Detail] *American White Pelican, Pelecanus Erythrorhynchos*, Gmelin. Havell plate no. CCCXI, engraving; Private Collection/[BAL].
Back cover: John Woodhouse Audubon (1812–62) *Portrait of John James Audubon c.*1840–1; oil on canvas, 44¼ x 33 in; [NYHS/BAL].
Endpapers: *Long-billed Curlew, Numenius americanus*. Havell plate no. CCXXXI, engraving; ©[NHM].
Frontispiece: John James Audubon (1758–1851) *Self-portrait* 1826; inscribed: 'Audubon at Green Bank/ <u>Almost</u> Happy!!/ Sepr 1826. Drawn by himself', pencil and black chalk, 5⅝ x 4¼ in;

Ref. No.: RPXXV.8.30. By courtesy of [ULL].
1. *Map showing Audubon's Travels 1828–1843*; [AMNH].
2. English School *The Princes Dock, Liverpool c.*1830; engraved by F.R. Hay; Private Collection/[BAL].
3. *Portfolio in which John J. Audubon carried specimens of his paintings while soliciting subscribers to his work on North American birds in Great Britain and France*, presented to the American Museum by Maria F. Audubon; [AMNH].
4. *Wild Turkey, Meleagris gallopavo*, Linnaeus. Havell plate no. I, engraving; [BL/BAL].
5. *Barred Owl, Strix varia*, Barton. Havell plate no. XLVI, engraving; Private Collection/[BAL].
6. Thomas Birch (1779–1851) *Mill Grove Farm, Perkiomen Creek, Philadelphia c.*1820; oil on panel, 16¼ x 24½ in; [NYHS/BAL].
7. *Blue Jay, Cyanocitta cristata*, Linnaeus. Havell plate no. CII, engraving; [NHM/BAL].
8. *Wired model of Blue Jays*, constructed for *John James Audubon: Science into Art* exhibition in 1985; Photographed by J. Beckett/D. Finnin; [AMNH].
9. After the miniature by F. Cruikshank *Lucy Bakewell Audubon* 1835; [AMNH].
10. *Portrait of Alexander Wilson*, frontispiece from *The Naturalist's Library. Ornithology*, Vol. 4 by W. Jardine; ©[NHM].
11. *Instructive Stories from the West: Audubon*, Japanese, Meiji era (1868–1928), 1875, woodblock print, ink on paper, 14¼ x 9½ in; Arthur M. Sackler Gallery, Smithsonian Institution, Washington, DC: Gift of the Daval Foundation – William and Florence Leonhart, S1996.97.
12. Constantine S. Rafinesque (1773–1840) *Devil-Jack Diamond Fish* 1818; pencil and ink; Smithsonian Archives.
13. *Northern Mockingbird, Mimus polyglottos*, Linnaeus. Havell plate no. XXI, engraving; Private Collection/[BAL].
14. John James Audubon (1758–1851) *Otter Caught in a Trap* 1826; oil on canvas, 28 x 36 in; [ULAG/BAL].
15. [Detail] John James Audubon (1758–1851) *Self-portrait* 1826; inscribed: 'Audubon at Green

Bank/ <u>Almost</u> Happy!!/Sepr 1826. Drawn by himself', pencil and black chalk, 5⅝ x 4¼ in; Ref. No. RPXXV.8.30. By courtesy of [ULL].

16. John James Audubon (1758–1851) *The American Wild Turkey Cock, Meleagris gallopavo,* oil on canvas, 60 x 48½ in; [ULAG/BAL].

17. *Canada Goose, Branta canadensis,* Linnaeus. Havell plate no. CCI, engraving; Private Collection/[BAL].

18. After W. Stewart *Robert Jameson,* lithograph by Frederick Schenck; By courtesy of [NPG].

19. William Home Lizars (1788–1859) *Self-Portrait*; chalk on paper, 17 x 14½ in; Scottish National Portrait Gallery.

20. *Peregrine Falcon, Falco peregrinus,* Tunstall. Havell plate no. XVI, engraving; ©[NHM].

21. John James Audubon (1758–1851) *Red-Shouldered Hawk Attacking Bobwhite Partridges*; oil on canvas, 26 x 39¾ in; [ULAG/BAL].

22. John Syme (1795–1861) *Portrait of John James Audubon 1826*; oil on canvas, 35½ x 27½ in; White House Historical Association (White House Collection).

23. Captain Edward Jones (*fl.* 1825) *Charles Waterton Capturing a Cayman 1825–26*; oil on canvas; Private Collection/[BAL].

24. After Sir John Watson Gordon (1788–1864) *Sir Walter Scott at Abbotsford*; engraving by Robert Bell; [MEPL].

25. *Passenger Pigeon, Columba migratoria* later *Ectopistes migratorius,* Linnaeus. Havell plate no. LXI, engraving; ©[NHM].

26. *Thomas Bewick at work in his studio*; engraving by John Eyre; [MEPL].

27. After Mosses *William Swainson*; stipple engraving by Edward Francis Finden, published 1840; By courtesy of [NPG].

28. *Box in which prints of Audubon's 'The Birds of America' were sent to subscribers*; [AMNH].

29. *Bonaparte's Gull, Larus bonapartii* now *Larus philadelphia,* Ord. Havell plate no. CCCXXIV, engraving; ©[NHM].

30. Prospectus for *The Birds of America,* 1831; Private Collection.

31. [Detail] *Northern Mockingbird, Mimus polyglottos,* Linnaeus. Havell plate no. XXI, engraving; Private Collection/[BAL].

32. *Turkey Vulture, Cathartes atratus* now *Cathartes*

aura, Linnaeus. Havell plate no. CLI, engraving; ©[NHM].

33. After Thomas H. Shepherd *Exeter 'Change, The Strand 1829*; engraving by T. Barber; [MEPL].

34. *Bald Eagle, Falco leucocephalus* now *Haliaeetus leucocephalus,* Linnaeus. Havell plate no. XXXI, engraving; Photograph by kind permission of Christie's, New York.

35. *Great American Hen and Young, Meleagris gallopavo.* Havell plate no. VI, engraving; Private Collection/[BAL].

36. Copper Plate of *Great American Hen and Young*; (see plate 35) [AMNH].

37. *Portrait of Baron Georges Cuvier,* engraving by Tardieu; [MEPL].

38. *Carolina Parrot, Psittacus carolinensis* also know as *Carolina Parrakeet, Conuropsis carolinensis* Linnaeus. Havell plate no. XXVI, engraving; Photograph by kind permission of Christie's, New York.

39. *Green Black-capped Flycatcher, Muscicapa pusilla* later *Wilson's Warbler, Wilsonia pusilla,* Wilson. Havell plate no. CXXIV, engraving; ©[NHM].

40. Letter from Audubon to Havell, 1831; John James Audubon Collection. Manuscripts Division. Department of Rare Books and Special Collections. Princeton University Library.

41. Artist Unknown *William MacGillivray*; oil on unknown support, possibly board, oval 15¼ x 12¾ in; University of Aberdeen.

42. *Blackburnian Warbler, Sylvia blackburniae* now *Dendroica fusca,* Müller; *Black-throated Green Warbler, Sylvia virens* now *Dendroica virens,* Gmelin; *MacGillivray's Warbler, Sylvia philadelphia* now *Oporornis tolmiei,* Townsend. Havell plate no. CCCXCIX, engraving; ©[NHM].

43. After George Cooke (1793–1849) *The City of Charleston,* engraved by W.J. Bennett, 1838, coloured lithograph; [NYHS/BAL].

44. *Brown Pelican, Pelecanus fuscus* now *Pelecanus occidentalis,* Linnaeus. Havell plate no. CCLI, engraving; ©[NHM].

45. [Detail] *Golden Eagle, Falco chrysaetos* now *Aquila chrysaetos,* Linnaeus 1833. Watercolour, pastel, graphite, gouache, metallic paints and selective glazing; 39¼ x 26¼ in; Collection of [NYHS], Accession # 1863.17.181.

46. *Golden Eagle, Falco chrysaetos* now *Aquila*

chrysaetos, Linnaeus. Havell plate no. CLXXXI, engraving; ©[NHM].

47. *Northern Gannet, Sula bassanus* now *Morus bassanus*, Linnaeus. Havell plate no. CCCXXVI, engraving; Private Collection/[BAL].

48. [Detail] *Bachman's Warbler, Sylvia bachmanii* or *Vermivora bachmanii*, Audubon. Havell plate no. CLXXXV, engraving; Private Collection/[BAL].

49. Broadside, June 1834, London; Collection of [NYHS]. Negative # 75821.

50. *Snowy Owl, Strix nyctea* now *Nyctea scandiaca*, Linnaeus. Havell plate no. CXXI, engraving; ©[NHM].

51. Title page of the *Ornithological Biography* by John James Audubon, 1831; Rare Books Division. Princeton University Library.

52. *Pileated Woodpecker, Dryocopus pileatus*, Linnaeus. Havell plate no. CXI, engraving; [NHM/BAL].

53. *Snowy Heron or White Egret, Ardea candidissima* now *Snowy Egret, Egretta thula*, Molina. Havell plate no. CCXLII, engraving; Photograph by kind permission of Christie's, New York.

54. Asher Brown Durand (1796–1886) *Portrait of President Andrew Jackson (1767–1845)* 1835; oil on canvas; 30 x 26 in; [NYHS/BAL].

55. *Night Hawk, Caprimulgus virginiana* now *Common Nighthawk, Chordeiles minor*, Forster. Havell plate no. CXLVII, engraving; ©[NHM].

56. *Roseate Spoonbill, Platalea ajaja* now *Ajaia ajaja*, Linnaeus. Havell plate no. CCCXXI, engraving; Photograph by kind permission of Christie's, New York.

57. A. D. Rinck *John Woodhouse Audubon (1812–62) c.1845*; miniature portrait, watercolour on ivory, 2¾ x 2½ in; [NYHS/BAL].

58. *American Flamingo* now *Greater Flamingo, Phoenicopterus ruber*, Linnaeus. Havell plate no. CCCCXXXI, engraving; ©[NHM].

59. After Thomas Herbert Maguire (1821–95) *Portrait of John Gould* 1849; lithograph, 11½ x 9½ in; The Royal Institution, London, UK/[BAL].

60. *American Dipper, Cinclus mexicanus*, Swainson. Havell plate no. CCCCXXXV, engraving; © [NHM].

61. *Hairy Woodpecker, Picoides villosus*, Linnaeus;

Three-toed Woodpecker, Picoides tridactylus; Linnaeus. Havell plate no. CCCCXVII, engraving; Private Collection/[BAL].

62. *Arctic Tern, Sterna arctica* now *Sterna paradisaea*, Pontoppidan. Havell plate no. CCL; engraving; Private Collection/[BAL].

63. Victor Gifford Audubon (1809–60) *View of Hudson River c.1840–5*; inscribed on reverse: 'View of the Hudson River at about 134th St. from a painting by Victor Audubon, a son of Audubon the naturalist, who is sitting on a rock in the foreground (about 1840–1845)', oil on canvas, 48 x 72 in; Gift of Miss Alice Lawrence, 38.188, Museum of the City of New York.

64. William Rickarby Miller (1818–93) *The House of John James Audubon: Minnie's Land* 1852; watercolour on paper, 15¼ x 10 in; Museum of the City of New York, USA/[BAL].

65. John Woodhouse Audubon (1812–62) *John James Audubon* 1843; oil on canvas, 35 x 27½ in; Photographed by Logan; [AMNH].

66. Mathew Brady (1823/4?–1896) *John James Audubon c.1848*; from a daguerreotype made by Brady in New York; [AMNH].

67. Abraham Bogardus (1822–1908) *Lucy Bakewell Audubon. Carte de visite*; albumen print; Collection of [NYHS]. Negative # 39786.

68. *Audubon's Coat*, skin coat made for Audubon by the Mandan Indians, or a closely related tribe, acquired by Audubon on the Upper Missouri River in 1843; pictured on display in 1985 exhibition; Photographed by Rick Sheridan; [AMNH].

69. *Whooping Crane, Grus americana*, Linnaeus. Havell plate no. CCXXVI, engraving; Victoria & Albert Museum, London, UK/[BAL].

70. John James Audubon's *The Birds of America*, The Early Subscriber's set of George Lane Fox, Property of the Marquis of Bute; Photograph by kind permission of Christie's, New York.

71. John Woodhouse Audubon (1812–62) & Victor Gifford Audubon (1809–60) *Audubon the Naturalist* 1848; inscribed and dated on belt, 'J.W.A. NY/1848', oil on canvas, 44 x 60 in; Photographed by Logan; [AMNH].

SOURCES

BOOKS

ALDINGTON, Richard, *The Strange Life of Charles Waterton, 1782–1865*. Evans Brothers, London, 1949.

AUDUBON, John James, *The Birds of America*. Four volumes double-elephant folio, published by the author, 1827–1838. 435 copperplate engravings, hand-coloured, no text except names of birds.

————*Ornithological Biography*. Five volumes and Synopsis, Adam & Charles Black, Edinburgh, 1831–39.

————Facsimile edition of all volumes published by the Abbeville Press & National Audubon Society, 1985.

————*The Journal of John James Audubon made during his trip to New Orleans in 1820–21*. Edited by Howard Corning. Cambridge Business Historical Society, Massachusetts, 1929.

————*The Journal of John James Audubon, 1840–43*. Edited by Howard Corning Cambridge Business Historical Society, Massachusetts, 1929.

————*The 1826 Journal of John James Audubon*. Edited by Alice Ford. University of Oklahoma Press, 1967.

————*My Style of Drawing Birds*. Introduction by Michael Zinman. The Haydn Foundation, Ardsley, New York, 1979. Facsimile and printed version of original 1828 paper, significantly different from the version given by Maria R. Audubon (below).

AUDUBON, Maria R., *Audubon and His Journals*, with zoological and other notes by Elliott Coues. Two vols, New York and London, 1898.

BACHMAN, C.L., *John Bachman*. Charleston, 1888.

BEWICK, Thomas, *A Memoir, Written by Himself*. Oxford University Press, 1975.

BLAUGRUND, Annette, and Stebbins, Theodore E., Jr., editors, *John James Audubon: the Watercolors for The Birds of America*. Villard Books, New York, 1993.

BUCHANAN, Robert, *Life and Adventures of Audubon the Naturalist*. J.M. Dent, London, and E.P. Dutton, New York, 1912.

CHANCELLOR, John, *Audubon: a Biography*. Weidenfeld & Nicolson, London, 1978.

CLARK, Taylor, and BANNON, Lois Elmer, *Handbook of Audubon Prints*. Pelican Publishing Company Inc., Gretna, Louisiana, 1985.

DALL, W. H., *Spencer Fullerton Baird: a Biography*. Lippincott, Philadelphia & London, 1915. Includes 18 of Audubon's letters to Baird.

FORD, Alice, *John James Audubon: a Biography*. Abbeville Press, New York, 1988.

FOSHAY, Ella M., *John James Audubon*. Harry N. Abrams Inc., in association with The National Museum of American Art, Smithsonian Institution, 1997.

FRIES, Waldemar H., *The Double Elephant Folio*. American Library Association, Chicago, 1973.

HERRICK, Francis Hobart, *Audubon the Naturalist*. Two vols., Appleton & Co., New York, 1917.

MacGILLIVRAY, William, *A History of British Birds*, five vols., London, 1837–52.

NOTTINGHAM, Lucie, *Rathbone Brothers: from Merchant to Banker*. Rathbone Brothers plc, 1992.

RALPH, Robert, *William MacGillivray: Creatures of Air, Land and Sea*. Merrell Holberton and the Natural History Museum, London, 1999.

RATHBONE, William, *A Sketch of Family History during Four Generations*. Privately published, Liverpool, 1894.

SCOTT: *The Journal of Sir Walter Scott* edited by W.E.K. Anderson. Oxford, 1972.

TREE, Isabella, *The Ruling Passion of John Gould*. Barrie & Jenkins, London, 1991.

TROLLOPE, Fanny, *Domestic Manners of the Americans*. First published 1832; Penguin edition, 1997.

WATERTON, Charles, *Essays on Natural History*. Edited by Norman Moore. Frederick Warne (London) and Scribner, Welford (New York), 1871. Includes many attacks on Audubon, first published privately or in journals.

————*Letters of Charles Waterton*. Edited by R.A. Irwin. Rockliff, London, 1955.

————*Wanderings in South America*. London, 1825.

PAPERS AND ARTICLES

ANON (Robert Jameson) 'Mr Audubon's Great Work on Birds of the United States of America'. *Edinburgh New Philosophical Journal*, Vol. 2, pp. 210–11. Edinburgh, 1826–27.

ANON. 'A Great Naturalist'. *Blackwood's Edinburgh Magazine*, Vol. 164, pp. 58–69. Edinburgh, 1898.

ANON. 'Wilson the Ornithologist'. *The Literary Gazette*, London, 3 September 1831, p. 574, and 15 October 1831. Erroneous report of the death of Audubon, followed by a correction.

ANON. Review of the *Ornithological Biography*. *Edinburgh Literary Journal*, p. 248–9. April, 1831.

AUDUBON, John James, 'Account of the Habits of the Turkey Buzzard (*Vultur aura*)'. *Edinburgh New Philosophical Journal*, Vol. 2. 1826–27.

———'Observations on the Natural History of the Alligator'. *Edinburgh New Philosophical Journal*, Vol. 2. 1826–27.

———'Account of the Carrion Crow or *Vultur atratus*'. *Edinburgh Journal of Science*, Vol. VI, 1826–27.

———'Notes on the Habits of the Wild Pigeon of America, *Columba migratoria*'. *Edinburgh Journal of Science*, Vol. VI, 1826–27.

———'Notes on the Rattlesnake (*Crotalus horridus*)'. *Edinburgh New Philosophical Journal*, Vol. 3. 1827. Reprinted without permission in *Journal of the Franklin Institute and American Mechanics' Magazine*, Vol. II, Philadelphia, 1828. Later repudiated by the Editor, Thomas P. Jones.

———'Account of the Method of Drawing Birds Employed by J.J. Audubon'. *Edinburgh Journal of Science*, Vol. VIII, pp. 48–54. Edinburgh, 1828.

———'Notes on the Bird of Washington (*Falco washingtonia*) or Great American Sea Eagle'. *Loudon's Magazine of Natural History*, Vol. 1, pp. 115–20. London 1828–29.

———'Hunting the Cougar, or the American Lion'. *Edinburgh New Philosophical Journal*, Vol. 11, 1831.

———'An Account of the Habits of the American Goshawk'. *Edinburgh Journal of Natural and Geographical Science*, Vol. 3, pp. 145–7. Edinburgh, 1831.

AUDUBON, Victor G., 'Reply to Mr Waterton's Remarks on Audubon's *Biography of Birds*'. *Loudon's Magazine of Natural History*, Vol. VI, p. 369. London, 1833.

———'Mr Audubon and His Work'. Ibid, pp. 550–3.

BACHMAN, John, 'An Account of Some Experiments' ... *Journal of the Boston Society of Natural History*, Vol. 1, pp. 15–31. Boston, 1834.

———'Remarks in Defence of the Author of the Birds of America'. *Loudon's Magazine of Natural History*, Vol. VII, pp. 164–75. London, 1834.

Blackwood's Edinburgh Magazine, Vol. XXX (July–December 1831), Vol. XXXVII (January–June 1835). William Blackwood, Edinburgh.

BLAND, D.S., *John James Audubon in Liverpool, 1826–27*. Published by the author, 1977.

BREWSTER, David, Review of Audubon's Edinburgh exhibition. *Edinburgh Journal of Science*, Vol. VI, p. 184. Edinburgh, 1827.

Caledonian Mercury (Edinburgh), 8 September 1831, 29 October 1831, 3 & 5 November 1831.

CHALMERS, John, 'Audubon in Edinburgh'. *Archives of Natural History*, Vol. 20, part 2, pp. 157–66, 1993.

COUES, Elliott, 'Ornithological Biography'. Proceedings of the United States National Museum, No 2, 1880.

JACKSON, Christine E., 'The Changing Relationship between J.J. Audubon and his Friends P.J. Selby, Sir William Jardine and W.H. Lizars'. *Archives of Natural History*, Vol. 18, part 3, October 1991.

LOUDON, J.C. (Editor), *The Magazine of Natural History and Journal of Zoology, Botany, Mineralogy, Geology and Meteorology*. Vol. 1., Vol. VI, Vol. VII, Vol. VIII. Longman, London, 1828, 1833, 1834, 1845. Numerous articles by Charles WATERTON.

NORTH, Christopher (pseudonym of John Wilson), 'Audubon's *Ornithological Biography*'. *Blackwood's Edinburgh Magazine*, Vol. XXX, pp 1–16 and *Wilson's American Ornithology*, pp. 247–80. Edinburgh, 1831.

————'Audubon's *Ornithological Biography*', Vol. 2. *Blackwood's Edinburgh Magazine*, Vol. 37, pp. 107–24. Edinburgh, 1835.

'ORNITHOPHILUS', Remarks on Audubon's *Birds of America* and *Ornithological Biography*', *Edinburgh New Philosophical Journal*, Vol. 10, pp. 317–32. Edinburgh, 1830–31

R.B. (Robert BAKEWELL), 'Observations on Mr Waterton's Attacks on Mr Audubon'. *Loudon's Magazine of Natural History*, Vol. VI, pp. 369–72. London, 1833.

SWAINSON, William (styled 'W.S.'), 'Some Account of the Work now Publishing by Mr Audubon'. *Loudon's Magazine of Natural History*, Vol. 1, pp. 42–52. London, 1828.

————'Mr Audubon and His Work, the Biography of Birds'. *Loudon's Magazine of Natural History*, Vol. VI, p. 550. London, 1833.

————'Taxidermy, Bibliography and Biography'. *The Cabinet Cyclopaedia*. Conducted by the Rev. Dionysius Lardner, pp. 116–17. London, 1840.

WATERTON, Charles, 'On the Faculty of Scent of the Vulture'. *Loudon's Magazine of Natural History*, Vol. V (April), pp. 233–41. London, 1832. The first of nineteen attacks on Audubon and his supporters, extending over five years.

————'The Means by which the Turkey Buzzard Traces its Food, and Remarks on Mr Audubon's Account of the Habits of the Turkey Buzzard'. *Loudon's Magazine of Natural History*, Vol VI, London 1833, pp. 162–71.

————'The Gland on the Rump of Birds'. Ibid, pp 274–77.

————'Mr Audubon Again'. Ibid pp. 465–8

————'A Letter to James' [he meant Robert] Jameson. Oblique attack on Audubon, privately printed 1835. Reprinted in *Essays on Natural History*, 1871 – see above.

————'Audubon's Plates of *The Birds of America*'. *Loudon's Magazine of Natural History*, Vol. VIII, pp. 236–8. London, 1835.

————'An Ornithological Letter to William Swainson'. Privately printed, 1837. Reprinted in *Essays on Natural History*, pp. 511–23, 1871 – see above.

UNPUBLISHED

The Rathbone Papers in the Department of Special Collections and Archives, the University of Liverpool.

Letters of Charles Waterton in the City of Wakefield Public Library.

Letters of J. J. Audubon to William Swainson in the library of the Linnean Society, London.

AUTHOR'S ACKNOWLEDGMENTS

My principal debt is to that excellent publisher DAVID BURNETT, whose idea it was to describe the creation of *The Birds of America* in detail, and who put the mountain of research material which he had collected at my disposal. I am grateful also to the expert print-maker JOE STUDHOLME for his advice on technical matters, and to ROBERT GILLMOR, fine bird-artist in his own right, for the loan of books and for ornithological expertise.

My thanks to the following for help of various kinds: ADRIAN ALLAN, archivist at the Liverpool University Library; ELAINE BLAKE, Curator of Art and Ethnography at Reading Museum; JANE CHEAPE, who combed through archives in Edinburgh on my behalf; GINA DOUGLAS, Librarian of the Linnean Society, London; JONATHAN ELPHICK; TOM GREENWOOD, Audubon House and Tropical Gardens, Key West, Florida; SUE HARRIS, Stark Museum of Art, Orange, Texas; BRIONY HUDSON, Assistant Keeper of Social History at the Wakefield Museum, who dug out many letters to and from CHARLES WATERTON; ED KENNEY, US Audubon expert; CHARLOTTE LORIMER, Bridgeman Art Library, London; Dr ROBERT RALPH, authority on William MacGillivray; MATT PAVLICK, American Museum of Natural History, New York; DAWN HATHAWAY at The Natural History Museum Picture Library; JENNY RATHBONE; BILL REESE; special thanks to BENDETTA ROUX, the Department of Printed Books and Manuscripts, Christie's New York; ERIC STANFORD; PRISCILLA THOMAS; MARGARET WESTWOOD and BRIDGET WRIGHT, who arranged for me to inspect Her Majesty the Queen's copy of *The Birds of America* in the Royal Library at Windsor Castle.

As always, I found the support and the service of the London Library beyond praise.

SUZANNE BAILEY, the picture researcher, showed exemplary ingenuity in hunting down illustrations. KEN WILSON, the designer, created the book's stylish appearance with his habitual flair, and my editors at Weidenfeld & Nicolson, MICHAEL DOVER and MARILYN INGLIS, gave invaluable support and encouragement.